Praise for *The Francis Effect*

"John Gehring takes a very perceptive look at how the Francis pontificate is challenging Catholic leadership in the United States after years of a narrow 'culture war' vision of the church's mission. The book offers fresh insight into the real 'Francis effect,' which involves a profoundly new understanding of the church's doctrinal tradition and its development." —**John Thavis**, former Rome bureau chief for Catholic News Service and author of *The Vatican Diaries*

"John Gehring provides the most thoughtful answer yet to the biggest question about America's biggest church: What has been 'the Francis effect,' both inside and outside Catholicism? While pundits and partisans provide their own superficial and self-serving conclusions, here the answer is grounded in rich historical context, careful nuance, and incisive observation. Anyone who wants to go beyond the headlines and understand the potential for—and constraints upon—change in the Francis era should read this book." —**David E. Campbell**, University of Notre Dame; author (with Robert Putnam) of *American Grace: How Religion Divides and Unites Us*

"Gehring provides an acute account of how a vocal minority of 'culture warrior' bishops and activists tried to reduce Catholic teaching to Republican talking points. More important, he also shows how Pope Francis is healing wounds and breathing new life into the Catholic Church in America." —**M. Cathleen Kaveny**, Darald and Juliet Libby Professor of Law and Theology, Boston College; author of *Law's Virtues*

"How the Francis era is received by an American hierarchy still clinging to the habits of the last two papacies will be a drama worth watching. For journalists and commentators, Gehring has written a first-class primer of events to come. For historians and ordinary Catholics in the pews, he also offers a rich chronicle of the throes the American church has struggled through over the past three decades." —**Drew Christiansen**, SJ, former editor of *America* magazine; Distinguished Professor of Ethics and Global Development, Georgetown University

"This timely book weaves historical analysis with up-to-date reporting and fresh insights to explain why Pope Francis's pontificate is 'a crossroads moment for the Catholic Church in the United States.'" —**Massimo Faggioli**, University of St. Thomas; author of *Pope Francis: Tradition in Transition*

"No other book better maps the painful division that two decades of culture war have wreaked upon the Catholic Church in America. Yet this is a book inspired by rising hope. The way forward from division, Gehring insists, is under way in the joyful and pastoral papacy of Pope Francis." —**Stephen Schneck**, The Catholic University of America

"Gehring's wide-ranging explorations detail both the tensions within the U.S. church and the movements that could make the 'Francis effect' one that re-energizes Roman Catholics. He shows just how Francis inspires hope for a church that can be united but diverse— engaging and challenging the secular culture, but not at war with it." —**Terrence W. Tilley**, Avery Cardinal Dulles, SJ, Professor of Catholic Theology, Fordham University

"John Gehring's essential book reminds us that 'the Francis effect' promises not a revolution for the Catholic Church, but rather a restitution. In the context of U.S. politics, this means returning to a broad, multi-issue defense of human dignity that will expand the church's public agenda and ensure that Catholic bishops will retain a prophetic voice in the United States long after today's 'culture war' politics have passed into history." —**Timothy A. Byrnes**, Colgate University; author of *Catholic Bishops in American Politics*

"It is well known that significant divisions for a century or more have existed among the U.S. bishops. This book documents the more recent differences so that each reader can evaluate the merits of these disputes. The radical, joyful, pastoral style of Pope Francis has already had a noticeable and welcome effect on the American church. Anyone interested in the far-reaching influence of Francis's papacy will find Gehring's book a valuable contribution to the Francis phenomenon and the bridge the new pope has formed between traditionally opposing groups." —**Joseph A. Fiorenza**, archbishop emeritus of Galveston-Houston

"Surveying the painful casualties of the church's involvement in the culture wars as well as the surprising hope unleashed by Francis's papacy, Gehring's book is a must-read for anyone interested in how politically engaged, progressive Catholics are responding to this new moment in both the church and society." —**Vincent Miller**, Gudorf Chair in Catholic Theology and Culture, University of Dayton; author of *Consuming Religion: Christian Faith and Practice in a Consumer Culture*

"John Gehring has written a wonderful book about how the culture wars have led both the left and the right away from what it really means to be Catholic, and how the 'Francis effect' is leading us all back united in the simple truths of the Gospel. For those devoted to their faith—or those who are simply interested in the topic—this is a must-read." —**Nicholas Cafardi**, former dean emeritus and professor of law, Duquesne University; editor of *Voting and Holiness*

"This supremely engaging book will be a cathartic read for progressives who are faithful Catholics—and tired of being told otherwise. This is the book to read for those who want to situate Francis's impact within the history and present politics of the U.S. Catholic Church." —**Lisa Cahill**, professor of theology, Boston College

"*The Francis Effect* is perfectly timed for this moment, when Pope Francis has both captured the world's attention and tossed something of a grenade into U.S. politics. In this deeply reported and indispensable book, John Gehring examines American Catholicism's tangled political history and the impact already felt by Francis's leadership. The result is a must-read for anyone who wants to understand American politics." —**Amy Sullivan**, author of *The Party Faithful: How and Why Democrats Are Closing the God Gap*

"Thoroughly researched and beautifully written, Gehring's book is a powerful analysis of the historic and existing tensions between conservative and progressive Catholics in the United States and the consequences of their continued divisions. Importantly, he offers not just a critique but also a path forward—one grounded in the teachings of Pope Francis—to unite Catholics for the common good." —**Mark J. Rozell**, George Mason University; coeditor of *Catholics and Politics: The Dynamic Tension between Faith and Power*

THE FRANCIS EFFECT

A Radical Pope's Challenge to the American Catholic Church

John Gehring

ROWMAN & LITTLEFIELD
Lanham • Boulder • New York • London

Published by Rowman & Littlefield
A wholly owned subsidiary of The Rowman & Littlefield Publishing Group, Inc.
4501 Forbes Boulevard, Suite 200, Lanham, Maryland 20706
www.rowman.com

Unit A, Whitacre Mews, 26-34 Stannary Street, London SE11 4AB

British Library Cataloguing in Publication Information Available

Library of Congress Cataloging-in-Publication Data

Gehring, John, 1974–
The Francis effect : a radical pope's challenge to the American Catholic Church / John Gehring.
pages cm
ISBN 978-1-4422-4320-0 (cloth : alk. paper) — ISBN 978-1-4422-4321-7 (electronic)
1. Francis, Pope, 1936– —Influence. 2. Catholic Church—United States. I. Title.
BX1378.7.G44 2015
282.092—dc23
2015019674

∞ ™ The paper used in this publication meets the minimum requirements of American National Standard for Information Sciences Permanence of Paper for Printed Library Materials, ANSI/NISO Z39.48-1992.

Printed in the United States of America

CONTENTS

FOREWORD

It's often said by social scientists and pundits that young Catholics come to the church today—if they show up at all—without the same baggage as previous generations. Often that view is delivered in a tone dismissive of past engagements and with the presumption that the time has come to rise above such acrimony and get on with simply being the church. A certain wisdom accrues to that view. No generation should feel bound to engage the quarrels or issues of its parents and grandparents, using the same language and dragging along the same effects, as if nothing in the world changes. Such a life would be unbearably tedious and stagnant. Successive generations of Catholics should no more be bound by such constraints than young women should be forced to use the language and arguments of their mothers and grandmothers who struggled for equality, nor young African Americans be required to use the tactics of those who navigated the treacherous waters of the civil rights era.

Yet, just as young women and African Americans play a dangerous game if they think the struggle for justice ended with previous generations, so young Catholics take unnecessary risks in believing that getting on with being the church today means wishing away the tensions that come with disagreements over important issues. Debates over the church's role in the world, theological differences regarding the place of women within the church, and questions on issues ranging from sexuality to the ethics of state violence are essential to the ultimate health of the community.

John Gehring is a rising voice among a new generation of Catholics who understand that the choice is not one of either taking up the arguments of his predecessors or maintaining silence in the false hope that calm and peace will then prevail. Such silence would hardly be fitting, or even possible, at this point in history, one Gehring refers to as a "crossroads moment for the Catholic Church in the United States."

If religion was once sequestered comfortably behind church doors with little effect on the public realm save for providing a well-mannered populace, its explosion on the public scene in the late twentieth century as an overt political force caused perverse distortions in the other direction. Religion became the thin veneer that covered everything, providing justification for all manner of state activity. It set up informal but very real tests for politicians. The rise of the religious right created a construct of Christianity theologically bounded by the most conservative strains of belief that led to an alignment with equally conservative secular forces.

A parallel movement occurred within the Catholic leadership in the United States. The church's once robust and complex engagement with the culture—from opposition to abortion to advocacy for workers' rights and challenges to U.S. militarism and unbridled capitalism—shrunk to a few "non-negotiable" issues that aligned neatly with a single political party. "Catholic identity" became shorthand for a narrow agenda that perceived orthodoxy largely through the lens of the church's teachings on sexuality. The splits within the Catholic community, especially in the United States, so deepened over the course of Pope John Paul II's nearly three-decade-long papacy that the prominent Vatican analyst John L. Allen Jr. observed that John Paul had left behind "the irony of a world more united because of his life and legacy and a church more divided." Conditions didn't change much during the years of Pope Benedict XVI's papacy.

And then along came Pope Francis. Those in the church who insist that a "hermeneutic of continuity" means that things cannot change surely wince at talk about how Francis is a radical reformer. Two years into his papacy, it is clear that while he is a traditionalist no more likely than his predecessors to advocate change in the fundamentals of Catholic faith, he also represents a distinct difference from the papacies of his two most recent predecessors in understanding how Catholicism should be projected into the wider culture.

In the brief time since his election, Pope Francis has firmly supplanted a rigidly legalistic approach to evangelism and Catholic identity with a far more pastoral style. The "art of accompaniment" has become the leading edge of Catholic engagement with the world, the phrase evoking something less precise than law, a skill requiring practice as well as flexibility and, above all, a willingness to journey with the other ahead of listing "non-negotiable" conditions for the journey.

If a word cloud descriptive of this papacy were to appear above St. Peter's Basilica, the terms competing for attention would be *mercy* and *poor*. Francis's emphasis on serving the poor and going to the margins recalibrates both the theological and the political conversation that emanates from the church today. It is appropriate to speak of a "Francis effect" and to attempt to understand how it will alter the way the Catholic Church moves in society and deals with the issues of this age. Ironically, this wildly popular pope has not attracted attention because he makes Christianity appear any less difficult. In fact, he challenges us almost daily in his homilies and public exhortations, and especially by his example, to understand that the call to holiness must move beyond self-concern, or even ecclesiastical obsessions with "small-minded rules," to service to others. Salvation is not to be found in the comfort of the sanctuary. The common good and our participation in it, including politics, "even if it is dirty," is mandatory.

The question is how the church will respond to this pope's critiques that appear aimed at the world's richest cultures—his blunt condemnation of war profiteering, of state-sanctioned violence, of environmental degradation, of the effects of unrestrained capitalism on the world's poor. What will we make of this pope whose most profound formation seems to have come late in his clerical career, and not in the academy or the secluded quarters of the Vatican Curia, but rather in Buenos Aires' *villas miserias* (misery villages), slums that were the primary locus of his ministry. The stakes are high because powerful and monied interests within the U.S. church and beyond clearly wish to keep expressions of faith confined to what's least unsettling to the economic and military status quo.

This book is important because of the landscape it surveys, for the dots in the narrative usually hidden from view that it connects with such detailed analysis, and for the questions that it raises about the future. Divisions and disputes, no matter how we choose to speak of them, are unlikely to disappear. In fact, this papacy seems to have also reversed previous Vatican attempts to shut down inconvenient discussions and pesky questions. Francis instead invites robust debate; he has said that no subjects are off the table and tolerates open disagreement at the highest levels of the hierarchy, claiming that out of such debate emerges the best pastoral theology.

The question is not whether we will debate with each other, but rather how we will conduct ourselves as a community amid the inevitable disagreements as we seek the truth and how to apply it in practical terms. Unity doesn't mean having the same answer in every circumstance, but rather agreement that we are propelled forward by an awareness of God's mercy and the insistent call to accompany the poor.

From the very first moment of his papacy, Pope Francis's language has been full of motion, of a sense of journey and change, always accompanied by his advice that we should never be afraid of failing. For U.S. Catholics interested in journeying with Francis into the future, this book is an excellent means for finding one's bearings.

Tom Roberts
Editor-at-large of the *National Catholic Reporter*
and author of *The Emerging Catholic Church:*
A Community's Search for Itself

PREFACE: WHY I WRITE

The headline jumping from my phone that early morning in February 2013 seemed implausible, or more likely pulled from *The Onion*—a satirical take on the scandals swirling around the Vatican. The pope resigned? I scratched away disbelief from bleary eyes. For Catholics around the world, and plenty of other observers and commentators outside the church, the next few weeks were heady days. Everyone from seasoned *vaticanisti*—experts who read the tea leaves inside the church's global epicenter—to armchair theologians and Catholics sipping coffee in the back of the parish hall had the upcoming papal conclave on their mind. When Cardinal Jorge Mario Bergoglio of Buenos Aires stepped out on to the balcony overlooking St. Peter's Square and greeted the world as Pope Francis, an unlikely revolution began that continues to shake up an ancient institution.

This story is personal for me.

I'm a cradle Catholic, writer, and social justice advocate. I've worked at a Catholic newspaper in Baltimore and the U.S. Conference of Catholic Bishops, and I now lead Catholic outreach at Faith in Public Life, an advocacy group in Washington. The sounds, smells, and symbols of the Roman Catholic Church are deep in my bones. As a kid, I was an altar boy. I walked the halls of Catholic schools from kindergarten through college, a passage of time marked by holy days of obligation and stark Lenten Masses. Nuns kept me on my toes. Jesuit priests in high school inspired me with daunting intellects and hearts on fire for justice. My faith is not only viewed through the mists of nostalgic memory. The beauty of the Catholic liturgy and the example of modern-day prophets who live out the Gospel in remote corners of the globe or just down the block also carve out prime real estate in my soul. At a time when one in ten Americans are now ex-Catholics—put together, the second largest "denomination" in the country—I never thought of leaving a faith tradition that comforts, challenges, frustrates, and inspires me (sometimes all in the same week). I'm anchored to a church whose teachings about human dignity, the sanctity of life, and the common good need to be heard more than ever. In a culture that deifies the market and makes an idol of individualism, my faith whispers in my ear reminding me of poverty, community, and solidarity.

When it comes to the intersection of faith and politics, I'm a progressive because of my Catholic faith. Lawmakers on Capitol Hill might not be able to get their act together to pass a modest increase in the minimum wage, but the Catholic Church has called for living wages that can support a family for more than a century now. Workers' rights are being rolled back in states across the country, and safety nets are shredded in the name of fiscal prudence. The *Compendium of the Social Doctrine of the Church* calls unions "indispensable," and I draw inspiration from my faith's emphasis on having a "preferential option for the poor." While some Americans and pandering politicians demonize immigrants and think higher walls are the solution, Catholic priests, sisters, and lay volunteers are on the front lines giving sanctuary to migrants and lobbying lawmakers to pass comprehensive immigration reform. As the stark gap between the wealthiest few and working families shapes up to be a front-burner issue in the 2016 presidential election, I'm grateful for a pope who has called inequality "the root of social evil" and raises timely questions about the moral dimensions of markets. However, the fact that Pope Francis has said, in his own words, that he's "never been a right-winger" does not make him a cheerleader for a conventional liberal agenda. Francis situates abortion as part of what he calls a "throwaway culture" that treats life in the womb, those on the economic margins, and the forgotten elderly as expendable. I'm grateful for a pope who challenges me and other Catholics across the political spectrum.

Even with the horrific clergy abuse scandals, the crass politicization of Communion in past U.S. elections, the Vatican's crackdown on American nuns, the heavy-handed policing of theologians, and the un-Christian way some Catholic schools have treated gay and lesbian teachers, many Catholic progressives who, like me, love our church refused to jump ship. We didn't pack it up and leave because, however flawed human institutions are destined to be, the best of Catholicism is worth the struggle. The election of Pope Francis signaled a refreshing new season for the church, full of hope and renewal. At once provocative and pastoral, Francis uses blunt language, vivid gestures, and even humor to remind us that the essence of faith is not a litany of prohibitions to be enforced by grim-faced watchdogs of orthodoxy. It's a living tradition made up of flawed human beings who imperfectly carry the joy of the Gospel into a messy world. Doctrine can't be reduced to ideology or simple checklists, the pope tells us, but is grounded in God's love and Jesus's radical message of good news for the poor.

The Francis papacy has been an unexpected gift in ways both spiritual and structural. While there has not been a stampede back to Sunday services, statistics or Mass attendance alone can't capture the intimate ways he is touching hearts and turning heads. "I'm telling you, brother, if you focus on the numbers, you're missing the story," a grizzled Boston pastor told a CNN reporter on the first anniversary of the pope's election. "There's an energy, a feeling, a spirit here. It's like a healing balm." This new moment also presents a unique opportunity to recast the role of the U.S. church in public life, where in recent years Catholic political debates have too often been narrowly framed and played out amid drearily predictable culture wars.

Even as a "Francis effect" begins to shift the power dynamics inside the church and has the potential to drive a better values debate in American politics, a well-oiled conservative Catholic movement in this country took more than three decades to build and won't fizzle easily. The leaders who shaped and continue to fuel this movement—a vocal minority of culture warrior bishops, like-minded Christian evangelicals, conservative intellectuals, and well-financed groups that act as the self-appointed watchdogs of orthodoxy—have forged a potent alliance that refashioned the church's public profile and engagement with politics. This remaking of the Catholic Church in the United States should not simply concern Catholics in the pews or academics. Since at least the 1960s, Catholics have been the largest denomination in Congress. Six of the nine U.S. Supreme Court justices are Catholic. One in six patients receives health care in a Catholic hospital. Nearly one in five voters are Catholic. While there is no monolithic Catholic voting bloc, presidential campaigns vie aggressively for Catholic swing voters in battleground states, and whoever does it the best usually ends up in the White House. Simply put, the Catholic footprint in U.S. culture and politics is wide and deep.

How did a church once known for laying the moral architecture that led to New Deal reforms and issuing widely covered national letters on economic justice and nuclear weapons in the 1980s earn a reputation—fair or not—for being perceived as "firmly on the Republican side in American politics," as a retired president of the U.S. bishops' conference warned in 2009? How did Catholic identity get reduced to a few hot-button issues? Why did the loudest voices drown out the sanity caucus? The first half of this book sets the stage for how the Francis papacy offers a particularly radical challenge to the church in this country, providing a historical overview of the major forces that influenced the church's posture in public life. In the second half, I examine how American bishops have been handed a rare opportunity to mirror the tone, style, and substance of Pope Francis in ways that could help untangle them from the culture wars and reclaim a broader moral agenda. I report on how the pope's call for a "poor church for the poor" is already found in faith-based community organizing in one of America's most challenged cities, analyze the potential for common ground between Catholic liberals and conservatives, and probe the ways a new generation of Catholic Millennials and Latinos might shape the future of the church.

A note about language is needed. I recognize that some readers may chafe at my use of "conservative" and "progressive" to describe certain individuals, organizations, and movements in the church. I share this tension. Labels by nature are problematic (if sometimes unavoidable) and often fail to convey nuance, especially within a Catholic context where the secular categories of left and right are frequently not well suited. "Liberal, conservative, moderate are words that describe factions in a polis, not members of a communion," the Jesuit magazine *America* stated in a 2013 editorial that drew attention for announcing a new policy of prohibiting those words in the publication "when referring to our fellow Catholics in an ecclesiastical context." There is much in this posture to admire and emulate. As someone who has been honored to write for that essential publication over the years, I appreciate the instinct for a journal edited by Catholic priests to transcend labels that surely can perpetuate division. Throughout this book, I do work hard to provide context, interview people who don't share my views, and go deeper than surface-level labels. I write not as a religious leader, priest, or academic theologian, but as an informed lay Catholic. In that context, I have made the choice to use these terms because labels, however incomplete, are not always without value in describing to a general readership outside the church the very real ways in which Catholics are divided over issues of theology, politics, religious identity, and the role of the church in the modern world.

To paraphrase F. Scott Fitzgerald, if holding two seemingly contradictory ideas in your mind without going crazy is one definition of genius, then perhaps it's possible to both lament how the toxic divisions playing out within the wider secular culture are mirrored in the church and not shy away from the real tensions that should be named. "Factionalism can indeed be a threat to the church (or to the country), but honest disagreement is not always destructive of ecclesial communion," the editors of *Commonweal*, a journal edited by lay Catholics, wrote in response to *America* magazine's new policy. "Nor does it do any good to pretend that the contemporary church is actually a community of harmony and virtue simply because ideally it should be. American Catholics belong to the church, but also to many other communities and organizations. They cannot, and should not, leave those attachments behind at the church door, nor should they regard their political commitments as peripheral to their Christian witness."

This is a crossroads moment for the Catholic Church in the United States. Will the example of Pope Francis and his key appointments in the American hierarchy usher in a new era for our nation's most influential religious institution? Will Catholics in the pews be energized to move beyond a kind of spectator-sport Catholicism—marveling from afar at the drama unfolding in Rome—to getting our hands dirty in building a better church in our own parishes and dioceses? It may take a decade to fully answer those questions. This book is my best, imperfect effort to offer a contribution to a subject that deserves further exploration by others in years to come.

John Gehring
Ad Majorem Dei Gloriam
Washington, DC, May 2015

I

THE FRANCIS REVOLUTION BEGINS

Hundreds of men file into a Baltimore hotel with the look of managers in town for the annual convention. Bleary-eyed from travel and huddled by coffee stations, they carry binders stuffed with agenda items and peck on iPhones inside the Hyatt Regency ballroom. Despite the familiar vibe, it's not your typical business meeting. This unusual fraternity of celibate men, wearing gold pectoral crosses and all dressed in black, represents the U.S. leadership of the world's most powerful religious institution. Just eight months earlier, the Catholic Church had been jolted by dramatic changes no one even in this room of clerical insiders would have predicted. The assembled bishops, spiritual shepherds charged with leading their flocks, could be forgiven if they seemed a bit whiplashed after the dizzying turn of events. An institution built on the rock of St. Peter now felt tempest tossed.

When Pope Benedict XVI resigned the papacy, breaking the news in Latin to a regularly scheduled meeting of cardinals gathered in the Sala del Concistoro inside the Apostolic Palace, many of the princes of the church were rusty enough in the ancient language or dozing off that they initially missed the bombshell drop. For the first time since the fifteenth century, a pope had done the unthinkable. "The single most revolutionary act committed by any pope in at least the last 600 years," wrote the veteran Vatican analyst John Allen. Facing a church bureaucracy known for turf wars and a media frenzy sparked by sensational leaks of secret papal documents that revealed a Vatican mired in dysfunction seemed too heavy a load for the slight shoulders of a shy, eighty-five-year-old theologian, who seven years earlier became pope after the death of the charismatic, globe-trotting John Paul II. Pope Benedict's resignation on February 11, 2013—rightly praised by many in subsequent days as a courageous act of humility—also cast an image of a wounded and weakened church. The lightning bolt that struck the dome of St. Peter's Basilica just hours after Benedict resigned offered a surreal backdrop for those raising existential questions about the church's future. Two conservative Catholic philosophers, writing in the French Catholic newspaper *La Croix*, called Benedict's resignation a "catastrophe," an act of "symbolic violence" that represented a "portrait of our time."[1]

"Veni, Sancte Spiritus!" the 115 scarlet-robed cardinals sang, summoning the Holy Spirit, as they entered the Sistine Chapel in March 2013 to elect a new pope. Two days later, Cardinal Jorge Mario Bergoglio of Buenos Aires, Argentina, became the 266th pope of the Roman Catholic Church. The first non-European pope in more than a millennium, the first from the Jesuit religious order, and the first to take the name Francis after the beloved saint of the poor, the new pontiff greeted hundreds of thousands gathered in St. Peter's Square with a simple "Buona sera!" (Good evening!) He then broke with custom for the first of soon-to-be-many diversions from church protocol. Looking out at the crowd, he made an unusual request: "Before the bishop blesses the people, I ask that you would pray to the Lord to bless me—the prayer of the people for their bishop. Let us say this prayer—your prayer for me—in silence."

The pope bowing to receive a blessing from the sea of hushed humanity below instantly became an iconic image. Captured on magazine covers and in newspapers around the world, a simple gesture, this literal posture of humility and symbolic inversion of power, set an immediate tone. Referring to himself as the "bishop of Rome" also sent a clear signal. A pope has a number of daunting titles at his disposal—"Vicar of Christ," "Successor of the Prince of the Apostles," "Supreme Pontiff of the Universal Church." Francis instead chose to ground himself in his pastoral role to the diocese of Rome. As the first Holy Father to take the name Francis, in honor of the thirteenth-century mendicant saint who was said to have received a direct message from God—"Francis, rebuild my church"—the pope explained in his first address to the media that he was inspired by what he called "the man of peace, the man of poverty, the man who loves and protects creation." Pope Francis then put a distinctive stamp on his papacy: "How I would love a church that is poor and for the poor!"[2]

In the most visible sign that a new era was dawning, Pope Francis broke with centuries of tradition a few days later when he declined to move into the Apostolic Palace. The leader of more than a billion Catholics around the world made his permanent residence a simply furnished room in the Vatican guesthouse where he and other cardinals resided during the papal election. "I need to live among people," he told an audience of Italian and Albanian schoolchildren a few days after making the decision. "If I was living alone, isolated, it would not be good for me."[3] The media quickly dubbed Francis "the cold-call" pope after he canceled his own newspaper subscription in Buenos Aires, phoned a pregnant Italian woman whose fiancé wanted her to have an abortion, and encouraged an engineering student who wrote to him about his fears of not finding work. On Holy Thursday, when the church commemorates the initiation of the priesthood with Jesus washing the feet of his disciples at the Last Supper before his Passion, the pope bucked tradition again. Instead of celebrating Mass at a Roman basilica and only washing the feet of priests as popes through the ages have done, Francis visited a juvenile detention center. He knelt down to clean the feet of inmates, including those of two Muslim women. It was the first time a pope had ever washed the feet of a woman in a Holy Thursday ceremony. Some traditionalists were scandalized. There would be more unconventional acts over the next two years that signaled a papacy stripped of pretense and grounded in servant leadership. Francis ordered showers to be installed in St. Peter's Square for the homeless and welcomed them to join him for breakfast on his birthday. He arranged a private tour of the Sistine Chapel for those who sleep in the streets around the Vatican. Greeting each of his guests individually, the most influential religious leader in the world played the unassuming role of hospitable tour guide: "This is everyone's house, this is your home," he told them. "The doors are always open for all."[4]

The world watches transfixed by these unexpected, poignant gestures. Some skeptics wonder if it is all just a polished public relations campaign. A master of conveying substance with symbols, Francis is surely aware that images matter, and he uses a global pulpit to skillful effect. But this is no mere smoke-and-mirrors show. For Jorge Mario Bergoglio, it's a way of life now projected on a far bigger stage. As cardinal of Buenos Aires, he earned a reputation as "the bishop of the slums" for his familiar presence in the *villas miserias*. As Paul Vallely chronicles in his book, *Pope Francis: Untying the Knots*, Bergoglio would show up unannounced to drink a traditional *mate* with people in the streets and deliver fearless homilies aimed at the drug dealers who ravaged neighborhoods. He lived in a modest apartment instead of a mansion reserved for the archbishop, cooked his own meals, and rode the bus. Bergoglio washed the feet of AIDS patients and drug addicts. The common touch is no act. When he departed Buenos Aires to attend the conclave of cardinals that would choose him as the next pope, Bergoglio ditched the polished new shoes his staff bought him to replace the scruffy pair on his feet. He left the new ones behind, along with a first-class ticket the Vatican sent for his trip. Jorge Mario Bergoglio would make the thirteen-hour flight to Rome in coach wearing the same fraying shoes that had carried him through the slums.[5]

Less than a year into his papacy, Pope Francis had already emerged as an unlikely global rock star—a spiritual troublemaker with a disarming style. In a riveting interview with his fellow Jesuit, the Rev. Antonio Spadaro of *La Civilta Cattolica*, an influential Rome-based journal, the pope quickly proved eager to shake up old ways of doing business and made headlines around the world.

> We cannot insist only on issues related to abortion, gay marriage and the use of contraceptive methods. This is not possible. I have not spoken much about these things, and I was reprimanded for that. But when we speak about these issues, we have to talk about them in a context. The teaching of the church, for that matter, is clear and I am a son of the church, but it is not necessary to talk about these issues all the time.
>
> The church's pastoral ministry cannot be obsessed with the transmission of a disjointed multitude of doctrines to be imposed insistently. We have to find a new balance; otherwise even the moral edifice of the Church is likely to fall like a house of cards, losing the freshness and fragrance of the Gospel.[6]

In the interview, published in Jesuit journals around the world, including *America* magazine in the United States, Francis took aim at a type of fortress Catholicism that guards institutional priorities above all else. "The church sometimes has locked itself up in small things, in small-minded rules," the pope said bluntly. Doctrine must never be divorced from engaging with the messiness of humanity and preaching the mercy of God, Francis insisted. "Those who today always look for disciplinarian solutions, those who long for an exaggerated doctrinal security, those who stubbornly try to recover a past that no longer exists—they have a static and inward-directed view of things," he said. [7]

While some Catholic liberals and media commentators draw too stark a contrast between Pope Francis and his immediate predecessor, it is difficult to imagine those words coming from Pope Benedict XVI. Before Cardinal Joseph Ratzinger became pope in 2005, he spent twenty-four years as prefect of the Vatican's powerful Congregation for the Doctrine of the Faith, the onetime office of the Inquisition. His role as chief guardian of doctrine—"God's Rotweiller," the media ungenerously branded him—shaped a narrative about Ratzinger long before he even became a pope who decried the "dictatorship of relativism" and sometimes gave the impression that he envisioned a smaller, "purer" church. [8] As pope, Benedict wrote a luminous encyclical about God's love, spoke powerfully about the church's commitment to social justice, and sat for engaging book-length interviews that showcased a brilliant intellect. For some Catholic conservatives, Benedict was never as hardline as they hoped for, even as some Catholic liberals experienced relief that he never lived up to their worst fears. Nevertheless, the man who worried that the reforms of the Second Vatican Council (1962–1965) that he supported as a young theologian had been too broadly misinterpreted as a rupture with church tradition, and who later spent decades policing orthodoxy, did see a church under siege from a hostile secular culture. Pope Francis shares many of these concerns, but he places a greater emphasis on mercy, joy, and engaging the broader culture. He insists that "the church is not a tollhouse; it is the house of the Father, where there is a place for everyone, with all their problems."

> I see clearly that the thing the church needs most today is the ability to heal wounds and to warm the hearts of the faithful; it needs nearness, proximity. I see the church as a field hospital after battle. It is useless to ask a seriously injured person if he has high cholesterol and about the level of his blood sugars! You have to heal his wounds. Then we can talk about everything else. Heal the wounds, heal the wounds. And you have to start from the ground up. [9]

Starting from the peripheries, Francis is not afraid to court those who have left the Catholic Church—including the nearly one in ten Americans who are former Catholics. [10] "Instead of being just a church that welcomes and receives by keeping the doors open, let us try also to be a church that finds new roads, that is able to step outside itself and go to those who do not attend Mass, to those who have quit or are indifferent," he said. "The ones who quit sometimes do it for reasons that, if properly understood and assessed, can lead to a return. But that takes audacity and courage." [11] His message to bishops is equally direct. Francis told papal nuncios from around the world, whose job includes nominating future bishops, that the hierarchy should "not have the psychology of princes." Bishops must be so "close to the people" that they have the "smell of the sheep." [12]

During his first overseas trip to Brazil, Pope Francis encouraged young Catholics gathered for World Youth Day to go back to their parishes and "make a mess" by challenging the status quo. "I want you to make yourselves heard in your dioceses," he said. "I want the church to go out onto the streets. I want us to resist everything worldly, everything static, everything comfortable, everything to do with clericalism." [13] A crowd estimated at more than one million packed Copacabana Beach for the closing Mass of World Youth Day. "The Gospel is for everyone, not just for some," the pope said in his final homily in Brazil. "It is not only for those who seem closer to us, more receptive, more welcoming. It is for everyone." On the flight back to Rome, the pope spoke to reporters and again made headlines by striking a tone different from previous popes and other Christian leaders when it comes to homosexuality. "If someone is gay and he searches for the Lord and has good will, who am I to judge?" Francis said as stunned reporters rushed copy to editors. His answer came in response to a question about an alleged "gay lobby" of Vatican priests referenced in documents leaked near the close of Benedict's papacy. While Pope Francis was echoing church teaching straight from the Catechism—some breathless pundits and fawning media took liberties to recruit the pope as a gay rights activist—his tantalizing sound bite was befitting a spiritual leader decisively reorienting the church toward pastoral leadership and the radical inclusion of the Gospel.

A BRAVE NEW WORLD

This was the brave new world that more than three hundred U.S. Catholic bishops found themselves suddenly thrust into as they met in Baltimore in the fall of 2013 for the first time as a group since the groundbreaking papal election eight months earlier. National media were in town to see if the "Francis effect" would impact the direction of an American hierarchy that in recent years had prioritized fights against same-sex marriage and contraception coverage in President Obama's signature health care reform law. The formal agenda did not inspire hope. Bishops heard a proposal to develop a statement expressing their opposition to pornography, received a briefing about their advocacy against same-sex marriage, and discussed an ongoing religious liberty campaign. No formal discussions about unemployment, income inequality, poverty, growing attacks on workers' rights, or grave threats to the environment were on the docket, despite the robust Catholic social tradition on these moral issues and the clear signals coming from Rome. It was business as usual taking place against the backdrop of a papacy redefining the Catholic narrative. The memo never made it to Baltimore.

One bishop did try to lay down a marker in advance of the meeting. In *America* magazine, San Francisco auxiliary Bishop Robert McElroy, whom Pope Francis would appoint two years later to lead the Diocese of San Diego, challenged his fellow bishops to wake up to the new reality. "Both the substance and methodology of Pope Francis' teachings on the rights of the poor have enormous implications for the culture and politics of the United States and for the church in this country," he wrote. "These teachings demand a transformation of the existing Catholic political conversation in our nation."[14] Speaking to *Vatican Insider*, McElroy offered a more direct assessment: "In recent years, the conference of bishops has labeled abortion and euthanasia as the preeminent issues in the political order, but not poverty. This had the effect of downgrading the perceived importance of poverty as a central focus for the Church's witness."[15]

While McElroy is not a lone wolf among bishops in his desire to revive the church's social justice voice and to chart a broader moral agenda, in recent years moderates and the few progressives in the hierarchy have found themselves elbowed aside by a vocal minority of culture warriors. Gathered in Baltimore along with McElroy that day were many representatives of that wing, such as Bishop Thomas Tobin of Providence, who in his diocesan newspaper had openly wondered why the pope wasn't speaking up more about abortion.

> I'm a little bit disappointed in Pope Francis that he hasn't, at least that I'm aware of, said much about unborn children, about abortion, and many people have noticed that. . . . It's one thing for him to reach out and embrace and kiss little children and infants as he has on many occasions. It strikes me that it would also be wonderful if in a spiritual way he would reach out and embrace and kiss unborn children.[16]

Tobin, who made headlines just a month earlier for publicly switching his party affiliation and becoming a registered Republican, also expressed discomfort over what he called "the unintended consequences" of the pope's "freewheeling style" and "off-the-cuff-comments."[17]

Days after the Catholic bishops' national meeting, Bishop Thomas Paprocki of Springfield, Illinois, celebrated a public exorcism to protest the state's Catholic governor signing a civil same-sex marriage bill into law. In the Cathedral of the Immaculate Conception, not far from the Illinois state capitol, Paprocki presided over what was formally billed as "Prayers in Supplication and Exorcism in Reparation for the Sin of Same-Sex Marriage." "I exorcise you, every unclean spirit, every power of darkness, every incursion of the infernal enemy, every diabolical legion, cohort, and faction, in the name and power of our Lord Jesus Christ," the bishop intoned from the pulpit.[18] Paprocki was one of three U.S. bishops appointed by the Vatican under Pope Benedict XVI to monitor the Leadership Conference of Women Religious, the umbrella organization representing most American nuns, after the Vatican's doctrine office issued a scathing 2012 report charging the nuns showed "certain radical feminist themes incompatible with the Catholic faith."

One wondered what Archbishop John Myers of Newark thought of the pope's refreshing vision for the church and his austere habits. As Pope Francis drew praise for refusing to move into the Apostolic Palace, Myers would soon face public backlash for his plans to make $500,000 in luxury renovations to a five-bedroom, three-car garage mansion he was preparing for his retirement residence on eight acres of land.[19] Bishop Robert Morlino of Madison, Wisconsin, also seemed cut from different clerical cloth than Francis. "I want the Lord to stir up the gifts of the Holy Spirit to fight the culture war," Morlino has said.[20]

The bishop deemed the popular Catholic hymn "All Are Welcome" inappropriate for use during Mass. "There's a sense that all are welcome, but I would submit that means, in fact, political liberals are especially welcome. And when a congregation is singing that song and meaning it like that, I don't think that's healthy for their salvation."[21]

Archbishop Charles Chaput of Philadelphia also mingled with his fellow bishops in Baltimore. An erudite thinker who writes thoughtful books about the role of faith in American democracy, he is regarded as an intellectual leader of conservative elements in the church. He is also no stranger to mixing it up in the political arena. In the 2004 presidential election, Chaput emerged as one of a small cadre of bishops who argued that a candidate's position on abortion trumps all other issues for Catholic voters. An outspoken proponent of denying Communion to Catholic politicians that don't support the criminalization of abortion, Chaput publicly scolded some Catholic social justice organizations and Catholic Obama supporters, including former Reagan-era official and pro-life advocate Douglas Kmiec, during the 2008 presidential elections. Chaput charged them with having done a "disservice to the church, confused the natural priorities of Catholic social teaching, undermined the progress pro-lifers have made, and provided an excuse for some Catholics to abandon the abortion issue instead of fighting within their parties and at the ballot box to protect the unborn."[22] Citing the need to uphold "the teachings of Jesus Christ," Chaput once defended a pastor in his diocese who refused to enroll two girls, ages five and three, in a Denver Catholic school after it became known their parents were lesbians. "Jesus did turn people away," the pastor argued, a statement never challenged by Archbishop Chaput, who instead assured Catholics that archdiocesan policy was followed.[23] A few months before the bishops' national meeting, Chaput acknowledged in an interview with the *National Catholic Reporter* that what he called "the right wing of the church . . . generally ha[s] not been really happy about his [Francis's] election."[24]

The angst caused by Pope Francis was not limited to some bishops who seemed more content to hunker down secure in their old ways than to hit the reset button. The editor of *First Things*, a conservative Catholic journal founded by the late Rev. Richard John Neuhaus, charged in an editorial that the pope's "naïve" and "undisciplined" rhetoric had been "used to beat up on faithful Catholics."[25] Germain Grisez, one of the most influential conservative theologians of the last fifty years, did not soft-peddle his complaint. Francis, he wrote, is "letting loose with his thoughts in a world that will applaud being provided with such help in subverting the truth it is his job to guard as inviolable and proclaim with fidelity." Grisez described Francis as "self-indulgent enough to take advantage of the opportunity with as little care as he might unburden himself with friends after a good dinner and plenty of wine."[26]

Some Catholic liturgical traditionalists, who favor the pre–Vatican II Latin Mass and saw Pope Benedict as a champion of their battles against the modernizing reforms of the Second Vatican Council, quickly expressed hostility toward Francis. "Of all the unthinkable candidates, Jorge Mario Bergoglio is perhaps the worst. . . . It really cannot be what Benedict wanted for the church," an Argentine wrote in a post at *Rorate Caeli*, a blog popular with Latin Mass enthusiasts. "Something is profoundly wrong when the winds of change can blow so swiftly through an immutable institution of God's own making," wrote a disgruntled American Catholic at *Creative Minority Report*, a conservative Catholic blog.[27]

Even longtime church observers cheering for Francis were floored by the unexpected signals being sent by the pope. Thomas Reese, a Jesuit priest and political scientist who has written extensively about the Vatican and U.S. Catholic bishops, once raised conservative eyebrows as editor of the Jesuit magazine *America* for publishing diverse theological perspectives on hot-button issues. In 2005, he was effectively pushed out as editor when Cardinal Joseph Ratzinger (later elected Pope Benedict XVI) made it known to Reese's Jesuit superiors in Rome that he should go.[28] "When I read Pope Francis's interview in *America* I had to laugh," Reese confesses. "If I had said what he was saying when I was editor I would have been fired quicker than I was! This pope invites debate and conversation." Sister Carol Keehan, the CEO of the Catholic Health Association, could hardly believe what she was seeing. "If you wrote this story about Pope Francis as a novel," she quipped, "you wouldn't be able to get it past a junior editor."

A BLUEPRINT AND A CHALLENGE

Just two months after his blockbuster interview with *America* magazine, Pope Francis released *The Joy of the Gospel*, a 142-page apostolic exhortation setting out his vision for the church. A document both profound in the depth of its spiritual insights and timely in its bold critique of economic inequality, the exhortation is a blueprint for the Francis papacy. It presents a challenging agenda for Catholic leaders in the United States and around the world:

> I prefer a Church which is bruised, hurting and dirty because it has been out on the streets, rather than a Church which is unhealthy from being confined and from clinging to its own security. I do not want a Church concerned with being at the center and then ends by being caught up in a web of obsessions and procedures. More than by fear of going astray, my hope is that we will be moved by the fear of remaining shut up within structures which give us a false sense of security, within rules which make us harsh judges, within habits which make us feel safe, while at our door people are starving and Jesus does not tire of saying to us, "Give them something to eat."[29]

The exhortation's searing assessment of unfettered capitalism, while in line with traditional Catholic social teaching, was delivered with a particular punch that landed squarely in the middle of U.S. political debates over growing inequality. Francis blasted the "idolatry of money" and warned that "an economy of exclusion and inequality" was undermining human dignity and respect for the sanctity of life. "Such an economy kills," the pope wrote.

> Some people continue to defend trickle-down theories, which assume that economic growth, encouraged by a free market, will inevitably succeed in bringing about greater justice and inclusiveness in the world. This opinion, which has never been confirmed by the facts, expresses a crude and naïve trust in the goodness of those wielding economic power and in the sacralized workings of the prevailing economic system. Meanwhile, the excluded are still waiting.
>
> As long as the problems of the poor are not radically resolved by rejecting the absolute autonomy of markets and financial speculation and by attacking the structural causes of inequality, no solution will be found for the world's problems or, for that matter, to any problems.

Conservatives in the United States erupted in outrage and condescending dismissals. "That's Marxism!" raged Rush Limbaugh. John Moody, executive editor of Fox News, railed that the pope "grievously exceeded his authority" and became "a robe-wearing politician." Francis should "stick to doctrine," Moody argued.[30] Fr. John Zuhlsdorf, a prominent conservative Catholic blogger, accused the pope of being "naïve" and "out of step with history."[31] Rep. Paul Ryan of Wisconsin, a prominent Catholic who has sometimes explained his policy ideas in the context of Catholic teaching, charged that the pope was simply ignorant of economic realities. "The guy is from Argentina, they haven't had real capitalism in Argentina," the 2012 Republican vice presidential nominee told the *Milwaukee Journal Sentinel*.[32]

Ken Langone, the billionaire cofounder of Home Depot who spearheaded a $180 million restoration of St. Patrick's Cathedral, was so miffed by the pope's words that he sought out Cardinal Timothy Dolan of New York. Langone explained to the cardinal that one of his wealthy friends was so upset by Francis's remarks that he was considering pocketing a donation for the renovation of the famed cathedral on Fifth Avenue. Cardinal Dolan told CNBC, a cable business news network, that he would assure the reluctant donor that he was "misunderstanding" Francis. "The pope loves poor people, he also loves rich people," the cardinal said in what came across as an awkward effort to soften the pope's pointed words.[33] Dolan later wrote an op-ed for the *Wall Street Journal*, "The Pope's Case for Virtuous Capitalism," offering a much sunnier assessment than Pope Francis.[34]

"Fortunately, few people subscribe to an inhumane philosophy of radical economic individualism," wrote a cardinal whose headquarters are not far from the offices of Wall Street banks and hedge fund managers whose greedy financial schemes played a role in the global financial crisis. When Larry Kudlow, a free-market cheerleader and CNBC commentator, tweeted that he had helped Cardinal Dolan with the op-ed, the optics were bad, to say the least. In an earlier interview with CNBC, Kudlow praised Pope John Paul II for having a "much more market friendly approach" and insinuating that Pope Francis's views on markets were flawed because of his experiences with capitalism as "state-run facism" and "cronyism" in Argentina.[35]

If Catholic bishops gathered in Baltimore for their national assembly had any doubts the status quo was no longer acceptable, the pope's apostolic nuncio to the United States made the case plain. "There has to be a noticeable lifestyle characterized by simplicity and holiness of life," Archbishop Carlo Maria Vigano told the gathered bishops. "The Holy

Father wants bishops in tune with their people . . . he wants pastoral bishops, not bishops who profess or follow a particular ideology."[36]

Indianapolis archbishop Joseph Tobin, who until 2010 served as the number two official at the Vatican congregation responsible for men's and women's religious orders around the world, gave voice to the discomforting questions many were asking when he spoke at a 2014 meeting of the College Theology Society:

> What I've seen is how disruptive Pope Francis has been within the hierarchy of the United States. I was talking to a couple of brother bishops a while back and they were saying that bishops and priests were very discouraged by Pope Francis because he was challenging them. I think there was a particular image, perhaps, of what it means to be a pastoral leader in this country, and Francis is disturbing it. I think there is some resistance to a different way of doing the Gospel mission of the church. . . . So, pray for Francis' health![37]

RADICAL SPIRITUAL RENEWAL AND INSTITUTIONAL REFORM

The Francis revolution, a radical spiritual renewal set out to more deeply root all aspects of ecclesial life in the soil of the Gospel and eradicate the virus of clericalism, is about more than a new style and tone. The pope's institutional reforms are intended to fundamentally reshape a Vatican culture that often resembles a self-serving Renaissance court. "Heads of the Church have often been narcissists, flattered and thrilled by their courtiers," the pope has said. "The court is the leprosy of the papacy. . . . This Vatican-centric view neglects the world around us. I will do everything I can to change it."[38] In an unprecedented move, Francis appointed a council of eight cardinals, dubbed the Gang of Eight by the media, to help him reform church governance. The idea came from cardinals themselves during prepapal election meetings know as General Congregations. (The council has since grown to nine cardinals.) Francis has criticized an "excessive centralization" and called for "a conversion of the papacy." He is looking outside of Rome for fresh perspectives. Only one of the cardinals on his advisory council is a Vatican official.

The first slate of new cardinals appointed by Francis in February 2014 also reflected his focus on the global South, where the new geopolitical heart of Catholicism is beating most strongly. Becoming a cardinal, Pope Francis told the nineteen men receiving the scarlet red biretta, "does not signify a promotion, an honor nor a decoration: it is simply a service that demands a broader vision and a bigger heart."[39] Francis reminded them to walk "the way of lowliness and of humility, taking the form of a servant." Among those named cardinals were bishops from Haiti and Burkina Faso, two of the poorest countries in the world. A year later, in 2015, Francis named twenty new cardinals, including appointing the first cardinals in history from Ethiopia, Myanmar, and Tongo. For the first time, there are now more non-European cardinals in the College of Cardinals than those from European ancestry.

The pope is continuing with efforts, started by Pope Emeritus Benedict XVI, to reform the scandal-ridden Vatican bank, formally the Institute for the Works of Religion (IOR). He has removed top officials in an effort to address allegations of money laundering, and the bank is now moving in line with international financial transparency standards. In a sign of progress, the Vatican and Italy reached an agreement to share financial and tax information, a move intended to crack down on corruption.

When it comes to the clergy sexual abuse crisis, Francis has established a special commission led by Boston cardinal Sean O'Malley that includes two survivors of clergy abuse, church officials, and experts in child protection. The panel has representation from every continent and is tasked with drafting recommendations for the pope, including policies to hold bishops who have shielded priests suspected of misconduct accountable. A major breakthrough came in the spring of 2015, when Pope Francis accepted the resignation of Bishop Robert Finn, who led the diocese of Kansas City–St. Joseph in Missouri. Finn was the first U.S. bishop to be convicted in criminal court for failing to report a former diocesan priest who was in possession of child pornography. Finn remained on the job for two and a half years after his 2012 conviction, a source of outrage for clergy abuse survivors and many American Catholics incensed that someone who would be prohibited from teaching Sunday school because he could not pass a background check was still a sitting bishop. Less than two months after Bishop Finn's departure, the Vatican also accepted the resignation of Archbishop John Nienstedt of Minneapolis–St. Paul, a diocese that faced criminal charges for its failure to protect children. And in June 2015, the Vatican took the most significant step to date in addressing the institutional nature of the clergy abuse crisis when Pope Francis approved the creation of a tribunal that will judge bishops accused of covering up or failing to act in the case of abuse from a priest.

NEW APPOINTMENTS, SHIFTING PRIORITIES

The balance of power inside the Vatican is shifting. Prominent cardinals who represented the most vocal conservative wing of the church in the United States once wielded considerable influence at the Vatican under Pope John Paul II and Pope Benedict XVI. Because of a major reshuffling under Pope Francis, this is no longer the case. Two American cardinals who sat on the all-important Congregation for Bishops, the thirty-plus-member Vatican committee that nominates new candidates for the episcopacy, are now gone. Despite an eight-year tenure in Philadelphia marred by grand jury investigations that exposed a culture of protecting abusive priests, Cardinal Justin Rigali—a longtime Vatican insider—maintained influence in Rome after his 2011 retirement and sat on several powerful congregations. His seat on the congregation that nominates bishops gave him a key role in shaping the American hierarchy. At the end of 2013, Pope Francis removed the former Vatican diplomat and onetime English-language translator for Pope John Paul II from that post.

While Rigali's departure was not surprising, given his impending eightieth birthday, the pope also removed the far younger Cardinal Raymond Burke, a former archbishop of St. Louis, from the Congregation for Bishops. The quintessential culture warrior, Burke supported denying Communion to pro-choice Catholic John Kerry in the 2004 presidential elections and has a penchant for head-turning liturgical vestments. He is one of the few cardinals in the world who still wears the *cappa magna*, a billowing train of silk that sends a decidedly regal message. Pope Benedict XVI brought Burke from St. Louis to Rome in 2008 and named him the prefect of the Vatican's highest court. Pope Francis removed Burke from that post and also from his seat on the influential bishops' congregation. He now has a largely ceremonial role as the patron of the Order of the Knights of Malta.

In another sign that personnel is policy, Francis replaced Burke on the bishops' congregation with Cardinal Donald Wuerl of the Archdiocese of Washington, widely regarded for his pastoral style more in line with that of Francis. As the leader of a high-profile diocese in the nation's political nerve center, he has rejected calls to deny Communion to pro-choice Catholic politicians and is a bridge builder between squabbling church factions. The most influential American church leader in Rome these days is Cardinal O'Malley of Boston, who, along with being the only American on the pope's select council tasked with reforming church governance, also leads the pope's clergy abuse watchdog commission. Known for dressing in a simple brown cassock and sandals, O'Malley is a heavyweight in American pro-life circles, and, like Francis, he has emphasized a broader pro-life ethic that includes respect for immigrants and economic justice. His predecessor in Boston, Cardinal Bernard Law, was forced to resign in 2002 after his widely criticized role in transferring pedophile priests. Law's departure from Boston did not mean the end of his influence. Sent to the Vatican, the cardinal was named the archpriest of St. Mary Major, considered to be one of the four most important basilicas in the world, and he continued to sit on several key Vatican congregations. Law reportedly was a leading voice in Rome pushing for the investigation of the main umbrella group for Catholic sisters in the United States.[40] The tense standoff between the nuns and the Vatican's doctrine office, which included a searing 2012 assessment that the sisters promoted "radical feminist themes" and didn't speak up loudly enough on abortion and same-sex marriage, led to the Vatican appointing a troika of American bishops to oversee the Leadership Conference of Women Religious. The controversial three-year crackdown ended with a whimper in the spring of 2015, with the Vatican praising the sisters for their work. Pope Francis met personally with the leadership of the nuns' group, and the sisters thanked the new pope for his "expression of appreciation for the witness given by Catholic sisters through our lives and ministry."[41]

The Francis papacy has also marked a swift rehabilitation of liberation theology.

Long held in suspicion during the pontificate of John Paul II, the movement coalesced during the 1970s and 1980s in Latin America as a response to the violence, inequality, and glaring social disparities in the region. John Paul, who came of age behind the Iron Curtain, viewed liberation theology as mixing dangerously with Marxist views. A 1984 document from the pope's doctrine chief, later Pope Benedict XVI, denounced it as "a perversion of the Christian message as God entrusted to His church."[42] During his papacy, liberation theologians were often investigated and censured for their writing and speaking. The Vatican's semiofficial newspaper, *L'Osservatore Romano*, now argues that with the first pope from Latin America, liberation theology can no longer "remain in the shadows to which it has been relegated for some years."[43]

The chief doctrine official at the Vatican, German cardinal Gerhard Müeller, praises liberation theology as "one of the most significant currents of Catholic theology of the 20th century."[44] Müeller spent years teaching theology to the poor in Peru, where he became friends with the Dominican priest and theologian Gustavo Gutiérrez, regarded as the father of liberation theology. Gutiérrez's classic 1971 work, *A Theology of Liberation: History, Politics, Salvation*, emphasized what he called "a preferential option for the poor," a focus clearly in line with Pope Francis's priorities.

When Archbishop Oscar Romero of El Salvador was gunned down while saying Mass in 1980, a day after delivering a sermon urging soldiers in his country to stop rampant human rights abuses, his assassination drew international attention. While Romero did not formally identify with liberation theology, his in-the-streets solidarity with those oppressed by the country's right-wing military and the archbishop's increasingly activist stance against the government made him a hero in the eyes of many Salvadorans. It also raised concerns in Rome that the church was mingling too closely with leftist political movements. For decades after his slaying, Romero's sainthood cause never moved forward even as John Paul II presided over a historic number of beatifications and canonizations. Pope Francis bluntly told reporters that in years past Vatican officials had stymied Romero's path toward official sainthood. He declared Romero a martyr of the faith in the winter of 2015, and a few months later the archbishop was beatified—the last step before sainthood—at an outdoor Mass in San Salvador.

Robert Mickens, a longtime Vatican observer based in Rome and editor of *Global Pulse* magazine, said the new mood has made the old guard deeply anxious. "There is a sense that they are just waiting for this pontificate to end and hoping the next pope will put things right," he said. "The conservatives also want things to drag on so the real reform, which is all about governance—synodality, episcopal collegiality and decentralization—does not come to fruition."

High-level Vatican shakeups, and the pope's future appointment of bishops in the United States, will ultimately form the slow work of refashioning the church. The unofficial beginning of a "Francis era" in the United States took shape with the pope's signature appointment of Bishop Blase Cupich as the Archbishop of Chicago in September 2014. Cupich led the small dioceses of Rapid City, South Dakota, and later Spokane, Washington, as a soft-spoken bishop with an aversion to culture war rhetoric and a focus on the poor and immigrants. His unexpected transfer to the third-largest archdiocese in the country with a storied history instantly elevated Cupich's profile and upended the power dynamics of the American church. Change is not likely to come quickly. Currently, of the 270 active bishops in the United States, Pope John Paul II and Pope Benedict XVI appointed 232 of them. At seventy-eight, Pope Francis is not expected to have the nearly three decades that Pope John Paul II had to shape the church with leaders who reflected his tone and priorities.

Massimo Faggioli is a Vatican analyst who has lectured widely in Europe and the United States. A generation of bishops, priests, and lay faithful in this country, he believes, are accustomed to a model of church leadership different from the kind Pope Francis imagines. The professor of theology at the University of St. Thomas in St. Paul, Minnesota, says the paradigm shift in part has to do with the pope's Latin American perspective, which grounds his approach in the need to accompany those living on the existential and economic margins. "It's impossible to understand Francis apart from this Latin American context," said Faggioli, the author of *Pope Francis: Tradition in Transition*. "You have to draw the picture upside down compared to how the European or U.S. church approach issues."

The U.S hierarchy will face a particular challenge because bishops here preside over a large, wealthy, and influential church that in recent years has been at the center of culture war battles in the political arena in a way not generally experienced in Europe. "There is no question U.S. bishops are the most difficult team Francis has to work with now," Faggioli observed. "Sociologically and culturally they are in a different place than how this pope sees the church."

To understand the challenge Pope Francis faces in America, one has to meet the architects who helped build a culture warrior church.

2

THE MAKING OF A CULTURE
WARRIOR CHURCH

In recent decades before the election of Pope Francis, a vocal minority of bishops, conservative intellectuals, and culture warriors wielded disproportionate influence in shaping the political voice of Catholicism in the United States. This is a story more than four decades in the making and includes a landmark U.S. Supreme Court ruling on abortion, the towering papacy of John Paul II, seismic cultural shifts in support for gay rights, and a new generation that rose to power at the U.S. bishops' national headquarters in Washington. Along the way, activist Catholics on the right funded think tanks, partnered with conservative evangelicals, and built influential networks that brought together church leaders, Republican politicians, and wealthy philanthropists in common cause. In stark contrast, progressives in the post–civil rights era often mistakenly conceded faith-based advocacy and values debates to a politicized Christian conservative movement that damaged the brand of religion in the public square. The Catholic Church in the United States found itself squeezed between the religious right and an increasingly secular-minded liberalism less comfortable with prophetic, Judeo-Christian justice claims that had animated earlier progressive movements.

During the thirty-five years that Pope John Paul II and Pope Benedict XVI led the Catholic Church, influential American Catholics baptized the Iraq War, made an idol of unfettered markets, and narrowed Catholic identity to a checklist that aligned neatly with the Republican Party. Quick to challenge a U.S. bishops' conference they perceived as too liberal and enjoying access at the top levels of the Vatican under the papacy of John Paul II, Catholic neoconservatives with intellectual chops and culture warriors with sharp elbows rose to prominence.

Riding the success of his 1999 biography of Pope John Paul II, George Weigel became a frequent commentator on Catholic issues in the mainstream media. His cheerleading for the invasion of Iraq found Weigel extolling the "charism of political discernment" that the Bush White House seemingly possessed. This charism—a particular gift of the Holy Spirit—was "not shared by bishops, stated clerks, rabbis, imams, or ecumenical and interreligious agencies," Weigel wrote in an audacious effort to diminish the voices of diverse religious leaders opposed to the war— including Pope John Paul II.[1] The senior fellow and Catholic studies chair at the Ethics and Public Policy Center in Washington offered his own distinctive Catholic stamp of approval on the doctrine of preventative war. The U.S. bishops' conference and other critics of invasion were complicit in what he called a "pattern of just war forgetfulness."

A week before the 2004 presidential election, Weigel extolled the Republican Party as "a more secure platform from which Catholics can work on the great issues of the day."[2] After Pope Benedict XVI released a 2009 encyclical that denounced the "scandal of glaring inequalities" and included passages about the prudent oversight of global markets that did not sit well with laissez faire economic dogma, Weigel knowingly assured us that the pope did not really believe what he said but "had to try and accommodate" the curial officials in the Pontifical Council for Justice and Peace who wanted them in the text. Weigel even offered his own helpful tutorial in navigating the encyclical. The discerning reader, he suggested, could underline in gold pen the passages that were Benedict's own and mark in red the offending parts forced on him by those lefty radicals in the Justice and Peace office.[3]

When several Catholic bishops, including Cardinal Sean O'Malley of Boston, celebrated Mass at the U.S.-Mexico border in 2014 to honor migrants who have died crossing the desert, the images of bishops distributing Communion through the slats in the fence offered a moving visual witness to a universal church that transcends any human boundaries. Weigel criticized the Mass as "an act of essentially political theater."[4] In contrast, there were no reservations aired from Weigel when the bishops' conference kicked off and ended their religious liberty "Fortnight for Freedom" campaign, sparked by debates over contraception coverage provisions in the federal health care reform law, with two high-profile televised Masses in Baltimore and Washington.[5] For all his endorsements of preventative war, personal editing of papal encyclicals, and political commentary, Weigel seemingly never had to worry about tarnishing his brand as an objective analyst. He became a regular presence on network news and is a syndicated columnist in sixty diocesan Catholic newspapers across the country.

Weigel learned many of his lessons from his close friend, the late Fr. Richard John Neuhaus. A onetime civil rights and antiwar leader of the left turned influential conservative thinker, Neuhaus converted to Catholicism from his childhood Lutheran faith in 1990, and that same year he founded the journal *First Things*. The publication gave Neuhaus, Weigel, and the prominent Catholic philosopher Michael Novak a platform for espousing hawkish foreign policy views along with a free-market triumphalism that strained traditional elements of Catholic social teaching. Neuhaus, whose 1984 book *The Naked Public Square* became a seminal and respected work beyond conservative circles, was an articulate and often caustic voice. He skillfully did battle with theological and political liberalism in print and television. Neuhaus's early bridge building with Christian evangelicals—*Time* magazine included the Catholic priest on a list of the nation's top twenty-five most influential evangelicals—caught the eye of Karl Rove, an adviser to then Texas governor George W. Bush. Neuhaus met with Bush in Austin to discuss how to effectively message the church's pro-life teachings to a diverse electorate. The priest, who died in 2009, became a close ally of the Bush White House, a frequent presence at conservative think tanks in Washington, and he rubbed shoulders with senators, judges, and other powerbrokers in the Republican establishment.

Neuhaus often admonished the U.S. bishops' conference for addressing economic justice, nuclear deterrence, environmental treaties, health care, and other issues with clear moral implications for how to order a just society. "The competence of bishops to speak on these questions is, to say the least, not self-evident," he said, while arguing that church leaders were unquestionably competent only when it came to what he called "the pro-life agenda"—abortion, physician-assisted suicide, and embryonic stem cell research. The Bush White House looked to Neuhaus as a high-profile religious voice on these issues, and the administration's choice of rhetorical framing often bore his imprint. Three months after the divisive 2000 presidential election that ended with a controversial U.S. Supreme Court decision awarding Bush the presidency, the administration surely found comfort in Neuhaus's sweeping description of the Democratic Party as "relentlessly hostile to the Church's public priorities" and his description of the Republican Party as a "champion" for the church.[6]

When Damon Linker, then an editor at *First Things*, knocked on Neuhaus's office door in 2002 with the idea of writing an essay making a conservative case against invading Iraq, the answer that came back illuminated much about the role the priest, his journal, and the neoconservative Catholic movement wanted to play. "Oh, Damon, that's really not a good idea," Neuhaus told him. "You don't want to get a reputation for being unreliable."[7] Linker soon left the journal and went on to write a critical book about the ways Neuhaus, Weigel, and Novak seamlessly integrated a selective reading of Catholic theology with the domestic and foreign policy pillars of the Republican Party. A past speechwriter for Rudy Giuliani, the former Republican mayor of New York City, Linker is no shill for the Democratic Party or a knee-jerk liberal. He is a frequent critic of how the mainstream media treats traditional religious believers and admires the classical political philosopher Leo Strauss, who challenged the exaltation of individual liberty as the highest goal of modern liberalism. But Linker saw in the Catholic right's theological attempts to sanctify one party's ideological end games a perversion of both religion and the ideals of democratic pluralism.

"The Catholic Church and the Republican Party almost blended together in their mind," Linker observed. "There was a confluence of events at a historical moment with Pope John Paul II, Margaret Thatcher and Ronald Reagan that made them feel like a corner had been turned in world history. If the pope was on our side in the Cold War then he must also side with us on American-style capitalism. To be a devout Catholic and a conservative Republican in the three decades separating Ronald Reagan's first term and the start of Pope Francis' pontificate was to feel virtually no tension between one's political and theological commitments." Those tensions, of course, clearly existed—John Paul II and Benedict XVI challenged the death penalty, highlighted the perils of unbridled capitalism, and spoke out against war—but Linker noted "there was always a theo-conservative writer at the ready, willing and eager to accentuate continuities with the GOP and explain away the difficulties."[8]

"THE CULTURE WAR IS UP FOR GRABS"

If George Weigel and the late Fr. Richard John Neuhaus represent two of the more formidable conservative Catholic thought leaders, Bill Donohue plays the role of gloves-off street fighter. The president of the Catholic League for Religious and Civil Rights, Donohue is a frequent commentator on cable news and most widely known for his screeds against gays and lesbians, liberals, and anyone who dares to question his role as guardian of all things Catholic. "The culture war is up for grabs," Donohue declares. "The good news is that religious conservatives continue to breed like rabbits, while secular saboteurs have shut down: they're too busy walking their dogs, going to bathhouses and aborting their kids."[9] During the 2004 presidential election, he called Sen. John Kerry "an idiot" who "never found an abortion he couldn't justify."[10] The culture wars are good business for the former college professor, who made just over $400,000 in 2013. Some members of the hierarchy are grateful for his particular brand of service.

Donohue counts among his fan club the cardinal of New York. "I am glad to express my encouragement for the work he does. Keep at it, Bill! We need you!" Cardinal Timothy Dolan wrote on his archdiocesan blog.[11] Archbishop Chaput of Philadelphia praises Donohue and the Catholic League for "the courage to speak up candidly and forcefully."[12] While Donohue is surely quick to speak up, his bluster is often less than factual. He has pointed to gay priests as one of the causes of the clergy abuse crisis, despite the fact that research from the John Jay College of Criminal Justice—commissioned by the U.S. Conference of Catholic Bishops—has consistently found no evidence to validate that claim.[13]

The Catholic League president who once claimed "most 15-year-old teenage boys wouldn't allow themselves to be molested" also repeatedly defended the first bishop in the country to face criminal charges for not informing authorities about a priest later convicted on child pornography charges.[14] Donohue called Bishop Finn "an innocent man" and said that "in an ideal world there would have been no charges."[15] When the Vatican accepted Finn's resignation in the spring of 2015, Donohue went out of his way to thank the bishop in a press release for "cleaning up the mess he inherited."[16] His selective outrage is also curious. When Rush Limbaugh blasted Pope Francis for having "gone beyond Catholicism" and preaching "pure Marxism," there was little of Donohue's usual bombast.

"He didn't like the pope's views on economics. Rush Limbaugh is entitled to that," he demurred with uncharacteristic restraint.[17]

While Donohue's fireworks might seem like a sideshow—a provocateur good for an outraged quote in the media—he is part of a sophisticated Catholic right movement in the United States, a nexus that includes top CEOs, Republican politicians, prominent cardinals, and wealthy philanthropists. All mingled together in 2012 at the Ritz Carlton Beach Resort in Naples, Florida, a five-star backdrop for the twenty-fifth anniversary of Legatus, an organization started by Domino's Pizza founder and Catholic billionaire Tom Monaghan.[18] The philanthropist, who has funded a plethora of conservative Catholic institutions and causes, was inspired to start the organization after a 1987 meeting with Pope John Paul II. Legatus is billed as the "only organization in the world designed for top-ranking Catholic business leaders and their wives." High-profile speakers at the Ritz included former president George W. Bush, a 2016 GOP candidate for president—Sen. Marco Rubio of Florida—and American cardinal Raymond Burke, now the most outspoken critic of Pope Francis's reform agenda. Legatus members received a copy of the organization's magazine a few months earlier, priming the pump for the silver anniversary gathering with a sleek cover photo of a smiling Cardinal Burke under the headline "Culture Warrior."[19]

Bill Donohue gave a speech to the well-heeled crowd and was granted the group's "Defender of the Faith" award. Reflecting back on the event a few days later, he buzzed with excitement. "They took to their feet to let me know how much they appreciated my remarks," Donohue wrote to his members. "Never have I seen our side as fired up as they are now. They've had it. Obama has unleashed a Catholic rebellion."[20] Two years before, in 2010, Legatus had given George W. Bush its prestigious Cardinal John J. O'Connor Pro-Life Award. "You could argue that he was the most pro-life president in our lifetime," gushed the group's executive director John Hunt.[21] There was no mention of the 152 executions that Bush presided over in Texas during his six-year gubernatorial term—more than any other governor in recent U.S. history—or the estimated half a million Iraqis and more than four thousand American soldiers killed during the war.[22]

Former Speaker of the House and later Republican presidential candidate, Newt Gingrich, was also on hand to talk about his conversion to Catholicism. Gingrich gave a screening of his documentary, *Nine Days*

That Changed the World, a film about Pope John Paul II's role in the collapse of the Soviet Union. The documentary was released by Citizens United, which financed a hit piece attacking Hillary Clinton before the 2008 elections that led to a historic and widely criticized U.S. Supreme Court decision that allowed corporations and unions to spend unlimited sums in political campaigns. Legatus usually keeps a low media profile, but in 2015 three scheduled speakers for their annual summit—Fox News host Bret Baier, actor Gary Sinise, and beer mogul Peter Coors—all withdrew after the organization invited a speaker who is a proponent of "conversion therapy," a widely discredited practice that claims to cure gays of their same-sex attraction. Baier of Fox News, who described himself as a "lifelong, Mass attending Catholic" and a lector at his parish, criticized Legatus in his explanation for withdrawing. "Describing homosexuality as a 'disorder' and talking about ways to 'cure" people from it does not seem to line up with the loving, accepting Church that I know," Baier said. "Nor does it match up with how Pope Francis has talked about the issue."[23]

The influence of the Catholic right is on display every spring at the National Catholic Prayer Breakfast in Washington, an event that brings together Catholic politicians, business leaders, and conservative activists. Although advertised as a nonpartisan affair, Catholics with close ties to the Republican Party founded the prayer breakfast in 2004 and dominate the board.[24] Joseph Cella, a cofounder of the gathering, served on John McCain's national Catholic steering committee. Founding board member Leonard Leo was the national cochair of Catholic outreach for the Republican National Committee. Other "founders circle" members of the prayer breakfast include the former Republican senator and 2016 presidential candidate Rick Santorum. During a difficult second term for the Bush administration, the event became a welcome date on the calendar for a president who could usually count on a friendly photo-op with a member of the Catholic hierarchy. Keynote speakers over the years have included President George W. Bush (who gave the address for four consecutive years), Supreme Court justice Antonin Scalia, Newt Gingrich, and Bishop Michael Sheridan of Colorado Springs.

The 2015 National Catholic Prayer Breakfast featured Greg Abbott, the Republican governor of Texas, and enthusiastically touted him as "a faithful pro-life Catholic." The prayer breakfast did not advertise that Abbott is a staunch supporter of capital punishment, which Pope Francis has described as "cruel, inhumane and degrading." Pope John Paul II called for an end to the death penalty, as has the U.S. Conference of Catholic Bishops. The Catechism of the Catholic Church does not exclude the use of capital punishment if it is the only recourse to protect society, but, citing John Paul II's encyclical the *Gospel of Life*, it says that those situations are "very rare, if practically non-existent."[25]

Board member Austin Ruse, who also served on McCain's national Catholic steering committee and praised President George W. Bush as the "second Catholic president,"[26] leads the Catholic Family and Human Rights Institute. The watchdog group monitors the United Nations on social policy. In 2015, Ruse made headlines when he said on a radio show that "the hard-left, human-hating people that run modern universities should be taken out and shot."[27] A Catholic priest who sat on his board and had previously served on the Pontifical Council for Justice and Peace resigned after Ruse's comments. Several prominent conservative Catholics are still on his board of patrons.

CONSERVATIVE CATHOLIC VOICES

Conservative Catholic activists are also well organized outside of elite Washington circles. The Cardinal Newman Society plays the role of self-appointed orthodoxy police by launching campaigns to blacklist speakers and stifle debate at Catholic universities across the county. In one petition drive coordinated with alumni of Gonzaga University and intended to bully the university into canceling a commencement invitation to Archbishop Desmond Tutu, the organization derided the anti-apartheid hero and Nobel Peace Prize winner as a "pro-abortion rights, pro-contraception Anglican."[28] The American Life League, a Virginia-based organization with a $6 million budget, has demonized social justice leaders in the church and ramped up efforts to undermine the U.S. bishops' signature national anti-poverty effort—the Catholic Campaign for Human Development—by conducting guilt-by-association witch hunts straight out of the McCarthy era.

Fr. Robert Sirico of the Acton Institute, a free-market think tank in Grand Rapids, Michigan, regularly gives Catholic cover to anti-union forces and libertarian-style economics in national media outlets. The institute's research director calls for a Catholic "Tea Party" movement.

Raymond Arroyo of the Eternal Word Television Network (EWTN)—the Birmingham, Alabama–based global Catholic media empire with an audience of more than 240 million in 140 countries—hosts *The World Over*, which has become a consistent platform for conservative Catholic leaders and politicians to criticize the Democratic Party. Republican policies that clash with Catholic teaching are rarely, if ever, highlighted. Arroyo once chatted amiably with a former official in the George W. Bush administration who defended "enhanced interrogation" techniques and failed to remind him that the church regards torture as an "intrinsic evil."[29] In another interview with Fr. Sirico of the Acton Institute, Arroyo exchanged chuckles with the priest about waterboarding. The two used the segment to downplay reports of CIA involvement in abusive interrogation of prisoners, and agreed the Catholic Church would not necessarily view waterboarding as torture.[30]

While Arroyo couldn't find the time to challenge Catholic apologists for torture, he scoffed that the funeral Mass of the late pro-choice Catholic senator Ted Kennedy was a "marvelous bit of political theater" and criticized retired cardinal Theodore McCarrick of Washington for his prayerful presence at Kennedy's grave.[31] Arroyo once compared President Obama's commencement address at the University of Notre Dame to "Ahmadinejad speaking at Yeshiva University."[32] (The former Iranian president had vowed Israel would "be wiped off the map.")

Buoyed by a generation of more conservative bishops appointed by Pope John Paul II, these Catholic activists, intellectuals, and media figures spoke loudly, organized strategically, and played a key role in influencing the American Catholic narrative. "Some conservatives hijacked Catholic identity by appointing themselves an alternative Magisterium," said Rev. Drew Christiansen, SJ, who directed the U.S. bishops' Office of International Justice and Peace for seven years in the 1990s. "They declared others unorthodox when they had few credentials to do so." Once at the forefront of moral debates over economic justice and military policy in the 1980s, moderate bishops and a handful of progressives in the hierarchy lost the steering wheel. The sharp turn came with a cost. An embattled posture and a politicized theology of "non-negotiables" have failed the church's broad pro-life mission, and it is in danger of marginalizing Catholic leaders who once operated at the center of American political and moral discourse.

When Archbishop Chaput, then of Denver, called Sen. Obama "the most committed abortion rights candidate in history" during the 2008 election, his speech was published in the online journal of an institute cofounded by Robert George, a Princeton professor of law and political philosophy who has played a major role in prodding the bishops to embrace the culture wars.[33] George is the reigning intellectual point man for conservative church leaders. In his battle against what he calls the "secularist orthodoxy" of "feminism, multiculturalism, gay liberationism and lifestyle liberalism," George weaves natural law philosophy dating back to Thomas Aquinas with hard-edged political analysis.[34] His varied admirers include Karl Rove, Glenn Beck, Supreme Court justice Antonin Scalia, and Newt Gingrich. "If there really is a vast right-wing conspiracy," the conservative Catholic magazine *Crisis* noted with tongue in cheek, "it's leaders probably meet in George's basement."[35]

"Whenever I venture out into the public square, I would almost invariably check it out with Robby first," Archbishop John Myers of Newark told the *New York Times* in 2009, noting that many bishops consider George "the pre-eminent Catholic intellectual."[36] Myers issued an edict to Catholics in his 1.3-million-member diocese in 2012, insisting that anyone who supported same-sex marriage should not receive Holy Communion. "Let's be honest about it," the archbishop told *National Public Radio*, "either you're with us on the important things or you're not."[37] The archbishop's stance is the kind of positioning favored by George. After the U.S. Supreme Court overturned the Defense of Marriage Act in 2012, George called for "a national rebellion" against gay marriage.[38] In the spring of 2015, as Indiana's Republican governor faced a national backlash from diverse sectors including corporate leaders, the National Collegiate Athletic Association, and some religious denominations over a religious freedom bill widely viewed as making it easier for businesses to refuse services to gays and lesbians, George wrote an essay equating critics of the legislation with a "lynch mob." The "mob," he wrote, "came first for the evangelicals and the Catholics and the Latter-Day Saints, but do not be deceived: it will not stop with them."[39] The extreme analogy did not dissuade two Catholic bishops—Archbishop Chaput of Philadelphia and Bishop William Lori of Baltimore—from that same week signing on to a joint religious liberty statement with George and two prominent Southern Baptists that was published in *Public Discourse*, an online journal of the Witherspoon Institute in Princeton, New Jersey, where

George is a fellow.[40] While Pope Francis accentuates the joy of the Gospel and encourages the faithful not to be "sourpusses," George is known for his somber warnings. "The days of acceptable Christianity are over. The days of comfortable Catholicism are past," he told more than eight hundred guests at the 2014 National Catholic Prayer Breakfast. "To believe in the Gospel is to make oneself a marked man or woman."[41]

Since the 2009 death of Fr. Richard John Neuhaus, George has been a driving force in bringing together conservative Christian evangelicals and Catholic leaders. Along with the evangelical Charles Colson, George was the catalyst behind a 4,700-word "Manhattan Declaration: A Call to Christian Conscience," which identifies abortion, same-sex marriage, and religious freedom as the defining issues for Christians. The 2009 manifesto, in part an effort to reinvigorate the political synergy of conservative Catholics and evangelicals that paved the way for the Reagan presidency and helped elect George W. Bush to two presidential terms, was signed by nine Catholic archbishops, including then Archbishop Charles Chaput of Denver and Cardinal Timothy Dolan of New York. Released at the National Press Club in Washington, the document is a rhetorical call to arms. "We pledge to each other, and our fellow believers, that no power on earth, be it cultural or political, will intimidate us into silence or acquiescence," the religious leaders declared.[42]

George is less animated when it comes to other moral issues. At a Washington conference attended by several American bishops in 2008, he advised church leaders that, instead of wasting much energy on advocating for living wages for workers, health care reform, and other justice issues central to the common good, they should focus on what he called "the moral social" issues—abortion, marriage, and embryonic stem cell research.[43]

THE POLITICS OF THEOLOGY

This kind of scaled-down political theology favored by George was prevalent in the 2004 presidential elections, when a San Diego–based group called Catholic Answers Action released *A Voter's Guide for Serious Catholics*, which argued Catholics should only vote based on a candidate's position on "five non-negotiable issues": abortion, euthanasia, embryonic stem cell research, human cloning, and same-sex marriage. Unlike war, poverty, and the death penalty, Catholic Answers argued, these were all "intrinsically evil." Ten million copies of the voter's guide were distributed during the campaign, the *New York Times* reported. While the guide served an obvious electoral goal, the effort was enough to make many theologians cringe and distorted the fullness of church teaching.[44]

"I have never understood the expression non-negotiable values," Pope Francis told the Italian daily *Corriere della Sera* in a 2014 interview. "Values are values, and that is it. I can't say that, of the fingers of a hand, there is one less useful than the rest."[45] Some high-profile Catholic politicians and a vocal minority of bishops in the United States seem to have a different vision. Rep. Paul Ryan, the chairman of the House Budget Committee, along with his fellow Catholic, House Speaker John Boehner, have pushed for budget proposals that slash programs for the working poor and give tax breaks to the wealthy even as the U.S. bishops' conference mobilized a coalition of Catholics and evangelicals to protect these targeted safety nets. Ryan went so far as to defend his budget proposals in specifically Catholic terms by cloaking his anti-government views in the finer vestment of subsidiarity, a principle in the church's social teachings that recognize civil society institutions closest to the ground—families, local charities, and churches—are essential. Catholic scholars and theologians quickly issued a public critique. "While you often appeal to Catholic teaching on 'subsidiarity' as a rationale for gutting government programs, you are profoundly misreading church teaching," they wrote. "Subsidiarity is not a free pass to dismantle government programs and abandon the poor to their own decisions."[46] The chairmen of the U.S. bishops' domestic justice committee said the House GOP budget that Ryan steered failed to meet a basic moral test, describing cuts to programs that assist children and other vulnerable populations as "unjust and wrong."[47]

Ryan quickly found help from more powerful figures in the church. Cardinal Timothy Dolan of New York, then president of the bishops' conference, called Ryan a "great public servant" and exchanged warm public letters with the congressman.[48] He praised Ryan for his "continued attention to the guidance of Catholic social justice in the current delicate budget considerations in Congress." Read carefully and with enough background knowledge of Catholic social thought, Dolan's letter to Ryan did not signal an endorsement of his budget.[49] Nevertheless, the cardinal's language was generic and his tone solicitous enough that Ryan and

Boehner issued public statements showcasing the letter as a seal of approval.[50] Secular media on Capitol Hill, not well versed in the finer points of Catholic theology, reported on Dolan's letter as a signal that the church had Ryan's back. "Paul Ryan Gets Boost from Catholic Bishops," *Politico* said in a misleading but telling headline that surely made the congressman smile.[51]

Ryan's hometown bishop offered the most unqualified support. In his diocesan newspaper, Bishop Robert Morlino of Madison, Wisconsin, wrote that the congressman's budget dealt with issues that Catholics of goodwill could disagree over because they involved matters of prudential judgment. Morlino listed what he called "the most fundamental issues for the formation of a Catholic conscience" as "the sacredness of human life from conception to natural death, marriage, religious freedom and the freedom of conscience, and a right to private property." Morlino contrasted the particular decisions involved in "how best to care for the poor" with black and white "intrinsic evils" that he said included "abortion, euthanasia and physician-assisted suicide, same-sex marriage, government-coerced secularism, and socialism."[52] The rather strange decision to include socialism in that list seemed to make more of a political than theological point given that the word had become a frequent epithet hurled at Obama by Fox News hosts and GOP politicians pandering to the Tea Party.

David Cloutier, a professor of theology at Mount St. Mary's University in Maryland, responded with a frank assessment. "Bishop Morlino's letter is problematic. There is no other way to say it," Cloutier wrote on the blog *Catholic Moral Theology*. "He suggests that Catholic teaching involves certain absolutes—such as the right to life and the right to private property—and beyond these, bishops have no competence to make moral pronouncements." Cloutier offered a helpful reminder that the church did not have quite such an absolute position on "private property" as the bishop expressed and noted that his use of "intrinsic evil," which in Catholic theology also includes masturbation, sent a confusing message to voters. "It should be repeated again and again: 'intrinsic' is not a word that denotes gravity," Cloutier wrote. "This is exactly the logic that disables the Church from speaking out on very serious issues like wars in Europe, economic and political oppression in Latin America, and environmental issues worldwide. If this logic is to hold, what are we to make of the statements of Paul VI and John Paul II on peace and the right to development? What are we to make of Benedict XVI's categorical insistence in *Caritas in Veritate* that advanced countries 'can and must lower their domestic energy consumption.' . . . Are these statements to be ignored by the citizens of the most militarized, richest and most consumptive nation in the world?"[53]

A vice presidential candidate in 2012, Ryan surely wasn't too worried about cogent analysis from academic theologians when he had cover in higher places. In an interview less than two months before the election, Archbishop Chaput said that he could not "vote for somebody who is either pro-choice or pro-abortion." While "Jesus tells us very clearly that if we don't help the poor, we're going to hell," the archbishop said, "Jesus didn't say that government has to take care of them, or that we have to pay taxes to take care of them. Those are prudential judgments."[54]

Theologian Meghan Clark of St. John's University in New York says that prudential judgment, an important tool in traditional Catholic theology, too frequently becomes a "get-out-of jail free card." Paired with the idea of "non-negotiable" issues, which she points out "does not come from Catholic theology," you have a recipe for misusing Catholic teaching in policy decisions and political debates. "This rhetoric is dangerous because it prioritizes political issues that are seen as uncomplicated in an attempt to circumvent conscience," Clark said. "There are no aspects of human life exempted from moral discernment, formation and judgments of conscience, and evaluation of the context. Poverty, hunger and homelessness are urgent and central to the Gospel. But they are also issues that require us to critically examine our own position, privilege and participation in structures of exclusion."

THE REPUBLICAN PARTY AT PRAYER?

When it comes to religion and politics, Americans today could be forgiven if they think of Catholic bishops as cheerleaders for a conservative ideology that lines up with the Republican Party. This is not because most bishops want to be shills for the GOP or even because Catholic social teaching blesses a right-wing agenda. In fact, traditional Catholic teaching dating back at least to Pope Leo XIII's 1891 social encyclical on capital and labor provides a vigorous affirmation of what are often viewed as "progressive" positions—living wages for workers, strong defense of unions, a robust role for government, and regulation of markets so that human dignity and the common good are at the forefront of economic decisions.

The U.S. Conference of Catholic Bishops objects to the death penalty, is a powerful voice for undocumented immigrants, views environmental stewardship as an urgent moral issue, criticizes federal budgets that slash social safety nets, and advocates for progressive taxation. None of this can be described as carrying water for today's GOP, which is increasingly defined by an ethos of radical individualism and a libertarian creed that is anathema to Catholic communitarianism. In contrast, the church's positions on abortion, contraception, sexuality, and marriage are opposed to many secular trends and mainstream liberalism. Simply put, Catholic social doctrine is expansive. It can't be easily squeezed into political or ideological boxes. The church's teaching on the sanctity of life, the common good, and the preferential option for the poor should cause heartburn for Democrats and Republicans alike. So what's the problem? Over the past few decades it's no secret that Catholic Democrats in elected office, progressive Catholic activists, Catholic nuns, and theologians have faced the most heat from the hierarchy and self-appointed guardians of Catholic orthodoxy. This glaring imbalance distorts Catholic political debates and hurts the church's essential role as a moral force in public life.

A view of the Catholic hierarchy as the "Republican Party at Prayer" is simplistic, but it is also an understandable perception. The increasingly zero-sum approach to public policy in concert with a combative posture during heated elections undermines the bishops' effectiveness as persuasive advocates and sends a message that the church favors one political party. Some in the American hierarchy have not helped the case by inflating the very real challenges all religious institutions face in an increasingly secular society with claims of anti-Catholic persecution. The image of a besieged Catholic Church under attack, the faithful oppressed by a hostile secular state, was captured well by the late Cardinal Francis George of Chicago, president of the U.S. Conference of Catholic Bishops from 2007 to 2010. "I expect to die in bed, my successor will die in prison, and his successor will die a martyr in the public square," the cardinal once told a group of priests as he reflected on the tensions between Catholic institutions and the wider culture. "His successor will pick up the shards of a ruined society and slowly help to rebuild civilization, as the church has done so often in human history."[55]

Some Catholic bishops' fevered reaction to the historic election of Barack Obama in 2008—and the eventual breakdown of trust between bishops and the Obama administration—encapsulates broader challenges the church faces in a cultural and political milieu that has undergone vast changes over the past half century. Two weeks after Barack Obama became the first African American to win the White House, an American cardinal at the Vatican described the election as "aggressive, disruptive and apocalyptic." Obama and Biden had campaigned on a "severe anti-life platform," Cardinal James Stafford proclaimed.[56] The cardinal's speech at the Catholic University of America in Washington was delivered on the fortieth anniversary of Pope Paul VI's controversial 1968 encyclical *Humanae Vitae*. The encyclical ignored the recommendations of the pope's own theological commission and upheld the ban on Catholics using birth control, which it described as an "intrinsic evil." The encyclical was met with opposition from Catholic theologians, many faithful in the pews, and some bishops around the world. In his postelection speech at Catholic University, Cardinal Stafford used the encyclical to offer a sweeping diagnosis of the zeitgeist that led up to Obama's victory.

> The encyclical arrived in Washington, DC in late July 1968. It had to contend with the chaos of assassinations, overseas wars, the conflicts surrounding the Democratic/Republican national conventions, indiscriminate killings, university strikes and riots, growing use of barbiturates, and ubiquitous insurrections within the cities. It was preceded by a one year *An Aquarian Exposition*, the for-profit, rock-music event staged on a Woodstock dairy farm in New York State. Since then, the chaos has become chronic, more insidious because partially hidden. If 1968 was the year of the year of "America's Suicide Attempt," 2008 is the year of America's exhaustion.[57]

While the cardinal's rhetoric toward the newly elected president was an extreme case and his cultural diagnosis alarmist, when Catholic bishops gathered for their national assembly a month after Obama's election the mood was also charged with suspicion and anxiety. Bishops lined up for a turn at the microphone. "This body is totally opposed to any compromise," one bishop proclaimed. "We are dealing with an absolute," said another. Others called for a "war" against abortion. The tone was so defensive and at times shrill that one church leader finally stood up to caution his brother bishops. "Keep in mind a prophecy of denunciation quickly wears thin," warned Bishop Blase Cupich, then of Spokane and now the archbishop of Chicago. "It seems to me what we need is a prophecy of solidarity, with the community we serve and the nation that we live in."[58]

His call for a more temperate, and ultimately smarter, approach to engaging with the democratically elected president of the United States would not win the day.

When Fr. John Jenkins, the president of the University of Notre Dame, invited Obama to deliver the commencement address in May 2009, Catholic bishops and conservative Catholic activists were outraged. Archbishop John C. Nienstedt of St. Paul and Minneapolis called it a "travesty." He blasted the president, whose work as a young community organizer in Chicago churches was partly funded by the U.S. bishops' Catholic Campaign for Human Development, as an "anti-Catholic politician."[59] Bishop John D'Arcy of South Bend, Indiana, refused to attend the graduation. Cardinal Francis George of Chicago, then president of the U.S. bishops' conference, initially described the invitation as an "extreme embarrassment."[60] Bishop Thomas Doran of Rockford, Illinois, called it "truly obscene."[61] Denver archbishop Charles Chaput, now of Philadelphia, warned of "prostituting our Catholic identity."[62] The Cardinal Newman Society accused Notre Dame's president of choosing "prestige over principles."[63]

One respected bishop saw the waves of condemnation as not only intemperate but also highly problematic for the credibility of the church. Writing in *America* magazine, the retired Archbishop Emeritus John Quinn of San Francisco offered a thoughtful and pointed warning:

> For most of our history, the American bishops have assiduously sought to avoid being identified with either political party and have made a conscious effort to be seen as transcending party considerations in the formulation of their teachings. The condemnation of President Obama and the wider policy shift that represents signal to many thoughtful persons that the bishops have now come down firmly on the Republican side in American politics. The bishops are believed to communicate that for all the promise the Obama administration has on issues of health care, immigration reform, global poverty and war and peace, the leadership of the church in the United States has strategically tilted in favor of an ongoing alliance with the Republican Party. A sign of this

stance is seen to be the adoption of a policy of confrontation rather than a policy of engagement with the Obama administration. Such a message is alienating to many in the Catholic community, especially those among the poor and the marginalized who feel that they do not have supportive representation within the Republican Party. [64]

While "the right to life," the archbishop insisted, is "a paramount and pre-eminent moral issue of our time," he spoke with rare candor about the challenge of moving from declarations of moral absolutes to the most effective way of winning hearts and minds in a diverse public square.

> There is no disagreement within this [U.S. bishops'] conference about the moral evil of abortion, its assault upon the dignity of the human person, or the moral imperative of enacting laws that prohibit abortion in American society. But there is deep and troubled disagreement among us on the issue of *how* we as bishops should witness concerning this most searing and volatile issue in American public life. And this disagreement has now become a serious and increasing impediment to our ability to teach effectively in our own community and in the wider American society. The bishops' voice has been most credible in the cause of life when we have addressed this issue as witnesses and teachers of a great moral tradition, and not as actors in the political arena.

Obama received a far warmer reception from Pope Benedict XVI than he did from many U.S. bishops when they met at the Vatican for the first time in 2009. The two leaders emphasized their broad agreement on Middle East peace, nuclear deterrence, poverty alleviation, interfaith dialogue, comprehensive immigration reform, and global climate change. Instead of vilifying the president, the pope gave Obama a signed copy of *Dignitas Personae*, a Vatican document on bioethics. Archbishop Quinn had raised a timely warning for the hierarchy not to fuel an image of partisanship, but the bruising political battle that ultimately led to the passage of national health care reform in 2010 marked a sharp escalation in conflict between the bishops and the Obama administration.

The U.S. Conference of Catholic Bishops, a longtime advocate for health care reform, opposed the final legislation that led to the Affordable Care Act because of fears that it would fund abortion. The Catholic Health Association, whose membership includes 600 hospitals and 1,400 long-term care and other health facilities in all fifty states, disagreed with the bishops' legislative reading and strongly supported the law, along with many Catholic nuns across the country. President Obama's executive order protecting existing limits on the federal funding of abortion did not mollify the bishops' concerns.[65] When the U.S. Department of Health and Human Services implemented guidelines for the law that required most insurance companies to cover contraception as part of "preventative" medical care, the dividing lines between the Obama administration and bishops hardened.[66]

The "contraception mandate," as it became known, was not hatched inside an anti-Catholic bunker under the White House. The independent Institute of Medicine recommended covering contraception with no co-pay along with cervical screenings, mammograms, and other medical care. Studies found that Americans use preventative services at about half the recommended rate because of prohibitive costs. Religious exemptions were included for churches and houses of worship. Original guidelines from the Obama administration did not provide any religious accommodations for Catholic hospitals or universities. This represented a significant blunder rightly challenged even by many of the president's strongest Catholic supporters, including Sr. Carol Keehan of the Catholic Health Association. Later modifications sought to respect Catholic theological principles regarding the "cooperation with evil." The new revisions would enable women at Catholic institutions to access the coverage directly though an insurance company or a third-party provider. Catholic institutions would not have to pay for the contraception. Finding the proper balance between honoring two moral goods (in this case, religious conscience objections and women's health) is a messy, difficult task. Catholic Charities USA, the Catholic Health Association, Catholic theologians, and many Catholic university leaders who appropriately criticized the Obama administration for its initial failure to provide any religious exemptions outside of churches were largely satisfied with the more robust, if imperfect, conscience protections and saw the revisions as generally workable. Opponents, including more than forty Catholic institutions, filed federal lawsuits seeking to block the contraception mandate.

Catholic bishops ramped up the fight. Less than a year before the 2012 presidential election, the U.S. bishops' conference launched a national "Fortnight for Freedom" campaign that kicked off with a high-profile Mass at the nation's first cathedral in Baltimore. The campaign was timed to begin when the liturgical calendar honored St. Thomas More and St.

John Fisher, who suffered political persecution and were executed by King Henry VIII. Evoking Christian martyrs of centuries past, the bishops argued that religious liberty was "under attack" and warned Catholics to "be on guard." The hierarchy asked for "all the energies the Catholic community can muster" and urged bishops and priests to take up the call from the pulpit.[67]

> In addition to this summer's observance, we also urge that the Solemnity of Christ the King—a feast born out of resistance to totalitarian incursions against religious liberty—be a day specifically employed by bishops and priests to preach about religious liberty, both here and abroad.

As if drafting the Mother of God herself into the Fortnight campaign, the official newspaper of the Brooklyn, New York, diocese featured a startling (and, for many, offensive) front-page image of the Blessed Mother wrapped in an American flag.[68] Speaking on a panel at the Ethics and Public Policy Center in Washington, Archbishop Salvatore Cordileone of San Francisco warned the nation was moving "in the direction of license and despotism."[69] It seems obvious to say that overheated references to "totalitarian incursions," martyrs, and the dangers of "despotism" are wildly out of step with the experiences of most Catholics in the United States. Some Catholics were so alarmed by the dire warnings surfacing in their parishes in the form of bulletin inserts and sermons that they began to speak up.

At the Shrine of the Most Blessed Sacrament in Washington, DC, where a diverse mix of liberals and conservatives had put aside political differences for many years, the "Fortnight for Freedom" became a source of sharp division. More than two dozen parishioners wrote to the pastor warning that the bishops' religious liberty campaign was a fight in search of a problem and had troubling political overtones so close to a presidential election. "We have been through trying times together—war, civil strife, scandals in the church, terrorist attacks on our nation, contested elections, and controversial legislation—but we have remained a community, with our parish serving as our refuge," the letter read. "For all of us, whatever our political philosophy, our church has been a welcoming home. This, we fear, may be changing."

We are deeply concerned that, under cover of a campaign for religious liberty, the provision of universal health care—a priority of Catholic social teaching from the early years of the last century—is being turned into a wedge issue in a highly-charged political environment and that our parish, and indeed the wider church, is in danger of being rent asunder by partisan politics. We, as a group, may have differing views as to the wisdom of the details of the Health and Human Services mandate, against which our archdiocese has now announced a lawsuit in federal court, but we are united in our concern that the bishops' alarmist call to defend religious freedom has had the effect of shutting down discussion.

It is a step too far. We, the faithful, are in danger of becoming pawns and collateral damage in a standoff between our church and our government. While HHS may have been tone-deaf and stubborn in its handling of the mandate, we believe that the points of disagreement have been grossly overstated by the bishops. In no way do we feel that our religious freedom is at risk. We find it grotesque to have the call for this "Fortnight" evoke the names of holy martyrs who died resisting tyranny. [70]

It was certainly easy to see why some Catholics were fed up. At the time the federal health care legislation was signed in law by President Obama, twenty-eight states already required that insurance coverage include contraception. Several Catholic universities—including Georgetown University, DePaul University, and Scranton University—had provided contraception coverage for years without any apocalyptic fallout. [71]

KNIGHTS OF COLUMBUS: "STRONG RIGHT ARM OF THE CHURCH"

In their religious liberty push, bishops relied on powerful allies who had the organizational muscle to mobilize the grassroots and the stomach to play hardball. The Knights of Columbus is the world's largest Catholic fraternal service organization with more than one million members. Founded in New Haven, Connecticut, in 1882 by an Irish American priest to help provide financial support for the widows and orphans of its members, the Knights' journey from hardscrabble defenders of Catholic immigrant families to power players in church politics is in large part due to the influential leadership of Carl Anderson. Elected as Supreme Knight in

2000, Anderson was a legislative assistant to segregationist Sen. Jesse Helms from North Carolina and held various posts in the Reagan administration. A consultant to the U.S. bishops' pro-life committee, Anderson was also appointed by Pope Benedict XVI to serve on the Vatican bank. The Knights have pumped hundreds of millions of dollars into projects to refurbish St. Peter's Basilica. Anderson has sat on several prominent boards, including the Catholic University of America in Washington. The *Tablet*, a London-based international Catholic newspaper, described Anderson as "one of the most influential Catholics in the world."[72] In 2012, the Knights' revenues and expenses exceeded $2 billion, largely raised through insurance plans it sells to members.

Anderson has given the Knights an assertive political voice. Two months before the 2008 presidential election—as campaigns were vying for Catholic voters in key swing states—Anderson took out a full-page advertisement in several major newspapers challenging vice presidential candidate Joe Biden. The ad took issue with the Catholic candidate's comments during an interview on *Meet the Press* in which Biden said that "as a matter of faith" he believed "life begins at the moment of conception," but it would be "inappropriate" for him to impose those beliefs "in a pluralistic society." Addressing Biden as a "fellow Catholic layman," Anderson urged the Delaware senator to "protect this unalienable right" and reminded him he was writing on behalf of "the 1.28 million members of the Knights of Columbus and their families in the United States." Biden's clunky phrasing—emblematic of how many pro-choice Catholic Democrats conveniently sidestep any public claims to their personal objections when it comes to abortion—was arguably ripe for criticism. The fact that the Knights' high-profile advertisement addressed no other issue bearing on human life and central to Catholic social teaching—war, torture, exploitation of migrants, environmental degradation—was also telling.[73]

While bishops did not specifically disclose who funded the "Fortnight for Freedom" campaign that began in 2011, it is widely viewed that the Knights played a leading role in financing the effort. The group's tax forms show that the Knights gave nearly $2 million to the U.S. bishops' conference in 2010 and $25,000 to the Becket Fund for Religious Liberty, which has led most of the legal challenges to contraception coverage requirements under the Affordable Care Act. "The strong right arm of the church," as Pope John Paul II once called the Knights, was ready for service. [74]

If any more confirmation was needed that the Knights and many bishops viewed themselves in an epic battle between good and evil rather than a prickly policy dispute, the May 2012 cover story of the Knights' magazine, *Columbia*, left little doubt. The cover featured an illustration of a cowboy on a black horse with a Winchester rifle in his right hand and a large crucifix around his neck. "Freedom Is Our Lives," the headline read. The special edition was devoted to mobilizing the Knights' more than one million members to fight against the Obama administration. Who was this determined cowboy? The image was a depiction of General Enrique Gorostieta Velarde, a 1920s guerilla leader in the Cristiada uprising against the dictatorial Mexican president Plutarco Calles. A zealot atheist, Calles outlawed Catholic religious orders and Catholic education, and he restricted the practice of faith, including participation in the sacraments. His anti-Catholic persecution led to the murder of thousands. The implication was as clear as it was stunning. Supreme Knight Carl Anderson wrote in the cover story:

> Today in the United States it is impossible to recall these events without thinking of current threats to religious liberty, including the Obama administration insistence that contraceptives, sterilization, and abortion-inducing drugs be included in the health insurance programs of Catholic organizations. [75]

Stephen Schneck, director of the Institute for Policy Research and Catholic Studies at the Catholic University of America, offered a sharp retort in *U.S. Catholic* magazine. "Such agitprop should frighten us all," Schneck wrote. "Given the illustrated cover and Anderson's connecting-the-dots, the implication is what? That it's time for armed resistance? A new Cristero War? Rifles with crucifixes? Let's note what's ridiculously obvious. There is no persecution of Catholics in the United States." [76]

HITLER, STALIN, AND OBAMA?

The hierarchy, which had never convinced the vast majority of Catholics that contraception was an "intrinsic evil," now framed the issue as one of government intrusion. In many respects, the bishops had a worthy case to make given the Obama administration's initial failure to offer broader religious liberty exemptions. However, bishops continued to back themselves into a corner with alarmist rhetoric. Cardinal Timothy Dolan, the president of the U.S. bishops' conference at the time, accused the Obama administration of "strangling" the church. Bishop Daniel Jenky of Peoria, Illinois, called it an "assault" on religious freedom that was "simply without precedent in the American political and legal system." In a homily that made headlines around the country, Jenky compared the Obama administration to some of the most notorious dictators of the twentieth century:

> Hitler and Stalin, at their better moments, would just barely tolerate some churches remaining open, but would not tolerate any competition with the state in education, social services, and health care. In clear violation of our First Amendment rights, Barack Obama—with his radical, pro abortion and extreme secularist agenda, now seems intent on following a similar path. Now things have come to such a pass in America that this is a battle that we could lose, but before the awesome judgment seat of Almighty God this is not a war where any believing Catholic may remain neutral. [77]

Archbishop William Lori of Baltimore, who chairs the U.S. bishops' ad hoc committee on religious liberty, defended the rhetorical fireworks. "Sometimes prophets are thought to be unduly alarmist," the archbishop told *National Public Radio.* "But that's what prophetic speech always has been." [78]

It was becoming harder by the day to tell whether bishops were acting like prophets or unflinching partisans. Less than two months before the presidential election, Bishop Thomas Paprocki of Springfield, Illinois, writing in his diocesan newspaper, warned Catholics that Democrats "explicitly endorse intrinsic evils." The bishop noted that he had "read the Republican Party platform and there is nothing in it that supports or promotes an intrinsic evil or a serious sin." And then came to real kicker: "A vote for a candidate who promotes actions or behaviors that are intrinsically evil and gravely sinful makes you morally complicit and places the eternal salvation of your own soul in serious jeopardy." [79] Bishop Paprocki was offering his flock a not-so-thinly veiled warning: vote for a Democrat and risk burning in hell. Some parish priests also crossed a line. At the Church of Siena on the Upper East Side of Manhattan, a priest devoted a page in the parish bulletin to the text of a letter written by six former ambassadors to the Vatican. "We urge our fellow Catholics, and indeed all people of good will, to join with us in this full-hearted effort to elect Gov. Mitt Romney as the next President of the United States," the statement read.[80]

If bishops or conservative Catholic leaders were aware that as governor of Massachusetts Romney had signed into law a health care reform bill that included taxpayer-funded abortions and gave Planned Parenthood a seat on a health care advisory board, not much of a fuss was raised.[81] There was only room for one "anti-life" politician in the presidential race, and Obama fit the bill. "Catholic Bishops Make Last-Minute Pitch for Romney," read one newspaper headline published just a few days before the 2012 election.[82] Melanie Sloan, the executive director of Citizens United for Responsible Ethics, a nonpartisan watchdog group in Washington, found the bishops' forays into election politicking alarming. "The IRS should immediately tell the Conference of Catholic Bishops that the conduct of its members is beyond the pale," Sloan wrote in a formal complaint.[83]

Meanwhile, the Romney campaign took advantage of the hierarchy's assertive posture to reach coveted Catholic swing voters in states like Michigan, Pennsylvania, and Ohio. "Who shares your values?" a narrator asked in a Romney advertisement that featured images of the late Pope John Paul II and the former Polish president and Solidarity movement leader Lech Walesa. "President Obama used his health care plan to declare war on religion," the narrator warns, "forcing religious institutions to go against the faith."[84]

THE COSTS OF PARTISAN RELIGION

While Barack Obama won Catholic voters in 2008 and again narrowly in 2012, the Catholic Church is in danger of losing a different numbers game. One in ten Americans is a former Catholic. A major report from the Pew Research Center, released in the spring of 2015, found that the number of Catholics in the United States has dropped by three million since 2007. For every Catholic convert, more than six Catholics leave the faith. There are now more Americans who identify as religiously unaffiliated than as Catholic.[85] Parish closures and priest shortages are common.

In 1975, there were 58,909 priests in the United States. Today, according to the Center for Applied Research in the Apostolate, there are 39,600, a drop of 33 percent.[86]

"This record makes the percentage of bad loans and mortgages leading to the financial meltdown look absolutely stellar," wrote the noted Catholic author and former *New York Times* religion reporter Peter Steinfels. "It dwarfs the bankruptcies of General Motors and Chrysler." Latino immigrants have kept the church's numbers growing, but even this bulwark is weakening. Nearly one in four Hispanics are now former Catholics. A Pew Research report found that the percentage of Hispanics who identify as Catholic declined from 67 percent in 2010 to 55 percent in 2014, a swift drop of twelve percentage points in just four years. The Catholic hierarchy is not alone in confronting a stark reality. One in five Americans—the "nones," as researchers call them—no longer identify with any religious denomination. The data is even more sobering for Millennials under the age of thirty-four. One in three Americans in that age group claim no religious affiliation. A third of young people (ages eighteen to thirty-three) who left organized religion said "negative teachings" or "negative treatment" of gay people was a "somewhat important" or "very important" factor in their departure, according to surveys from the Public Religion Research Institute.[87]

When lapsed Catholics were asked why they left the church in the Diocese of Trenton, New Jersey, a 2012 study led by a Jesuit Catholic priest and the Center for the Study of Church Management at Villanova's School of Business found that Catholics cited a lack of pastoral sensitivity, including unwelcoming attitudes toward gays and lesbians, as factors driving them away.[88] The Diocese of Springfield commissioned professors at Benedictine University to find out why Catholics were leaving the church. The professors surveyed 575 lapsed Catholics from November 2012 to March 2013. Results found several major reasons why they left: disagreement with church doctrine regarding birth control, homosexuality, and the all-male clergy; the perception that the church faced too many scandals; and a feeling that parishioners were being judged harshly by the church and are not welcomed. "I have visited many parishes in the Springfield community trying to find a priest that seems dedicated to his parishioners and the word of God," wrote one lapsed Catholic as part of the survey. "All of the priests seem too wrapped up in themselves and the 'power' they perceive they hold. They all seem more wrapped up in themselves, much like politicians."[89]

The church's teachings on homosexuality and same-sex marriage will continue to be a flashpoint in the United States. A 2015 survey from the Public Religion Research Institute found that 60 percent of Catholics now support civil marriage for same-sex couples.[90] Younger Catholics are even more supportive. Three-quarters of Catholics under the age of thirty support legal same-sex marriage. Pope Francis and future popes are unlikely to endorse gay marriage, of course, but Francis has emphasized human dignity and God's love for all when discussing homosexuality. "A person once asked me, in a provocative manner, if I approved of homosexuality," the pope said in an interview. "I replied with another question: 'Tell me: when God looks at a gay person, does he endorse the existence of this person with love, or reject and condemn this person?' We must always consider the person."[91]

As archbishop of Buenos Aires, the pope joined his fellow Argentine bishops in opposing a same-sex marriage law—even calling it "of the devil"—but did signal support for civil unions for gay couples as a compromise measure.[92] When asked if Jesus would support gay marriage, one of the pope's friends, retired Brazilian cardinal Claudio Hummes, said in a 2014 interview, "I don't know. I formulate no hypothesis on this. Who must answer this is the Church in its entirety . . . I think we must get together, listen to people, those who have an interest, the bishops. It is the Church that must indicate the ways, and there must be a way for all."[93] In a 2014 interview, a Belgian bishop urged the church to consider ways to recognize same-sex couples. "Just as there are a variety of legal frameworks for partners in civil society, one must arrive at a diversity of forms in the church," said Bishop Johan Bonny of Antwerp. "The intrinsic values are more important to me than the institutional question. The Christian ethic is based on lasting relationships where exclusivity, loyalty and care are central to each other."[94]

Meanwhile, the U.S. hierarchy and conservative allies have doubled down in opposing civil marriage for gays and lesbians. Catholic bishops and the Knights of Columbus invested considerable resources in the 2012 elections—a losing effort, as three states endorsed marriage equality that year and another rejected a proposal to amend its state constitution to prohibit same-sex unions. Between 2005 and 2012, the Knights spent $6.5 million to oppose same-sex marriage.[95]

In *American Grace: How Religion Unites and Divides Us*, Robert Putnam of Harvard University and David Campbell of the University of Notre Dame draw on extensive research to show the costs of these kinds of efforts. In particular, they demonstrate how the perception of Christian leaders as anti-gay is driving away young people from churches.

> Throughout the 1990s and into the new century, the increasingly prominent association between religion and conservative politics provoked a backlash among moderates and progressives, many of whom had previously considered themselves religious. . . . This backlash was especially forceful among youth coming of age in the 1990s and just forming their views about religion.
>
> Just as this generation moved to the left on most social issues—above all, homosexuality—many prominent religious leaders moved to the right, using the issue of same-sex marriage to mobilize electoral support for conservative Republicans. In the short run, this tactic worked to increase GOP turnout, but the subsequent backlash undermined sympathy for religion among many young moderates and progressives. Increasingly, young people saw religion as intolerant, hypocritical, judgmental and homophobic. If being religious entailed political conservatism, they concluded, religion was not for them.[96]

Mark Rozell, an acting dean and professor of public policy at George Mason University, who writes frequently about religion and politics, worries that Catholic bishops have risked more than they have gained. "The real danger is they are becoming perceived as a wing of one political party," said Rozell, who is Catholic and taught at the Catholic University of America for a decade. "It is utterly confusing to many Catholics that bishops take strong partisan-type stands in a pluralistic society where there is serious disagreement over contentious issue. I think that approach backfires. There is no evidence in Catholic voting behavior that bishops are really influencing Catholic voters. I respect they have deeply held beliefs and from their standpoint there can be no compromise on these issues, but the language of absolutes does not work well in a pluralistic society. They are not persuading people."

Retired archbishop Joseph Fiorenza of the Archdiocese of Galveston-Houston, president of the U.S. bishops' conference from 1998 to 2001, hopes that Pope Francis will help motivate church leaders in the United States to reclaim a more effective public voice. "Bishops have a lot to learn from Pope Francis," Fiorenza acknowledges. "Catholic identity is far broader than opposition to abortion and same-sex marriage. Catholic identity is a commitment to living the Gospel as Jesus proclaimed it, and this must include a commitment to those in poverty." He thinks that conservatives who deflect attention from the pope's bold critique of inequality and those in the pro-life community who insist that abortion is the only "life issue" face a real test from the Francis papacy.

> The pope's very clear teaching condemning the "economy of exclusion" and the structures of sin that are involved strikes at the heart of some conservative Catholics who are so wedded to the unfettered free market that they think the pope's talk is naïve. Well, the pope sees it as realistic. The poor of the world who suffer from that type of economic philosophy see it as realistic. The pope is on a steady course. He is not naïve. He knows what he is doing.
>
> Pope Francis makes it clear that he is opposed to abortion, but that can't be the only thing we talk about. What he said early on in his papacy struck the heart of people who make abortion the whole agenda. The pope is saying we have to oppose abortion but there must be a broader agenda. Some pro-life advocates don't like to hear that and think if you take the focus off abortion, you weaken your position. The pope is saying you weaken your pro-life position when you don't take a broader view of issues that attack human life. Some people think there are only sins that are intrinsic evil, but the pope is saying the economy has built in a structure that strongly impacts against the humanity of people and that is an evil too.

Archbishop Fiorenza, who is now in his eighties and marched with Rev. Martin Luther King Jr. as a young priest, represents something of a bygone voice. As a new generation of bishops has been less vocal about a broad array of economic and social justice issues, Fiorenza calls to mind an era when Catholic leaders were at the forefront of shaping a faith-infused progressive movement that had a decisive impact on the arc of American politics.

3

CATHOLIC PROGRESSIVISM ON THE MARCH: THE NEW DEAL TO VATICAN II

Nearly three decades before President Franklin D. Roosevelt was elected president in 1932 and began digging America out of the depths of the Great Depression, a twenty-nine-year-old priest toiled away on his doctorate in moral theology at the Catholic University of America in Washington. No one knew it at the time, but Fr. John Ryan was just beginning to sow some of the first seeds that would later blossom in Roosevelt's New Deal reforms. Born to Irish immigrant parents in Minnesota, John Ryan grew up in a family where the priority of labor, workers' rights, and solidarity with those struggling in the shadows of capitalism's bright promise were an integral part of Catholic identity. He had the support of Archbishop John Ireland of St. Paul, an often fiery leader who lamented the church was not doing more to address social injustice. "What has come over us that we shun the work which is essentially ours to do? These are days of action. . . . Into the arena, priest and layman! Seek out social evils, and lead in movements that tend to rectify them," Ireland declared.[1]

In 1891, a year before Ryan entered the seminary, Pope Leo XIII issued the church's first social encyclical—*Rerum Novarum*, which addressed capital and labor. It provided a clear moral response to the savage inequalities that defined an industrial era in which workers had virtually no power and the state provided no checks on unbridled capitalism. The pope rejected socialism, but he specifically defended workers' rights to organize, endorsed a living wage that could support a family, and envisioned a more equitable distribution of wealth. "The oppressed workers, above all, ought to be liberated from the savagery of greedy men, who inordinately use human beings as things for gain," the pope wrote.[2] The encyclical became a foundational text for Catholic social thought.

This Catholic vision of the common good, which rejects an ideology of radical individualism and anti-government activism resurgent in today's political battles, includes a robust role for the state in helping to safeguard human dignity. "Whenever the general interest or any particular class suffers, or it is threatened with evils which can in no other way be met, the public authority must step in to meet them," Leo XIII insisted. For the young Ryan, the encyclical added the formidable weight of papal authority to his own analysis that the Catholic Church should take an active role in pursuing justice in the political and policy realm. His 1906 doctoral dissertation at Catholic University, *A Living Wage*, applied core principles outlined by Pope Leo XIII in arguing for the state to ensure workers were paid a wage that allowed their families to live in dignity.[3] After the publication of *A Living Wage*, Ryan was recognized as the most prominent Catholic priest writing and speaking out on a range of progressive issues. He became a tireless voice in the fight for minimum wage legislation in several states. "American Catholicism's foremost social reformer," the historian David O'Brien called him.[4]

Ryan released his most influential book, *Distributive Justice*, in 1916. He again applied principles articulated by Pope Leo XIII to examine industrial production, profits from enterprise, and the relationship between workers and owners. *The New Republic* praised Ryan for his "unimpeachable" scholarship and described the book as "the most comprehensive and dignified existing treatise on the ethics of economic reform."[5] After the First World War, Catholic bishops formed the National Catholic Welfare Conference, the first time the U.S. hierarchy had a coordinated body to address national issues. Ryan was named the director of the Social Action Department, and he drafted the Bishops' Program for Social Reconstruction in 1919. The Catholic hierarchy threw its moral weight behind what were then viewed by many as radical social reforms: a minimum wage; public housing for workers; labor participation in management decisions; and insurance for the elderly, disabled, and unemployed that would be funded by a tax on industry. The bishops' program ended with a stern warning to the "capitalist":

He needs to learn the long-forgotten truth that wealth is stewardship, that profit-making is not the basic justification of business enterprise, and that there are such things as fair profits, fair interest and fair prices. Above and before all, he must cultivate and strengthen within his mind the truth which many of his class have begun to grasp for the first time during the present war; namely, that the laborer is a human being, not merely an instrument of production; and that the laborer's right to a decent livelihood is the first moral charge upon industry. . . . This is the human and Christian, in contrast to the purely commercial and pagan, ethics of industry.[6]

These bold proposals, which historian Joseph M. McShane credited with launching "the American Catholic search for social justice," never took root during the Roaring Twenties. Americans elected three Republican presidents, and a bullish Wall Street left most political leaders in no mood for reform. But after the 1929 stock market crash and the beginning of the Great Depression, the nation's politics changed. Presidential candidate Franklin D. Roosevelt wrote to Ryan in 1932 and asked him to be an informal campaign adviser. Roosevelt, a nominal Episcopalian, would soon be steeped in perspectives from the Catholic social tradition. Another papal encyclical issued at the time, *Quadragesimo Anno* (In the Fortieth Year)—released four decades after Pope Leo XIII's labor encyclical—provided another round of Catholic moral thinking on questions of economic and social justice that seemed far from abstract at a time when more than 20 percent of U.S. workers were unemployed and more than half of all elderly lived in poverty.[7] As Lew Daly writes in his seminal essay, "In Search of the Common Good: The Catholic Roots of American Liberalism":

It was arguably the most radical and controversial church-wide statement in all of Catholic history to that point and the political culmination of the natural-law revival in Catholic thought that began under Leo XIII. As Pius XI explained, *Rerum Novarum* "completely overthrew" the tenets of economic liberalism, "which had long hampered effective interference by the government," and had a galvanizing effect on Catholic social reform.

Most controversially, *Quadragesimo Anno* proposed (in a section specifically designated "Reconstruction of the Social Order") the establishment of a corporatist industrial order built around occupational councils comprising industry, labor, and government representatives.

Charged with negotiating fair wages, hours, prices, and business practices, the councils would replace pure market forces with mandatory bargaining.

A year after the encyclical was released in 1932, Roosevelt gave a speech in Detroit sponsored by a key Catholic ally, Mayor Frank Murphy. The presidential candidate argued:

> It is patent in our days that not alone is wealth accumulated, but immense power and despotic economic domination are concentrated in the hands of a few, and that those few are frequently not the owners but only the trustees and directors of invested funds which they administer at their good pleasure. . . . This accumulation of power, the characteristic note of the modern economic order, is a natural result of limitless free competition, which permits the survival of those only who are the strongest, which often means those who fight most relentlessly, who pay least heed to the dictates of conscience.

Roosevelt won in a landslide. The social reforms Msgr. John Ryan first proposed in his doctoral dissertation and later for the Bishops' Program for Social Reconstruction in 1919 now had a chance to move from proposal to reality. Roosevelt appointed Ryan to the Federal Advisory Council of the U.S. Employment Service, established by the progressive Wagner Act, which guaranteed workers the right to organize unions. He became a leading figure in the brain trust of Frances Perkins, the influential Secretary of Labor, who led the charge for unemployment and elderly insurance, a massive public works program, and a minimum wage. Fr. Francis Haas, a Ryan protégé, was appointed to the National Labor Board and the Labor Advisory Board of the National Recovery Administration.[8]

At Roosevelt's second inauguration in 1937, Msgr. John Ryan gave the invocation. It was the first time a Catholic priest had been asked to do so. Two years later, Labor Secretary Perkins toasted Ryan on his seventieth birthday and retirement from the Catholic University of America. Supreme Court justices, members of Roosevelt's cabinet, and senators were on hand to hear Perkins praise Ryan that day in a banquet at the Willard Hotel.

> We have still not caught up with Father Ryan's thinking . . . but we are coming closer to it. Only lately has business begun to realize that economic policies are subject to ethics, and that a moral obligation to

pay a good wage falls on the employer of labor as a consequence of his position of power over the fruits of the earth. . . . There is no greater tribute I can give his persistent influence on American thought and action than to quote his own words. "Never before in our history," he says, "have Government policies been so deliberately and consciously based on the conception of moral right and social justice."[9]

President Roosevelt sent a message to the banquet: "With voice and pen, you have pleaded the cause of social justice and the right of the individual to happiness through economic security, a living wage, and an opportunity to share in the things that enrich and ennoble human life."[10] "Catholic social teaching had revolutionized the moral landscape of capitalism," Lew Daly wrote. "It was a turning point that made the welfare state morally necessary and, because of that, politically possible." Nearly all of the recommended reforms in the U.S. bishops' 1919 Program for Social Reconstruction were eventually enacted into law during Roosevelt's presidency.[11]

Outside the corridors of power in Washington, Catholics were leading movements to support workers, challenge unchecked capitalism, and respond to the masses of urban poor. After Roosevelt's election in 1932, Catholic institutions mobilized what the *New York Times* called a "crusade for social justice." The National Catholic Alumni Federation hosted conferences that called for a radical new way of thinking about the status quo. "The immediate goal of the crusade," the newspaper wrote, "is the education of industrialists and workmen to the realization that capitalism, in its present form, 'has failed and must continue to fail.'"[12] In New York, Boston, Philadelphia, and other cities, "labor priests" organized parish labor schools where workers were taught Catholic social teaching about workers' rights and connected it to principles of collective bargaining. On May 1, 1933, the first copies of a newspaper that sold for a penny were handed out in Union Square in New York City. "In an attempt to popularize and make known the encyclicals of the Popes in regard to social justice and the program put forth by the Church for the 'reconstruction of the social order,' this news sheet, *The Catholic Worker*, is started," Dorothy Day wrote in the paper's inaugural edition. "It's time there was a Catholic paper printed for the unemployed."[13] Inspired by Catholic teaching and Jesus's mandate to clothe the naked and feed the hungry, Day and Peter Maurin developed houses of hospitality that were serving the poor, unemployed, and homeless throughout the city.

AN IMMIGRANT CHURCH GROWS UP

While Roosevelt and Ryan teamed up to put a distinctive mark on American history during the New Deal era, Catholics and their church were still viewed by the dominant Protestant culture with suspicion and hostility in the decades preceding World War II. When an Italian archbishop sailed to America in 1853 with a gift of marble for the completion of the Washington Monument, he was met by a riot, and the marble was tossed into the Potomac River. The acclaimed political cartoonist Thomas Nast frequently drew Catholics as drunken, violent hordes. His infamous 1871 cartoon "The American River Ganges" depicted Catholic bishops' miters as crocodiles waiting to attack public schoolchildren. Anti-Catholic animus has deep roots that can be traced back to America's founding. The fear that Catholicism and democracy were incompatible—and that a surge of Catholic immigrants redefining the nation's cultural landscape would be loyal to the pope in Rome—dogged Catholics up until John F. Kennedy Jr. became the first (and so far only) Catholic to win the presidency in 1963. Al Smith, the first Catholic candidate to seek the White House, faced ugly attacks in his 1928 campaign because of his religion. The popular New York governor quickly learned his faith would be a stumbling block as he courted a national electorate beyond his urban and heavily immigrant base. "If he is elected President, you will not be allowed to have or read a Bible," read a note sent to parents by the school board of Daytona Beach, Florida. If Smith was elected, flyers warned, all Protestant marriages would be annulled. Opponents pinned up photos of the recently completed Holland Tunnel, the caption describing it as a secret passage being built between Rome and Washington.[14]

Smith was trounced by Herbert Hoover.

Catholics gradually moved into the mainstream of American life. Their fierce anti-communism and support for the U.S. military ingratiated them to the wider culture. When the United States entered World War II in 1941, Catholic bishops and the faithful in the pews saw the occasion as an opportunity to demonstrate their patriotism by rallying behind the flag. Cardinal Francis Spellman of New York, in particular, became the most important Catholic validator for the war effort, declaring that "our President and our Holy Father have combined the forces of our great country and the forces of religion in a battle for peace."[15] As the Catholic military vicar of the United States, Spellman became the unofficial head chaplain to the armed forces, and his close relationship with Pope Pius XII made him a key link between the pope and Roosevelt. If there were any lingering suspicions about Catholics' loyalty to America, they seemed to be thawing. "Catholic patriotism in the great crusade would be so shining that never again would anyone dare to question their Americanism," wrote George Flynn in *Roosevelt and Romanism*.[16] While that assessment turned out to be optimistic—ugly strains of anti-Catholicism would resurface during John F. Kennedy's run for the White House—the war effort largely solidified Catholics' standing in a once deeply suspicious Protestant culture.

The postwar 1950s are often regarded as the Golden Era of American Catholicism. Vocations to the priesthood surged. Catholic schools were packed. Archbishop Fulton Sheen of New York brought Catholicism into the living rooms of Americans with his hugely popular television show, *Life Is Worth Living*, which drew as many as thirty million weekly viewers. Sheen, dressed in a scarlet cape, used his theatrical flair and erudition to entrance audiences from 1951 to 1957. Such was the archbishop's reach into popular culture that he twice won an Emmy award and appeared on the cover of *Time* magazine.[17]

While Catholics were increasingly becoming part of mainstream America, a tightly woven Catholic subculture still imbued the faithful with a distinctive identity. Most Catholics lived in urban neighborhoods, went to Catholic schools, and grew up memorizing the tenets of the faith as spelled out in question-and-answer format in the Baltimore Catechism. Bishops presided over a thriving ecosystem of schools, parishes, and social service organizations that still represented the local interests of an immigrant church. Some bishops emerged as influential figures in urban cities like Boston—mayors and governors courted the largely Democratic flock of Catholic voters—but the church was not a major player in national politics.[18] An unexpected and transformative event set in motion by an unlikely pope would soon catapult U.S. Catholic leaders from these parochial confines on to the national stage.

THE VATICAN II REVOLUTION

When Cardinal Angelo Roncalli was elected pope in 1958, most Catholics did not expect anything dramatic from this humble son of Italian sharecroppers. At seventy-eight, Pope John XXIII was the oldest pope elected in two centuries. Most Vatican insiders and Catholics in the pews expected a fairly brief, uneventful papacy. John XXIII would indeed die just shy of five years after his election, but the prognosticators were wrong: his papacy would be revolutionary. Just three months after his election, the pope shocked everyone by convening the historic Second Vatican Council and calling for *aggiornamento*—an "updating" that would signal a new era for the church's posture toward the modern world. A monarchial institutional that had established a Holy Office of the Inquisition and late into the nineteenth century condemned the evils of modernism and liberalism would now, as Pope John put it, "throw open the windows of the church and let the fresh air of the Spirit blow through." In his opening address before more than two thousand bishops and theologians assembled in St. Peter's Basilica, the sunny optimist known by many adoring faithful as "The Good Pope John" said the church must look to the future "without fear." He challenged "prophets of gloom who are always forecasting disaster as though the end of the world is near."[19] It was a heady time. Pope John inspired a new spirit of possibility for global Catholicism just as the nation's first Catholic president, John F. Kennedy, marked a watershed moment for Catholics in the United States.

The council, which met in four consecutive sessions in the fall from 1962 until 1965, produced a prodigious volume of work and adopted groundbreaking reforms. Mass would now be permitted in the vernacular, instantly sweeping aside centuries of liturgical tradition with a priest intoning Latin with his back to the congregation. Ecumenical dialogue with other Christian denominations was stressed. After centuries of Christian animosity and violence toward the Jewish people, who were demonized as "Christ killers," the council issued a major document that denounced anti-Semitism and urged "mutual understanding and respect" between Catholics and Jews. The council declared the entire "people of God," not simply the hierarchy of bishops and cardinals, integral to the church's pilgrim journey. The lay faithful were recognized as essential. The American Jesuit priest and theologian John Courtney Murray, who had earlier faced Vatican censure for his writings, became the architect behind the council's affirmation of religious freedom and conscience. The opening words of the council's "Pastoral Constitution on the Church in the Modern World" showed a church that would now engage with the broader society with a newfound spirit: "The joys and the hopes, the griefs and the anxieties of the men of this age, especially those who are poor or in any way afflicted, these are the joys and hopes, the griefs and anxieties of the followers of Christ."[20]

The mandate of *Gaudium et Spes* (Joy and Hope) to have the church read "the signs of the times" and "interpret them in light of the Gospel" also came with specific instructions for Catholic bishops around the world to create national or regional conferences. These were not to be toothless associations that would simply rubber-stamp orders from Rome, but robust episcopal bodies empowered to enhance the church's voice in public debates. U.S. bishops, at the time largely focused on local and diocesan matters, moved to beef up their national operations. The hierarchy's existing National Catholic Welfare Conference in Washington was not designed for the new challenge. U.S. bishops did not have to be members in this voluntary association, collective statements from the episcopacy were rare, and it lacked any authoritative voice. In 1966, a year after Vatican II ended, the National Conference of Catholic Bishops was officially designated as the hierarchy's collective body. In addition, bishops established the U.S. Catholic Conference, which would serve as the church's policy arm in the nation's capital.

Catholic leaders around the country threw themselves into struggles for civil rights and economic justice. A young priest named Bernard Law, who later became an influential cardinal before leaving Boston disgraced in the wake of clergy abuse scandals, edited a diocesan newspaper in Mississippi as an eloquent voice for racial equality. After Medgar Evers, an NACCP field secretary in the state, was assassinated in 1963, Law stepped up his advocacy and became such a frequent presence in black churches and on civil rights commissions that his name appeared on a KKK hit list.[21] When in 1968 the National Advisory Commission on Civil Disorders named "white racism" as an underlying cause of violence in cities, Cardinal John Dearden of Detroit affirmed the report's conclusions and called for urban strategies focused on housing, education, and employment. Speaking as the first president of the U.S. bishops' conference just after the 1968 assassination of Rev. Martin Luther King Jr., Dearden pledged to raise $1 million for his archdiocesan development fund to make anti-poverty grants. "We do not intend to set up a program in any patronizing or paternalistic way that tells people what they need and provides it for them," the cardinal declared. "We want to know what they need. . . . They will tell us what they need."[22]

The U.S. bishops' conference approved *A Statement on the National Race Crisis* and formed an Urban Task Force to be "an instrument of Catholic involvement in inter-religious programs and civic programs to affect solutions to the twin crises of race and poverty." In 1969, the bishops' annual Labor Day statement for the first time called for the church to make "a generous portion of its limited resources available for the development and self-determination of the poor and powerless." This was not to be a simple charitable endeavor or a safety-net program. It would tackle structural injustice head on. A year later, bishops passed a resolution creating a national anti-poverty effort, which called for the church to help impoverished communities "develop economic strengths and political power . . . through specific projects aimed at eliminating the very causes of poverty." The first national collection for the campaign in 1970 raised more than $8 million, the largest single collection in the Catholic Church in the United States at the time. The bishops' Campaign for Human Development, a shining pillar of the post–Vatican II church, became the church's most systematic response to social injustice, and to this day it is one of the most important funders of grassroots community organizing.

As Catholic bishops flexed their muscles on racial and economic justice issues, the sexual revolution brought a jarring challenge to Catholicism's traditional teachings on sexuality and gender. The birth control pill, released on the market the same year that Betty Friedan's 1963 classic *The Feminist Mystique* awakened the conscience of a generation of women, underscored the deep fissures between the Catholic Church and a liberalizing culture. In the summer of 1968, Pope Paul VI reaffirmed the church's teaching against contraception. Ignoring the guidance of his own theological advisory commission, the pope's encyclical affirmed artificial contraception as an "intrinsic evil" prohibited even for married couples. *Humanae Vitae* (On Human Life) sparked bitter recriminations. Theologians around the world challenged the encyclical. Fr. Charles Curran of the Catholic University of America in Washington spoke out against the encyclical, and the Vatican later prohibited him from teaching Catholic moral theology. Even some national bishops' conferences signaled that they found the document flawed. The distinguished theologian, Jesuit priest, and later cardinal Avery Dulles warned that it would be a "serious mistake to use the encyclical as a kind of Catholic loyalty test. Nothing could so quickly snuff out the spirit of personal responsibility, which has done so much to invigorate American Catholicism in the past few years."[23]

Hardliners were in no mood for debate. Cardinal John Krol of Philadelphia, who emerged as a pivotal figure in the church as president of the U.S. bishops' conference and was regarded by many as influential in the election of Karol Wojtyla as Pope John Paul II in 1978, described the birth control encyclical as "divine law."[24] Just three years after Vatican II opened the church to the modern world, the Catholic hierarchy found itself in an isolated corner defending a position rejected by nearly every other Christian denomination. However, an even bigger earthquake was looming on the horizon that would reshape the U.S. bishops' public advocacy and upend the nation's political alignment.

4

THE RISE OF THE RELIGIOUS RIGHT AND A POWER STRUGGLE IN THE CHURCH

Just as American Catholics were absorbing the jolting changes unleashed by Vatican II reforms and a divisive birth control encyclical, the political ground under their feet was also shifting. The sturdy New Deal coalition, anchored by ethnic Catholics and southern whites that fueled Democratic victories from Roosevelt to Johnson, was tearing apart at the seams. Catholics whose parents and grandparents found a home in a party defined by immigrants, unions, and populist challenges to the excesses of capitalism were now growing increasingly disillusioned with the party's shifting identity. Racial unrest, sexual liberation, and antiwar fervor shaped a strain of liberalism that alienated blue-collar Catholics and traditional voters. Many Catholics who found the church's centuries-old teachings about solidarity and the common good reflected in the Democratic Party for so many years were chafing at a liberalism that seemed more focused on individual rights, personal choice, and identity politics.

Conservative leaders seized an opening. By dismantling the old political alignment, they hoped to build what the Nixon strategist and author Kevin Phillips called an "emerging Republican majority." Catholics and their bishops were swept up in the currents of this political upheaval. In particular, the clash over abortion rights thrust church leaders into a newly activist role on the national stage and provided a burgeoning conservative movement with powerful allies. The unexpected election of a Polish pope who emphasized a muscular orthodoxy and spoke boldly against a "culture of death" would bring a decisive shift in church politics as well.

When Richard Nixon rose to deliver his second inaugural address on a cloudy, windswept day in January 1973, he could take satisfaction in driving a nail in the coffin of the New Deal coalition by winning a majority of Catholic voters—a feat that had eluded Republican presidential candidates for more than three decades.[1] Cardinal Terence Cooke of New York delivered the benediction, as he had four years earlier at the president's first inaugural. Nixon courted the cardinal and other Catholic leaders to help validate his appeals to traditional values and to peel Catholic voters away from the Democratic Party at a time when 60 percent of Catholics were registered Democrats. Seven months before the election, another prince of the church, Cardinal John Krol of Philadelphia, warmly welcomed Nixon as the keynote speaker at the annual convention of the National Catholic Education Association in Philadelphia. Nixon reminded the audience that Krol had participated in Sunday worship services at the White House and praised the cardinal as a "great religious leader" with a "deep understanding of philosophy and government."[2]

Nixon proved especially appealing to a Catholic hierarchy fighting efforts in state legislatures to expand abortion rights. While his opponent George McGovern was branded the candidate of "acid, amnesty and abortion," the president rejected the pro-choice findings of his own population commission, and on May 16, 1972, just shy of six months before the presidential election, sent a letter to New York's Cardinal Cooke applauding the church's efforts in the state capitol in Albany to roll back one of the most liberal abortion bills in the country. Noting that the issue was "a matter for state decision outside federal jurisdiction," Nixon wrote, "I would personally like to associate myself with the convictions you deeply feel and eloquently express. . . . The unrestricted abortion policies now recommended by some Americans, and the liberalized abortion policies in effect in some sections of this country seem to me impossible to reconcile with either our religious traditions or our Western heritage."[3] It was the first time a president had waded into the abortion debate with such vigor.

Two days after Nixon's second inaugural ceremony at the U.S. Capitol, a judicial thunderbolt struck across the street at the U.S. Supreme Court. In a 7–2 ruling, the Court found that a right to privacy under the due process clause of the Fourteenth Amendment protected a woman's right to terminate her pregnancy in the first three months. In an instant, state laws limiting the procedure were swept away. The bishops' reaction to *Roe v. Wade* was immediate and decisive. Cardinal John Krol, the president of the bishops' conference, denounced the ruling as "bad logic and bad law," calling it an "unspeakable tragedy."[4] By coincidence, the bishops' newly created ad hoc committee on pro-life activities was scheduled to have its first meeting the day after the momentous ruling. Speaking as a collective body, the bishops for the first time in U.S. history called for civil disobedience. "We cannot accept the Court's judgment," the bishops declared, and "we urge people not to follow its reasoning or conclusions."[5] The hierarchy issued a flurry of statements, testified on Capitol Hill, and focused on lobbying Congress to overturn *Roe* through a constitutional amendment. Bishops soon realized that statements and testimony would not be enough. A sophisticated political strategy was needed.

Plans mapped out by the U.S. bishops' conference called for "coordinated political action by citizens at the national, state and local levels," which would include "the development in each congressional district of an identifiable, tightly knit and well organized pro-life unit." Catholic scholar Mary Seegers described the ambitious effort as "the most detailed and explicit proposal for political action ever to emanate from the offices of the American Catholic hierarchy."[6] The bishops' administrative board spent considerable time trying to figure out how to distance this political blueprint from the tax-exempt church. In the end, the plan defined the pro-life lobbying groups targeted to congressional districts as independent agencies of citizens that were not "operated, controlled or financed by the church."[7]

A few bishops raised warning flags. Bishop Thomas Gumbleton of Detroit noted the political risks of pouring so much of the church's resources behind a single-issue strategy. He questioned why similar "elaborate procedures" had not been developed to address other moral issues. Some of the bishops' key staffers, including Msgr. George Higgins, a towering social justice figure in the church, worried the plan would constrict the bishops' ability to impact political debates when it came to a more expansive set of concerns. "I was afraid it was too much of a one shot, one issue affair, and it might involve the bishops in one issue politics," he said. "I think in the minds of some of the people who were responsible for it, it was a one issue thing. They were going to move on that one issue and they were going to use whatever political clout they could muster."[8] The plan passed overwhelmingly.

A FOUNDATIONAL PRINCIPLE AND
A POTENT WEDGE ISSUE

It's hard to fathom today, but abortion in the years before *Roe* was not cemented as a rigid partisan issue. Sharp clashes over abortion played out at the state level to be sure, but the political and ideological cleavages that would soon define the abortion debate at the national level had not yet broken wide open. Several high-profile Republicans were pro-choice. As governor of California, Ronald Reagan—who by 1980 would ride a wave of pro-life Catholic and evangelical voters to the White House—signed the Therapeutic Abortion Act, a bipartisan measure, just six months after his gubernatorial election in 1966. Prominent Democrats, including Sen. Ted Kennedy and future Speaker of the House Tip O'Neill, opposed abortion. "While the deep concern of a woman bearing an unwanted child merits consideration and sympathy," Kennedy wrote in a letter to a constituent just a year before *Roe*, "it is my personal feeling that the legalization of abortion on demand is not in accordance with the value which our civilization places on human life. I believe that human life, even at its earliest stages, has certain rights which must be recognized—the right to be born, the right to live, the right to grow old."[9] By 1972, the power base of the Democratic Party had shifted to such an extent that the heavily Catholic AFL-CIO chose not to endorse the Democratic ticket for the first time in its history. Pro-choice activists and fundraisers for the Democratic Party became so central in shaping the party's agenda in subsequent decades that Pennsylvania governor Robert Casey, a Catholic liberal who championed social justice policies but opposed abortion, was denied a speaking slot at the 1992 Democratic National Convention.

A Gallup poll in June 1972 found that more Republicans than Democrats supported leaving the decision to have an abortion to a woman and her doctor, a position then endorsed by a sizable majority of voters—including Catholics—from both parties.[10] Nevertheless, most Catholics did recognize that abortion raised profound moral questions distinct from the issue of contraception, a fact that some leaders in the Democratic Party and the liberal establishment failed to grasp. "Abortion rights supporters assumed that ordinary Catholics would reject the Church's teaching on abortion the same way they had with contraception," wrote Amy Sullivan in *The Party Faithful: How and Why Democrats Are Closing the God Gap*. "They had little patience for those who expressed concerns about abortion as they had with those who questioned the morality of birth control. When the American Civil Liberties Union (ACLU) came out in support of legalized abortion in the late 1960s, an ACLU member—and Notre Dame law professor—who complained was told that the organization equated 'anti-abortion positions with anti-birth-control ones, and the defenders [of abortion restrictions] with an effort to enact theological positions into law.'"

Efforts to politicize abortion began in the years before *Roe*. When parishioners arrived for Mass at St. Barbara's Catholic Church in Santa Ana, California, on the last Sunday in August in 1970, voting registrars were seated in front of the church. Fr. Michael Collins, the pastor, explained in his homily that he had invited the registrars. The priest asked all Democrats in his congregation to join him after Mass and change their party affiliation to Republican to protest an "abortion on demand" plank in the Democratic State Convention.[11] At the end of the day, 530 members of the parish had changed their party affiliation. The Democratic candidate for California Secretary of State investigated and found that St. Barbara's Republican voter registration drive was not an isolated case. Fourteen of the twenty-nine Catholic churches in Orange County had requested registrars to visit their parishes the following Sunday. This was no spontaneous uprising. The Republican State Central Committee had orchestrated the effort to see whether abortion could be used as a wedge issue to drive Catholics away from the Democratic Party.

National Republican strategists were closely watching the state-level experiment. The same year Orange County Catholic churches were persuading parishioners to ditch the Democratic Party, the U.S. Department of Defense adopted a policy that doctors on military bases could perform abortions in some instances. Patrick Buchanan, a Catholic and key Nixon aide, urged the president to reverse the policy. Abortion, Buchanan noted, was "a rising issue and a gut issue for Catholics." A week later, Nixon sent a statement to the Defense Department and drew heavily from the language of the Catholic Church when he spoke of his "personal belief in the sanctity of human life—including the life of the yet unborn." A Nixon strategist had a less lofty ideal in mind. "Favoritism toward things Catholic is good politics," the aide wrote in "Dividing the Democrats," a 1971 memo to H. R. Haldeman. "There is a trade-off, but it leaves us with the larger share of the pie."[12] In a strategy guide put together before the 1972 presidential election, Buchanan named "abortion and contraception" first under a list of "Social Issues—Catholic/Ethnic Concerns." When a New York Republican complained about President Nixon's increasingly vocal opposition to abortion, Buchanan chortled, "He will cost himself Catholic support and gain what, Betty Friedan?"[13]

For the Catholic Church, abortion is an intrinsic evil that transcends political or ideological categories. The bedrock principle that all life is sacred because human beings are created in the image of God is fundamental. "Our defense of human life is rooted in the biblical prohibition, Thou Shall Not Kill," the U.S. bishops wrote in 1970, three years before the *Roe* decision. "The life of an unborn child is a human life."[14] Catholic teaching is clear that all rights flow first from the foundational right to life. Contrast that absolute claim with the competing absolute claim articulated in 1969 by feminist icon Betty Friedan: "There is no freedom, no equality, no full human dignity and personhood possible for women until we assert and demand the control over our own bodies, over our reproductive process." A clash of worldviews with little room for complexity or compromise seemed inevitable.

Abortion became a national political issue in the United States less than a decade after bishops departed from the Second Vatican Council with the clear charge to engage the "whole of humanity" and apply church teachings to the "signs of the times."[15] While Vatican II is most widely known for creating a revolution in Catholic liturgy, interfaith dialogue, and empowerment of the laity, the council's landmark document, the "Pastoral Constitution on the Church in the Modern World," also insisted "from the moment of conception, life must be guarded with the greatest of care." The document called abortion and infanticide "unspeakable crimes."[16] When the U.S. Supreme Court found that a right to privacy protected a woman's access to legal abortion, Catholic bishops suddenly faced a momentous political and cultural challenge they could not ignore.

On a late summer day in August 1976, Democratic presidential nominee Jimmy Carter met with a delegation of Catholic bishops at the Mayflower Hotel down the street from the White House. A born-again evangelical who taught Sunday school, Carter had a felicity with biblical themes and moral arguments that left him at ease with religious leaders. Eight days before the election, televangelist Pat Robertson draped his arms around Carter on his national broadcast, *The 700 Club*, and offered what amounted to a political baptism for his "Christian brother." Despite his bonhomie with the faithful, Carter expected and received a grilling about his views on abortion as he sat down with Catholic bishops that day in the nation's capital. It was the first presidential race after the *Roe* ruling. Catholic voters would be decisive in the election.

Led by Archbishop Joseph Bernardin, the bishops sized up Carter and President Ford's positions. As president of the bishops' conference in Washington, Bernardin would become in the next decade the nation's most influential Catholic leader and the architect of a "seamless garment" ethic of life that regarded abortion as part of a broad pro-life witness that included economic justice, nuclear disarmament, and capital punishment. For now, abortion dominated the discussion inside the hotel suite. A few weeks later, President Ford invited Bernardin and five members of the bishops' conference executive committee to the White House. As Carter had done, the president assured the bishops of his personal objection to abortion. Unlike the Democratic candidate, Ford could point to specific language in the GOP platform calling for a constitutional amendment to overturn *Roe*.[17] After the meetings, Bernardin told reporters he was "encouraged" by Ford and "disappointed" with Carter. The media had its story. Russell Shaw, a spokesperson for the bishops' conference at the time, describes the fallout. "All hell broke loose," Shaw recalled. "It was hot and heavy for a few weeks. The bishops took a pounding for sticking their noses in the presidential election. We had to call a press conference saying we're not endorsing anyone. Conference staff threatened to resign. Bernardin got chewed out by some of his brother bishops. He learned a lot from that moment."

While the mainstream media had not picked up on internal tensions starting to divide Catholic leaders, the U.S. bishops' public stumble during the 1976 presidential election underscored emerging fissures over how to address abortion as it related to other moral issues in politics. The public impression that Catholic bishops viewed abortion as the defining issue in the election belied the fact that the conference's first official election-year political responsibility statement released that year was anything but a single-issue manifesto. "The church's concern for human rights and social justice," it declared, "should be comprehensive and consistent." Insisting they did "not seek the formation of a religious voting block," the bishops listed "a broad range of topics," including education, the economy, food policy, housing, human rights, U.S. foreign policy, and military expenditures, as issues Catholics must weigh in the voting booth. Nevertheless, the media could be forgiven for interpreting Bernardin's comments as a de facto endorsement. No bishop stood in the glare of television cameras expressing disappointment in President Ford and the Republican Party. Despite the lengthy list of moral issues the bishops' political responsibility statement highlighted for Catholic voters, there was no detailed political game plan for ending poverty or homelessness. In the end, the election was not a referendum on abortion. Carter cruised to victory.

The conservative dream of an "emerging Republican majority" was put on ice for now. The onetime peanut farmer won Catholics back to the Democratic Party. Evangelicals put their trust in one of their own. The public expressed cautious hope that an outsider could bring ethical leadership back to Washington after the Watergate scandal. The religious right's moment had not yet arrived. While plenty of evangelicals opposed abortion, the Catholic bishops' full-throated advocacy and unique ability to marshal the resources of a hierarchical church wired for coordinated action meant that abortion was still largely regarded as a Catholic issue. Rev. Jerry Falwell expressed "horror and disbelief" at the *Roe* decision, but he did not preach a sermon against abortion until five years after the Supreme Court ruling. "Jerry Falwell couldn't spell 'abortion' five years ago," the founder of the American Life League, a grassroots Catholic organization, declared in 1982.[18]

A Catholic political strategist with an uncanny instinct for uniting disparate religious leaders across the theological spectrum was determined to write a new playbook. It was with no little hint of irony that a once divorced former Hollywood actor, who as governor signed one of the nation's most liberal abortion bills into law and opposed a ballot initiative barring homosexuals from teaching in public schools, would have a powerful Christian conservative movement, anchored by Catholics and Protestant evangelicals, to thank for his ticket to the White House.

CATHOLICS AND THE MORAL MAJORITY

The late Rev. Jerry Falwell is both revered and reviled for mobilizing millions of conservative Christians into an electoral force that helped elect Republicans. The Southern Baptist preacher who founded the Moral Majority and changed the public face of Christianity in the 1980s didn't set out to be a political crusader. In a 1965 sermon, "Ministers and Marches," he criticized the Rev. Martin Luther King Jr. and other preachers for being too politically active. Getting souls to heaven (not the polls), Falwell insisted, should be the "higher calling" of a minister. This reluctance to engage in the political arena reflected a long-held belief among Christian fundamentalists that separating from a secular culture rife with corruption and sin was essential to keeping a straight path to salvation.

This tenet was reinforced after the famous 1925 Scopes "Monkey Trial," when creationists won a high-profile court case but faced widespread ridicule and backlash in the court of public opinion. Fundamentalists retreated from the public square and hunkered down in a vibrant subculture where Christian bookstores, colleges, and media outlets nurtured them in a self-protected cocoon. "Many evangelicals were not even registered to vote because politics is dirty and unseemly," observed the historian of American religion Randall Balmer. "And besides, Jesus is coming back at any time to get us out of this mess, so why should we worry about the temporal order. That was a very, very real sentiment among America's evangelicals for the middle decades of the 20th century. This was an alternate universe within the larger American culture."[19]

By the late 1970s, Falwell and other conservative Christians felt less belittled by the wider culture than under siege. The days of retreat and withdrawal from politics were over. In their view, unelected judges on the Supreme Court had already kicked prayer out of the public schools, enshrined the killing of a fetus as a protected right, and curtailed government aid to religious schools. Jimmy Carter's presidency was the final straw. His championing of the Equal Rights Amendment (ERA), and, more important, the IRS challenge to the tax-exempt status of all-white Christian academies that had opened across the South in the wake of the Supreme Court's desegregation order in *Brown v. Board of Education*, awakened a sleeping giant.[20] Falwell was ready to act but worried that launching a political organization would distract him from his ministry and divide his congregation. Paul Weyrich, a Catholic political strategist who earned his stripes during Sen. Barry Goldwater's insurgent 1964 presidential campaign and later cofounded the Heritage Foundation, stepped in to make the case.

In a key meeting that led to the creation of the Moral Majority in 1979, Weyrich came prepared with results from a national poll he commissioned. It showed Americans were not worried about mixing religion and politics. In fact, as Weyrich described it, "they were chomping at the bit to do so."[21] Weyrich proposed that abortion should be "the keystone of their organizing strategy, since this was the issue that could divide the Democratic Party."[22] He also knew that opposition to abortion by itself could not bring together Catholics, Southern Baptists, Pentecostals, and Mormons into a broad coalition. "I had discussions with all the leading lights of the movement in the late 1970s and early 1980s, post–*Roe v. Wade* and they were all arguing that the decision was one more reason why Christians had to isolate themselves from the rest of the world," Weyrich said in an interview in the early 1990s. "What changed their mind was Jimmy Carter's intervention against the Christian schools, trying to deny them tax-exempt status on the basis of so-called de facto segregation."[23]

In order to construct a big-tent movement, Weyrich and other architects of the New Right framed their argument with accessible appeals to rebuild America's "Judeo-Christian" tradition. The language of moral absolutes and the need for a united culture war against a common secular enemy struck a chord with conservatives across a wide swath of Christian denominations. "We are talking about Christianizing America," Weyrich explained. "We are talking about simply spreading the Gospel in a political context."[24] Even if Weyrich knew that abortion would never be the only issue to politicize Christians, he recognized its electoral efficacy. Conservative Catholics had already scored a victory for Republicans in 1978, a year before the Moral Majority was founded, when they helped defeat a liberal Iowa senator by leafleting cars parked at Catholic churches the Sunday before Election Day with anti-abortion literature. Backed by Catholics, pro-life candidates also won three Senate seats and the governor's mansion in Minnesota. If blue-collar Catholics could be mobilized around abortion, Weyrich said, they could be "the Achilles's heel of the liberal Democrats."[25]

Along with the direct-mail guru Richard Viguerie, Conservative Caucus chairman Howard Phillips, and Ed McAteer, the head of the Religious Roundtable, Weyrich huddled with Falwell at his Lynchburg, Virginia, home in an effort to convince the preacher that if they acted fast, they could impact the 1980 presidential election. Falwell was sold. Now all the organization needed was a name. The group struggled to come up with something that would stick. "What we really need is a moral majority of Americans with a name like—" Weyrich began before Falwell cut him off. *Moral Majority*. The phrase hit the mark perfectly. Only two decades after John F. Kennedy faced virulent anti-Catholic attacks organized by leading evangelicals to keep him out of the White House, Catholics and Southern Baptists were now building what the Baptist theologian and founding dean of the Beeson Divinity School later called "an ecumenism of the trenches." Falwell had fully shed his earlier unease about politics. "We're fighting a holy war," he preached at his Thomas Road Baptist Church in 1980.[26]

In its first year, the Moral Majority had organized in forty-seven states with the goal of mobilizing ten million voters for the presidential election.[27] Thousands of preachers participated in political and media training seminars. Falwell claimed that four million voters had been registered as Republicans.[28] The organization played a key role in four Senate races in 1980, and in three of those races it backed pro-life Catholic candidates who went on to win.[29] By Falwell's estimate, nearly a third of his members were Catholic. Weyrich later recalled Falwell acknowledging the political marriage of convenience that fueled their efforts together. "He said, 'If you and I were discussing theology we'd probably come to bloody blows,'" Weyrich told *Catholic News Service* in 2007. "But we were not; we were discussing politics and so we were blood brothers."[30]

Ronald Reagan, who rarely darkened the door of a church, was no fundamentalist Christian. But he did know the fundamentals of electoral math. Winning evangelicals in the South and Catholics in the Northeast would secure the White House. Reagan's frequent defense of traditional family values, staunch anti-communism, aversion to government activism, and free-market enthusiasm endeared him to Christian conservatives eager to restore American triumphalism at home and abroad. He jettisoned his past support for abortion rights and supported a constitutional amendment to overturn *Roe*. When Reagan stood before eighteen thousand evangelicals and other Christians at a Dallas conference less than three months before the election, he sealed the political marriage between religious conservatives and the Republican Party. "I know this is a nonpartisan gathering and you can't endorse me. . . . But I want you to know that I endorse you and what you are doing," Reagan said to a roaring crowd that hung on his every word. "Religious America is awakening perhaps just in time for our country's sake."

Reagan steamrolled to victory with a clean sweep of the South, and he carried 51 percent of Catholics. Blue-collar Catholics in places like Macomb County in suburban Detroit rallied behind the Republican ticket, spawning a new species in the political ecosystem: the Reagan Democrat. Jimmy Carter's share of the Catholic vote plummeted nearly fifteen points from 1976.[31] The religious right was now a force to be reckoned with in American politics.

THE BERNARDIN ERA AND
A CONSISTENT ETHIC OF LIFE

The U.S. bishops' conference in Washington hummed with energy during the Reagan era, emerging as a vocal critic of the president's economic policies and nuclear arms agenda and an ally in his opposition to abortion and support of federal tax credits for Catholic schools. Archbishop Joseph Bernardin of Chicago recovered from his awkward foray into national politics during the Carter-Ford campaign, determined to never again let the church's opposition to abortion be viewed as a single-issue partisan cause. Soon he would find himself embroiled in an unusual, and highly public, power struggle with several influential bishops emboldened to fight the culture wars by John Paul II, whose surprising 1978 election gave firepower to conservative Catholic activists and church leaders equally determined to keep abortion at the center of political debates.

By the time Archbishop Bernardin stood to deliver the annual Gannon Lecture at Fordham University at the end of 1983, he was already the public face of the U.S. church. A year earlier, *Time* magazine featured him on its cover. "God and the Bomb—Catholic Bishops Debate Nuclear Morality," read the headline. The archbishop had steered the complex and often contentious three-year drafting process of a landmark national pastoral letter on nuclear weapons. Even before its formal release in the spring of 1983, the effort spooked Ronald Reagan enough that he sent his national security adviser William Clark, a Catholic, to head off potential criticism. *The Challenge of Peace: God's Promise and Our Response* did not endorse nuclear abolition, but, in calling for an end to the development of any new weapons systems, the bishops offered a clear challenge to the administration's plans for nuclear buildup. A decade later, the *New York Times* praised the bishops' public letter as "a theologically and militarily sophisticated document that has become a standard resource for study and discussion in military circles."[32]

At Fordham, church leaders, theologians, and national media packed into a student center as Bernardin used the pastoral letter to advocate for what he called a "consistent ethic of life" framework that included issues of poverty, abortion, war, euthanasia, and capital punishment. This expansive vision for defending the sanctity of life defined the church's concern for life in the womb as woven together in what Bernardin described as a "seamless garment" bearing on "the multiple ways in which human life is threatened today." "We intend our opposition to abortion and our opposition to nuclear war to be seen as specific applications of this broader attitude," Bernardin explained. Noting that he had just been appointed the chairman of the U.S. bishops' pro-life committee, the archbishop said he was committed to "shaping a position of linkage among the life issues."[33]

> When one carries this principle into the public debate today, however, one meets significant opposition from very different places on the political and ideological spectrum. Some see clearly the application of the principle to abortion but contend the bishops overstepped their bounds when they applied it to choices about national security. Others understand the power of the principle in the strategic debate, but find its application on abortion a violation of the realm of private choice. I contend the viability of the principle depends upon the consistency of its application. . . . If one contends, as we do, that the right of every fetus to be born should be protected by civil law and supported by civil consensus, then our moral, political and economic responsibilities do not stop at the moment of birth. Those who defend the right to life of the weakest among us must be equally visible in support of the quality of life of the powerless among us: the old and the young, the hungry and the homeless, the undocumented immigrant and the unemployed worker. Such a quality of life posture translates into specific political and economic positions on tax policy, employment generation, welfare policy, nutrition and feeding programs, and health care. Consistency means we cannot have it both ways. We cannot urge a compassionate society and vigorous public policy to protect the rights of the unborn and then argue that compassion and significant public programs on

behalf of the needy undermine the moral fiber of the society or are
beyond the proper scope of governmental responsibility.

It was a speech with far-reaching implications for the church's role in
politics and public policy. As Reagan's 1984 reelection campaign began,
Bernardin's "seamless garment" approach would quickly be put to the
test. Bishop John O'Connor of Scranton, Pennsylvania, then largely unknown on the national stage, had just been appointed by Pope John Paul
II to lead the nation's most high-profile diocese after only six months in
the working-class Pennsylvania city. Even before moving into the archbishop's residence next to St. Patrick's Cathedral, the vocal leader had
already angered the Jewish community by declaring that abortion was
"precisely the same" as the murder of six million Jews in the Holocaust. [34]
He would rarely be seen without a red rose lapel, a symbol of the pro-life
movement.

In the archbishop's first year in New York, Democrats nominated a
pro-choice Catholic, the Queens assemblywoman Geraldine Ferraro, as
the party's vice presidential candidate. A public showdown in the hot
spotlight of the city's ubiquitous media seemed almost inevitable. "I do
not see how a Catholic in good conscience can vote for an individual
expressing himself or herself as favoring abortion," the archbishop said
during a televised news conference. [35] Asked by a reporter whether he
might excommunicate New York governor Mario Cuomo, a pro-choice
Catholic, the new archbishop demurred but refused to rule it out. At a
convention in Altoona, Pennsylvania, O'Connor again plunged in to the
fray, telling a crowd of 450 members of the Pennsylvania Pro-Life Federation that the vice presidential candidate had misrepresented Catholic
teaching on abortion. Before the archbishop spoke, a seven-minute message from President Ronald Reagan was aired at the banquet. "For this
fight, God will bless you," the president told the convention. "The time
has come for Congress to act and pass a human life amendment. Abortion
is a tragedy that can't wait." After the president's message, Archbishop
O'Connor quipped, "I didn't tell you to vote for Ronald Reagan, did I?" [36]

Speaking to reporters after the convention, O'Connor explained that
Catholic teaching on abortion was clear. "There is no variance and no
flexibility. There is no leeway as far as the Catholic Church is concerned," he said. "Pope John Paul II has said the task of the church is to
reaffirm that abortion is death. Geraldine Ferraro doesn't have a problem

with me," the archbishop added for dramatic effect. "If she has a problem, it's with the Pope." O'Connor praised Reagan as a "friend of the unborn."[37]

Ferraro was later forced to pull out of the annual Columbus Day parade in Philadelphia after Cardinal Krol threatened to withdraw all the marching bands and Catholic school students from the event if she made an appearance.

Another archbishop appointed that year by Pope John Paul II to lead the Archdiocese of Boston also turned up the heat. Bernard Law, who two decades later would resign in disgrace after media revelations of widespread clergy sexual abuse of children, called abortion "the critical issue in this campaign." At a press conference at his stately residence, Law released a statement signed by seventeen other Catholic bishops from Maine, Vermont, New Hampshire, and Massachusetts declaring it "irresponsible" to downplay the centrality of abortion in the presidential campaign "on the pretext that this is only a matter of personal opinion and morality." The bishops acknowledged that "nuclear holocaust is a future possibility," but added, "The holocaust of abortion is a present reality." Law insisted the church was not endorsing any candidate. "This statement is directed at all the candidates and all voters," he said, before adding coyly, "I think Geraldine Ferraro is a candidate."[38]

The rising prominence of abortion in the presidential race likely pleased more than Ronald Reagan. "I think it is quite possible that the Holy Father conveyed his feelings on the matter [abortion] to some of the more prominent American bishops," the late auxiliary Bishop Joseph Sullivan of Brooklyn told *New York* magazine during the 1984 election. "I think there is a great concern in Rome that America, which could be a force for moral strength in the world, is in danger of becoming a force for moral chaos."[39] While it's unlikely that John Paul II discussed campaign particulars with leading American prelates, the pope played a decisive role in shaping the tone and direction of the U.S. church with his appointment of bishops and stark challenge to fight what he later described vividly as a "culture of death."

THE CHURCH JOHN PAUL II BUILT

When the fifty-eight-year-old Cardinal Karol Wojtyla of Krakow, Poland, stepped on to the balcony overlooking St. Peter's Square as the newly elected pope on October 16, 1978, the curtain opened on a monumental papacy that spanned nearly three decades. The onetime youth actor who risked his life performing in underground theater during the Nazi occupation of Poland almost seemed destined to become a towering presence on the global stage. The dramatic arc of his life and pontificate were so epic that his biographer, Jonathan Kwitny, described him without much hyperbole as "the man of the century." His support of Poland's Solidarity movement and searing moral critique of communism helped put an end to the Soviet Union. The first pope in the age of CNN, his papal trips to no less than 129 countries were international events covered in real time. A giant of interfaith dialogue, John Paul was the first pope to visit a synagogue and a mosque, and, in a move that discomforted traditionalists at the Vatican, he hosted a historic interfaith prayer service at Assisi, Italy. He canonized eighty-two new saints, plus 1,338 beatifications—more than all his predecessors combined.[40] The pope's massive World Youth Days took on the feel of rock concerts in cities including Sydney, Toronto, and Denver, where hundreds of thousands of young people became part of the "JP2 generation."

For all of his undeniable spiritual depth and talent as a global evangelizer, the pope also became a polarizing figure. His vision of a heroic papacy, muscular orthodoxy, and authoritarian style served as the model for a generation of "JP2" priests and bishops. "Inside the church, he tolerated a form of absolutism that some critics could not help comparing with the Soviet system he helped bring down," the veteran Vatican analyst John Allen wrote in the pope's 2005 obituary. What Allen described as his "unapologetically hierarchical and clerical papacy" buoyed the spirits of traditionalists looking for doctrinal order to be restored after what they perceived as the chaos of liturgical relativism and theological liberalism infecting the church in the aftermath of the Second Vatican Council. The pope attended the council as a bishop and viewed himself as a guardian of its legacy, but his definitive moves to centralize authority and silence theological debate undermined many of the council's reforming impulses. Like popes before him, John Paul kept a close eye on the church in the United States.

Because of its size, wealth, and political potency in international affairs, the American church has a big footprint. The Vatican historically viewed U.S. democracy, anchored in the principles of pluralism and church-state separation, with deep suspicion and even outright hostility. Pope Leo XIII's 1899 encyclical, *Testem benevolentiae nostrae* (Witness to Our Good Will), was addressed to Archbishop James Gibbons of Baltimore and challenged ideas that "would give rise to the suspicion that there are among you some who conceive and would have the Church in America to be different from what it is in the rest of the world." Leo saw in America the "confounding of license with liberty" and "the assumed right to hold whatever opinions one pleases upon any subject," serving as proof that there was "a greater need of the Church's teaching office than ever before." The idea that Catholicism was incompatible with democratic principles persevered in large part until the American Jesuit priest and theologian John Courtney Murray, once censured by the Vatican, helped develop the church's tradition so that religious pluralism and freedom of conscience were explicitly affirmed during the Second Vatican Council. Because of his personal experience with Nazism and communism, John Paul admired the American experiment even as he challenged a culture increasingly defined by rampant consumerism, military interventions, sexual liberation, and a sometimes blind faith in unfettered capitalism. In many ways, he was a paradoxical figure. John Paul shook off the strictures of the Vatican's European insularity and did more than any of his predecessors to preach the Gospel in nearly every corner of the globe. When it came to the world outside the church, he reached out with a wide embrace. Inside the church, his posture could be rigid and at times even reactionary.

The new pope moved to tighten the reins on American Catholicism, where dissent from the birth control encyclical, *Humanae Vitae*, was rampant. Rev. Charles Curran, a theologian at the Catholic University of America in Washington, had led a scholarly revolt against the birth control encyclical just days after its release in the summer of 1968. Along with more than a dozen other faculty members at the Vatican-chartered university in the nation's capital, Curran publicly challenged the teaching that artificial contraception was an intrinsic evil. In a statement eventually signed by over six hundred theologians and other academics, including the well-known Jesuit priest Walter Burghardt, they argued that faithful Catholics could "decide according to their conscience that artificial contraception in some circumstances is permissible and indeed necessary to preserve and foster the value and sacredness of marriage."[41] The theologian's own bishop came to his defense. "If Father Curran's status as a Roman Catholic theologian is brought into question," said Bishop Matthew Clark of Rochester, "I fear a serious setback to Catholic education and pastoral life in this country."[42]

John Paul took action. The Vatican's Congregation for the Doctrine of the Faith, led by the future pope Cardinal Joseph Ratzinger, prohibited Curran from teaching theology at a Catholic university in 1986. The Curran affair unfolded only three years after the Vatican began an investigation of Archbishop Raymond Hunthausen of Seattle, an outspoken antiwar prelate who withheld half his income tax in 1982 to protest the U.S. stockpiling of nuclear weapons, which included a submarine-based nuclear missile program in Puget Sound. Hunthausen became a lightning rod for encouraging the Vatican to consider ordaining women, his public support for gay Catholics, and his belief that divorced Catholics should be able to receive the sacraments even if they did not secure a church annulment. The Vatican's doctrine office eventually stripped Hunthausen of much of his diocesan authority.

Along with clamping down on theologians and individual bishops, John Paul also weakened the scope of national bishops' conferences in an effort to consolidate doctrinal authority and make sure local bishops who felt empowered by Vatican II knew their real marching orders came from Rome. "The problem in the American church," the pope's longtime Vatican spokesman Joaquin Navarro-Valls once explained, "is a problem about the structure of the church and where authority comes from. The Catholic Church says their bishops get their power as successors of the Apostles and the Pope as successor of St. Peter. That is the central issue."[43] John Paul didn't hesitate to use his power even in sensitive cases. In 1983, when the legendary Superior General of the Jesuit order, Pedro Arrupe, had to resign because of a debilitating stroke, he followed the order's protocol and appointed a temporary replacement. John Paul overruled his pick of an American Jesuit and imposed his own delegate.

In one apostolic letter, he decreed that bishops' conferences had no doctrinal authority unless they had a two-thirds majority of their members supporting a particular issue and received approval from the Vatican. The pope later issued a pastoral letter on Catholic colleges that required theologians to receive approval from their local bishop to teach. Critics feared that academic freedom would be threatened. When U.S. bishops passed a compromise plan, Rome vetoed it, and a few years later a new set of rules more to the pope's liking were adopted. John Paul also released a new Catechism of the Catholic Church, partly in an effort to replace more liberal national catechisms that had emerged in the wake of Vatican II.

A pope can wield influence in myriad ways, but the power to align the church with his own priorities and steer the ship in a defined direction is most clearly exercised by the power to appoint bishops and cardinals. Not unlike presidents selecting Supreme Court justices who share their consti-tutional, if not political, sympathies, popes put their distinctive mark on the church by the kind of leaders whom they choose. When it came to naming bishops, Pope John Paul II above all valued obedience to the Magisterium, the teaching authority of the church. He wanted the secular equivalent of "company men" who followed orders handed down from the top. As John Paul himself told U.S. bishops in 1983, ideal candidates to the episcopacy would be "priests who have already proven themselves as teachers of the faith as it is proclaimed by the Magisterium of the Church."[44] Specifically, he wanted bishops who would defend the church's ban on birth control, as well as candidates who were rock solid when it came to the church's teaching regarding all-male clergy and priestly celibacy.

"For a man who saw the church at war with communism and later secularism and relativism, John Paul prized unity," said Rev. Thomas Reese, a longtime church analyst and author of *Inside the Vatican: The Politics and Organization of the Catholic Church*. "When it came to appointing bishops loyalty was the most important thing for him. He remade the hierarchy in the United States." It was often repeated, but never confirmed, that when John Paul was looking for a successor to take over the Archdiocese of New York after the death of Cardinal Terence Cooke, he said, "I want a man like me in New York." Whether the pope spoke those exact words or not, John O'Connor's meteoric rise from auxiliary bishop for the Archdiocese for Military Services to the bishop of Scranton, Pennsylvania, and then to archbishop of New York in just six years reflected the pope's desire to restore doctrinal and organization-al discipline to the American church. The pick also reflected the pope's desire to reinvigorate the church's anti-abortion voice, which, a decade removed from *Roe v. Wade*, some conservative Catholics and bishops saw as muffled.

For Catholic activists on the right, the U.S. bishops' conference in the 1980s had become the "Democratic Party at Prayer," issuing detailed statements on nuclear policy and economic justice widely regarded as causing heartburn for the architects of the Reagan revolution. Indeed, only three years removed from provoking a debate about the morality of nuclear deterrence, the bishops again waded into contested terrain. The 1986 pastoral letter, "Economic Justice for All," was released after a period of lengthy consultation and collaboration that included town hall forums with economists, struggling families, and leaders across the ideological spectrum. At a time when the Reagan administration slashed spending on social welfare, challenged unions, and demonized government, the bishops offered a timely reflection grounded in traditional Catholic social teaching about the need for economic systems to serve human dignity and the common good. The document affirmed a positive role for government, a "preferential option" for the poor, and the importance of labor unions in helping "workers resist exploitation"; it also recognized the limits of free markets and called for a more progressive tax system in which "those with relatively greater financial resources pay a higher rate of taxation."[45]

Just as conservatives organized counterstatements to challenge the bishops' letter on nuclear weapons, William Simon, a former Treasury secretary under Nixon, led a committee of high-profile Catholics who criticized the bishops' positions and released their own analysis that touted limited government and market solutions. Five years after the bishops' economic letter, John Paul released *Centesimus Annus*, an encyclical conservatives cheered as the most market-friendly reflection ever written by a pope. In the *Wall Street Journal* the day after its release, Fr. Richard John Neuhaus of *First Things* argued that the American bishops' economic pastoral "must now be recognized as unrepresentative of the church's authoritative teaching." Under the headline "The Pope Affirms the 'New Capitalism,'" Neuhaus even went so far as to bless capitalism as "the economic corollary of the Christian understanding of man's nature and destiny."[46] He argued that the encyclical should bring "a careful, and perhaps painful, rethinking of conventional wisdoms about Catholic social teaching." This response offered a selective reading of the pope's frequent challenges to unbridled capitalism and his warning against "an idolatry of the market." Just a few years earlier, the same conservatives now trumpeting the pope's supposed free-market bullishness had taken issue with John Paul's assertion of "the priority of labor over capital" as part of their counterresponse to the bishops' economic pastoral.

Archbishop Bernardin's "seamless garment" framework situating abortion as part of other attacks on human life, critics argued, only diluted the church's commitment to protecting innocent life in the womb. Deal Hudson, who led Catholic outreach for President George W. Bush, described it this way in his book *Onward, Christian Soldiers: The Growing Political Power of Catholics and Evangelicals in the United States*:

> In spite of Bernardin's intentions, the broadening of the pro-life position enabled the Catholic Conferences to back away from the abortion issue and distance themselves from pro-life activists who were demanding more action from the bishops. The American bishops, who truly can be credited for helping to lead the pro-life movement after *Roe v. Wade*, gradually withdrew from grassroots involvement to attend to what they considered larger matters. John Cardinal O'Connor of New York City, the pope's point man in the United States, was one obvious exception among others, including Bernard Cardinal Law of Boston. While the American bishops were moving left, there was a different wave of change in the Vatican. The election of Reagan may have alarmed the Conference staff in Washington, DC, and led to a series of anti-Reagan pastoral letters, but the election of Karol Cardinal Wojtyla as pope in late 1978 had consequences they could not thwart.

The prominent conservative and papal biographer George Weigel, who had entrée to top officials at the Vatican during John Paul II's papacy, also viewed the election of the Polish pontiff and the appointment of John O'Connor to New York as watershed moments signaling a new direction in the American church. "O'Connor's staunch and unyielding pro-life activism as archbishop of New York was crucial in keeping that issue alive at a moment when the pro-life energies of the American episcopate showed some signs of flagging," Weigel wrote in "The End of the Bernardin Era," a 2011 essay for the journal *First Things*. "In doing so, O'Connor . . . set in place one of the markers that would eventually help displace the Bernardin approach to the Catholic Church's interaction with the U.S. public-policy debate." When Pope John Paul II released his 1995 encyclical *Evangelium Vitae* (The Gospel of Life), he offered a stirring defense of human life from the moment of conception and presented a stark image of a "culture of life" in battle with a "culture of death." The pope spoke out strongly against a broad spectrum of threats to life and human dignity, including euthanasia and capital punishment, as well as what he called "disgraceful working conditions, where people are treated as mere instruments of gain."[47] But with its emphasis on abortion, the encyclical quickly became a key text of the pro-life movement.

Six months after its publication, the pope visited the United States. "Resist the pressures and temptations of a world that too often tries to ignore a most fundamental truth: that every life is a gift from God," the pope told a crowd estimated at 120,000 people who gathered on the Great Lawn in Central Park for an outdoor Mass. After praying the rosary with three thousand invited guests at St. Patrick's Cathedral, the pontiff shocked the crowd when he waved off his Popemobile and started walking down Fifth Avenue and then east on 50th Street to Madison Avenue, where he entered the residence of Cardinal O'Connor.[48] While other popes had condemned abortion, John Paul II's papacy in many ways elevated anti-abortion advocacy as the lynchpin of Catholic identity. The church, he believed, was called to be an unwavering witness that confronted a relativistic and dehumanizing culture. The prophetic stance modeled by John Paul became the blueprint for a generation of bishops and pro-life Catholic activists. The lines of debate hardened as the increasingly uncompromising rhetoric of the Democratic Party and pro-choice donors who made abortion rights a litmus test of their own liberal orthodoxy clashed with an anti-abortion movement that saw abortion as nothing less than murder of a human being.

The public battles Cardinal O'Connor and Cardinal Law waged against Geraldine Ferraro were just the beginning. Sen. John Kerry, another pro-choice Catholic, faced intense scrutiny from the hierarchy during the 2004 presidential election as a minority of bishops grabbed headlines by declaring Kerry unfit to receive Communion. "Wafer watch," the traveling press corps dubbed it. Newark archbishop John Myers took to the pages of the *Wall Street Journal*: "Certain policies on issues such as welfare, national security, the war in Iraq, Social Security or taxes, taken singly or any combination, do not provide a 'proportionate reason' to vote for a pro-abortion candidate." Colorado Springs bishop Michael Sheridan wrote in a pastoral letter less than a year before the 2004 election that abortion "trumps all other issues." Catholic public officials who opposed criminalizing abortion, he said, "jeopardize their salvation," and Catholics who vote for them will "suffer the same fatal consequences."

Cathleen Kaveny, a professor of theology and law at Boston College who recognizes the implications of what she regards as *Roe*'s flawed legal reasoning, worries about the efficacy of this posture. "To make their point, pro-lifers understandably appropriated a time-honored form of American political rhetoric: the jeremiad," Kaveny wrote in a 2011 *Commonweal* essay. "In American history the form goes back to the Puritans, and it has been appropriated by every major moral reform movement since, most notably the abolitionists. The jeremiad is of course modeled on the scathing denunciations of violations of divine law by the Hebrew prophets, and has been used effectively by political liberals as well as conservatives. The jeremiad's *expressive* function is clear and powerful. . . . Ironically, however, its *persuasive* function is far more questionable. Most self-proclaimed Jeremiahs give you two options: agree with them completely or be consigned to everlasting damnation. A discerning, nuanced conversation about a complicated issue is not an option." Kaveny argues that when we situate "pregnant women and the unborn child within a supportive society rather than consigning them to an all too isolating intimacy," a true culture of life is being built "rather than merely castigating a culture of death."[49]

As abortion reconfigured American politics, it also created an increasingly tribal American Catholic Church during the John Paul era. Bernardin's "seamless garment" was being ripped to shreds in the meat grinder of politics, both secular and ecclesial. Catholic activists and even institutional church leaders came to identify with competing camps whose labels obscured as much as they revealed. It became "social justice Catholics" versus "pro-life Catholics." On my first day on the job at the U.S. bishops' conference in 2005, a grizzled veteran offered some humorous shorthand by way of describing the factions in the building I would need to navigate. "It's the social justice socialists on that floor," she explained wryly, "and the pro-life fascists down there." Bernardin saw this internecine tug-of-war breaking out inside the church and tried to call a ceasefire. In 1996, a year after *Evangelium Vitae* and John Paul's U.S. visit, the cardinal launched a common-ground initiative designed to provide a forum for constructive dialogue that might begin to heal divisions between left and right. The Catholic Common Ground Project's foundational document—"Called to Be Catholic: Church in a Time of Peril"—didn't mince words about the fractured state of American Catholicism:

> A mood of suspicion and acrimony hangs over many of those most active in the church's life; at moments it even seems to have infiltrated the ranks of the bishops. One consequence is that many of us are refusing to acknowledge disquieting realities, perhaps fearing that they may reflect poorly on our past efforts or arm our critics within the church. Candid discussion is inhibited. Across the whole spectrum of views within the church, proposals are subject to ideological litmus tests. Ideas, journals, and leaders are pressed to align themselves with preexisting camps, and are viewed warily when they depart from those expectations. There is nothing wrong in itself with the prospect that different visions should contend within American Catholicism. That has long been part of the church's experience in this nation, and indeed differences of opinion are essential to the process of attaining the truth. But the way that struggle is currently proceeding, the entire church may lose.[50]

The project included a committee of nearly two dozen prominent Catholics—theologians, nuns, judges, academics, and others—who would host discussions on topics that included women's roles in the church, the nature of human sexuality, the responsibility of theology in relation to authoritative church teachings, and Catholic identity in education. Charter members included both the prominent conservative Mary Ann Glendon, a Harvard Law professor the Vatican named to lead the Vatican's delegation to the 1995 World Conference on Women in Beijing, and Sister Elizabeth Johnson, a noted feminist theologian. It also included the conservative Catholic Michael Novak, who championed free-market capitalism and butted heads with the bishops on economic issues. Along with Bernardin, the committee included seven other bishops. "This was a committee of moderate liberals and conservatives, men and women with strong disagreements who could be counted on to discuss rather than denounce. . . . It was hardly a group to start endorsing heresy," wrote Peter Steinfels, the widely respected Catholic writer and a former *New York Times* religion columnist.[51] The balanced makeup of the committee and the modest goal of probing obvious fissures in the church made the instant blowback against the initiative from powerful forces in the hierarchy even more shocking.

Within hours of its release, several of John Paul's stalwarts in the United States denounced the effort in stinging terms. "The church already has common ground," Cardinal Law of Boston bristled in a statement. "It is found in sacred Scripture and tradition. . . . Dissent from revealed truth or authoritative teaching of the church cannot be 'dialogued away.'"[52] The next day Cardinal James Hickey of Washington echoed Law's unusually pointed challenge and broke with the standard church protocol of not airing grievances in the public spotlight. "We cannot achieve church unity by accommodating those who dissent from church teaching," Hickey said.[53] Cardinal Bevilacqua of Philadelphia and Cardinal Adam Maida of Detroit weighed in with similar statements that appeared on the front pages of their archdiocesan newspapers. The pushback amounted to a coordinated effort to kill the initiative before it ever got off the ground. Bernardin was personally stung by the episode. He offered thoughtful responses and assurances that tradition and doctrine would not be tossed aside. It was a lost cause. The power dynamics inside the church had shifted.

Just three months after Bernardin launched the common ground effort, cancer ended his life at the age of sixty-eight. For three days and nights in the bitter Chicago winter, people waited five hours to pay their respects at Holy Name Cathedral. A leader some considered to be the most influential American bishop of the twentieth century was now gone. A new era was dawning. In the decade after the cardinal's death, a consistent ethic of life framework and calls for common ground began to lose traction. While church leaders still lobbied Congress to protect the social safety net and advocated for immigration reform, the clearest expressions of Catholic identity in politics and culture were narrowing. If the spirit of Vatican II set aflame a hopeful vision of engaging with the modern world, the church also now seemed hunkered down for a long fight with the enemy of secularism. At the U.S. Conference of Catholic Bishops, where a generation of social justice advocates drew inspiration from the *aggiornamento* of the Second Vatican Council and extolled Bernardin's broad pro-life vision, a quiet revolution was also transforming the church's institutional presence in Washington.

THE CONSOLIDATION OF CONSERVATIVE POWER AND A NEW DIRECTION FOR BISHOPS IN WASHINGTON

It's hard to know who was more stunned: the backslapping bishop with a big personality or the soft-spoken protégé of Cardinal Bernardin he had just defeated to become president of the U.S. Conference of Catholic Bishops. The 2010 election of Cardinal Timothy Dolan of New York was not exactly front-page news—even most faithful were surely not paying much attention—but Dolan's upset victory over Bishop Gerald Kicanas of Tucson signaled a telling shift in the church's power dynamics. "Not to elect Kicanas," the Jesuit priest and veteran bishop watcher Thomas Reese wrote on the eve of the vote, "would be an ecclesial earthquake of monumental proportions."[54]

As vice president, Kicanas was all but assured of making the jump to the presidency under the unwritten rules of conference protocol. Only once since the 1960s had a vice president not risen to the top post. A pastoral leader mentored by Bernardin, the understated bishop had instincts for consensus building, viewed politics as the art of the possible, and welcomed social science research about the church as a source of dispassionate analysis. In short, he was exactly the wrong kind of leader if you were a bishop who viewed the church under constant threat and wanted someone who would throw a punch.

Kicanas faced an aggressive campaign to derail him. One bishop, commenting after the vote, acknowledged hearing rumblings of a "putsch" in the days leading up to the election at the bishops' national assembly but dismissed the possibility.[55] Kicanas became a target of criticism for his alleged lax oversight of a seminarian once under his care in Chicago who went on to abuse several children. Survivors of clergy abuse and conservative activists who disliked the moderate bishop lobbied hard to defeat him. Flyers were slid under the doors of bishops' hotel rooms. Text messages were sent. Phone calls were made. Tim Drake of the *National Catholic Register*—a conservative publication then owned by the Legion of Christ, a Catholic religious order plagued by revelations of sexual abuses by its late founder, Father Marcial Maciel Degollado— wrote an essay calling for the bishops to reject Kicanas.[56] Ironically, the allegations of negligent oversight of the abusive priest had begun years earlier and were originally directed against Cardinal Francis George of Chicago, a favorite of conservatives. Catholic activists on the right did not mobilize against the cardinal as they did with Kicanas, and he became president of the conference in 2007. Thomas Peters, a conservative Catholic blogger with a wide following, warned that "vibrant orthodoxy" would be threatened if Kicanas won. "Can we expect Bishop Kicanas to defend the teachings and prerogatives of the church when they come into conflict with the President and Democrats' liberal agenda?" he wrote.[57]

The specter of the Obama presidency was also clearly on the minds of bishops. Only three years earlier, a year before Obama won the White House, Kicanas beat Dolan out in the conference's vice presidential race. What changed in just a few years? For a vocal contingent of conservative bishops, Obama's 2008 election was viewed less as a watershed moment in the nation's history than a foreboding sign. Weeks after his election, bishops took aim at the Freedom of Choice Act (FOCA), legislation that had floundered in Congress for years and showed no sign of going anywhere. As Washington focused on digging out from the worst economic crisis since the Great Depression, bishops pledged to "mobilize the resources of the USCCB, dioceses and the entire Catholic community" to oppose the act. Bulletin inserts in parishes across the country warned about FOCA. Priests delivered sermons encouraging the faithful to write to the administration in protest. Emails of unknown origin began popping up in the inboxes of Catholics claiming the proposal would force Catholic hospitals to shut down, and even lead to "a future amendment that would force women by law to have abortions in certain situations."

The anti-FOCA hysteria that religion commentator Amy Sullivan described as the "Catholic crusade against a mythical abortion bill" reached such a fevered pitch that *Catholic News Service* felt compelled to tamp down the furor. "Internet rumors to the contrary," one story clarified, "no Catholic hospital in the United States is in danger of closing because of the Freedom of Choice Act."[58]

When the University of Notre Dame invited Obama to give the commencement address less than a year after his election, more than one hundred bishops spoke out in protest. Bishop Kicanas was not one of them. Cardinal Dolan, in contrast, called the Notre Dame invitation "a big mistake." His brother bishops viewed Dolan as a happy warrior not afraid to mix it up. Gregarious and press savvy, Dolan had folksy charm along with the gravitas that came with being a cardinal and leader of an influential diocese in the nation's media capital. He impressed some bishops with his willingness to publicly challenge the *New York Times* for what they viewed as the paper's anti-Catholic bias. After Dolan's surprise election, conservatives were triumphant. "What a splendid choice!" gushed Bill Donohue of the Catholic League. "He'll get the job done and will not disappoint practicing Catholics who are loyal to the Magisterium."[59] The election "almost certainly means increased determination to fight the culture war outside the church and face up to dissent within," observed Russell Shaw, a respected conservative Catholic author and former spokesman for the bishops' conference. "That is very much the case on abortion and also on same-sex marriage, where the bishops, late in the game, have finally begun gearing up for a serious fight. Cardinal Bernardin's famous 'common ground' for dissenters and loyalists alike won't have many bishops occupying it in the years just ahead."[60]

A more subtle but significant changing of the guard had already been taking place among the lay staff that directs the daily educational and policy work at the bishops' conference. In 2006, a major restructuring upended the conference. A wave of veterans with institutional memory and experience in leading the conference through the heady days of post–Vatican II social activism and the landmark national pastoral letters on the economy and nuclear weapons took retirement incentives. More than two dozen staffers at the conference left, including the executive director of the Catholic Campaign for Human Development, the bishops' national anti-poverty program; the government affairs director; and two longtime policy advisers in the International Justice and Peace office.[61]

Thomas Quigley, the bishops' senior point man on Latin America for more than four decades, watched the conference's identity change toward the end of his tenure. "In my time, we were overrun with Domers—great young Notre Dame grads. Now it's the Christendom crusaders," Quigley said, referring to Christendom College in Virginia, a small conservative school that is a flagship for traditionalists and pro-life activists. Quigley played a key role in advising U.S. bishops responding to human rights struggles and solidarity movements in Chile, Brazil, Bolivia, and Argentina. Church leaders took center stage at international conferences and led delegations. Conference staff was frequently in the media speaking about global justice issues. Because of geopolitical changes and the rise of the culture wars, the U.S. church has played a less central role on the international stage, Quigley observed, but the bishops' conference has been widely recognized for its leadership in advocating for comprehensive immigration reform in the United States. "It's still hard to see how many of today's John Paul II culture warriors will reset their clocks to Francis time—and maybe buy some shirts without French cuffs—but I have to be hopeful," Quigley said. "The sheer dynamism of Francis and the impact he has already had tells me, given the years needed, his vision will become that of the church in the United States."

When Frank Monahan arrived at the bishops' conference in 1971 from Chicago, the place crackled with energy. Vatican II had concluded six years earlier. Catholic leaders were poised to play a public role in a wide range of policy debates. The longtime director of the bishops' government affairs office, Monahan led the church's advocacy and lobbying on Capitol Hill before retiring in 2007. "The Catholic Church was one of the few church agencies that was active in the policy arena in Washington," he recalled. "We always took on the issues as they came. The right and the left came to us when they were building coalitions. We were able to reach across the aisle to a lot of different people." Bishops made common cause with groups that did not always share the church's teachings on every issue and navigated through the complexity. In the 1980s, the conference was part of a broad coalition pushing major civil rights legislation that would restore federal protections for minorities, women, the elderly, and the disabled. Abortion funding soon divided the coalition. Civil rights groups balked when the bishops' conference refused to push ahead unless abortion-neutral language was included.[62]

It was added, the legislation passed, and the bishops joined the same civil rights group that were miffed over the abortion funding squabble to ultimately help Congress overturn Reagan's veto. Again in the 1990s, the bishops teamed up with the Children's Defense Fund, led by the prominent civil rights leader Marian Wright Edleman, to ensure passage of the first major childcare legislation since the Nixon era. "We convinced a lot of Republicans to support a child care program they would not otherwise have supported," Monahan said. As the church's internal politics shifted, this kind of bridge building with groups that parted ways with the bishops on abortion and other hot-button issues grew increasingly unwelcome. "Today we probably could not have joined Marian Wright Edleman because she would be viewed as a liberal activist," Monahan said. "You can't go near coalitions that are viewed as suspect on abortion. We used to say 'let's agree or disagree on some issue, but let's find common ground.' This still happens, but the coalition work is more difficult. It means a diminishment in our effectiveness in the public policy arena."

The atmosphere at the conference became more suspicious and divisive, he recalls, when Sen. John Kerry ran for president in 2004. "Kerry was just not seen as acceptable," he said. "I think that was the beginning of a serious effort on the part of some in the conference's leadership to say the conference is being run by liberal staff, and it's time to rein everyone in."

Dolores Leckey, who served at the bishops' conference for two decades and was the founding executive director of the Secretariat for Family, Laity, Women and Youth until she retired in 1997, also observed this shift. "For most of the time I was there we could get someone from the government to come give a talk, but there came a point when there was almost no woman in Congress who could pass muster with the pro-life office," Leckey said. "There is now a kind of unspoken test and if anyone has a perceived taint of not being on target with every single element of Catholic doctrine, it just doesn't fly. The church gets cut out of all kinds of effective partnerships. It's crimping our ability to make a difference."

As the old guard was exiting the conference, a new wave of leaders came on board. Anthony Picarello, who carved out a reputation as one of the nation's most prominent young conservative legal stars at the Beckett Fund for Religious Liberty, was named general counsel of the bishops' conference in 2007. He was later promoted to associate general secretary for policy and advocacy, a key position that gives him a hand in shaping the bishops' agenda. Religious liberty has been the defining issue for the hierarchy in recent years, a guiding framework that covers everything from the bishops' battles with the Obama administration over contraception coverage to legislative disputes over the rights of gay employees and same-sex marriage. Picarello's former employer represents many of the Catholic institutions suing the government over the birth control requirements, which exempts churches and provides accommodations to religious nonprofits like hospitals and universities that critics say still force Catholic institutions to violate church teaching. The Beckett Fund also represented the evangelical owners of the giant crafts store chain Hobby Lobby, who won a controversial 2014 U.S. Supreme Court case that, for the first time in the Court's history, found some for-profit corporations have religious rights. "There came a point when you could not distinguish between the agenda of the Beckett Fund and the bishops' agenda," said

Rev. Drew Christiansen, a Jesuit priest who led the U.S. bishops' office of International Justice and Peace for seven years in the 1990s.

Along with Picarello, the new guard included Jayd Hendricks, hired away from the Family Research Council to join the bishops' government relations staff. The Family Research Council is widely known for its culture-war rhetoric and an annual "Values Voter Summit" in Washington, where socially conservative Republicans test the waters for a presidential run. FRC leaders have claimed that gay men become Boy Scout leaders for "predatory purposes" and argued that homosexual behavior should be criminalized.[63] The Southern Poverty Law Center in 2010 designated the organization a "hate group" for its consistent pattern of demonizing the LGBT community.[64] When John Carr left the conference in 2012 after two-and-a-half decades, the bishops lost their most experienced social justice advocate, an anti-poverty lobbyist highly respected on Capitol Hill and in dioceses across the country. As director of the department of Justice, Peace and Human Development, Carr skillfully led the drafting of the bishops' election-year statements on political responsibility and was widely viewed as a leader out of the Bernardin mold who sought common ground between feuding church factions. He was frequently attacked by the most extreme voices in the pro-life movement.

Perhaps the clearest sign of a sea change at the conference is the bishops' staggering failure to assert a strong collective voice on issues of economic justice during a time when Americans suffered through the worst financial crisis since the Great Depression and a dramatic rise in income inequality. While the domestic justice office at the bishops' conference frequently sends letters to Congress on budget issues and formed a "Circle of Protection" initiative with evangelicals and other faith groups as part their advocacy efforts to safeguard the social safety net, the conference has not spoken in a unified way since the "Economic Justice for All" pastoral letter in 1986. Five months after launching a "Fortnight for Freedom" campaign with a coordinated national effort to rally Catholics in the pews to fight contraception coverage in the Affordable Care Act, bishops meeting in Baltimore for their 2012 national assembly were sharply divided over a draft economic justice statement. "The Hope of the Gospel in Difficult Times" never saw the light of day.

The unusually testy debate over the document during a public session of the meeting underscored generational and ideological splits in the hierarchy. Older bishops, many of whom grew up in working-class families with ties to unions, panned the draft for its failure to substantively address the structural causes of poverty or to offer a clear response through the lens of the church's century of Catholic social teachings. "Why don't we address the growing gulf between the haves and have-nots?" asked retired Archbishop Joseph Fiorenza, a former conference president. He noted there was only a single reference to the right of workers to unionize. "It's almost like it was an afterthought," he said. "But when you look at the compendium of the social teachings of the church, there are three long paragraphs on the right to organize, the right to collective bargaining, and the right to strike." Fiorenza also pointed out that there was "not even a footnote" about the bishops' 1986 pastoral letter on the economy. Instead, the proposed statement highlighted the church's opposition to gay marriage and abortion and support for school vouchers in ways critics worried distracted from the intended focus.[65] Other bishops seemed to wonder why there was a need for an economic justice statement at all, a view emblematic of a generation of more conservative church leaders. "The best thing we can do is to scrap the document and go home and find some tangible and practical ways to help the poor," said Bishop Thomas Tobin, of Providence, Rhode Island.[66] Tobin and other bishops who prefer a low profile for the church when it comes to economic issues stand in stark contrast not only to Pope Francis but also to Pope Benedict XVI, whose timely reflections on the moral hazards of unfettered corporate globalization included a critique of the "scandal of glaring inequalities" in his 2009 encyclical *Caritas in Veritate* (Charity in Truth).

A year before the bishops met for their national meeting and failed to muster any reflection on economic justice, the Vatican's Pontifical Council for Justice and Peace issued a detailed analysis so timely it addressed "the speculative bubble in real estate" and the "tendency to deregulate banking and financial activities." It called for a financial transaction tax that would pay for a "world reserve fund" to support the economies of countries hard hit by the economic crisis, and a "minimum, shared body of rules to manage the global financial marketplace."[67] The Vatican critique of neoliberal economic orthodoxy was far to the left of even most Democrats in Congress. Rick Santorum and Newt Gingrich, two conservative Catholics then running in the Republican presidential primary, tuned out the Vatican as they bashed government and waxed poetic about the free market.

If bishops struggled to find a unified voice on poverty and inequality, they had no such trouble when it came to issues of gender and sexuality. A year after departing from their national meeting without addressing the growing economic insecurity felt by many Americans, the bishops' conference strongly opposed legislation reauthorizing the Violence Against Women Act, designed to protect women against domestic violence, sexual assault, and human trafficking. No less than the chairmen of four committees and one subcommittee at the bishops' conference issued a joint statement opposing the legislation because it included language about sexual orientation and gender identity, which the bishops called "unnecessary" and warned could be "unjustly exploited for purposes of marriage redefinition." Just four months later, the bishops also opposed the Employee Non-Discrimination Act, a legislative effort to ban workplace discrimination against gay and transgender employees that passed the Senate with bipartisan support. Even though ENDA included a religious exemption and under the Civil Rights Act of 1964 religious organizations maintained the right to use religious background as a factor in hiring, the conference saw the accommodations as insufficient and again viewed the bill as a backdoor effort to legitimize same-sex marriage.[68] Some Catholics were surely left wondering how the bishops' position on ENDA comported with the Catechism of the Catholic Church, which says that "every sign of unjust discrimination" against homosexuals "should be avoided."[69]

When President Obama signed a 2014 executive order that prohibited federal contractors from discriminating on the basis of sexual orientation or gender identity, the bishops' conference did not simply express restrained concern. Archbishop William Lori of Baltimore, the chairman of the bishops' religious liberty committee, and Bishop Richard J. Malone of Buffalo blasted the order as "unprecedented and extreme . . . with the stroke of a pen, it lends the economic power of the federal government to a deeply flawed understanding of human sexuality, to which faithful Catholics and many people of faith will not assent."[70] The response, devoid of any pastoral tone and echoing Fox News rhetoric about an oppressive federal government, was coldly legalistic. It also failed to mention that the order did maintain Bush-era rules that permit religious agencies that receive federal contracts to give preferential hiring status to coreligionists. The bishops' response also strangely faulted the administration for not considering Catholic teaching regarding the difference between homosexual *inclinations* and homosexual *acts*, a Catholic theological distinction a government should not be expected to make.

In contrast, Rev. Larry Snyder, then president of Catholic Charities USA, offered a more sober assessment than the hierarchy. "As has always been the case, Catholic Charities USA supports the rights of all to employment and abides by the hiring requirements of all federal contracts. We are pleased that the Executive Order signed today by the President upholds already existing religious exemptions that will allow us to maintain fidelity to our deeply held religious beliefs. Specifically, we are pleased that the religious exemption in this Executive Order ensures that those positions within Catholic Charities USA that are entrusted with maintaining our Catholic identity are to be held exempt."[71] Later that year, when the U.S. Supreme Court declined to hear challenges to several state same-sex marriage laws—allowing gay marriage to stand in Virginia, Utah, Oklahoma, Indiana, and Wisconsin—the bishops' conference called the decision a "grave concern for our entire nation," and said the Court's decision "fails to resolve immediately the injustice of marriage redefinition."[72]

Beyond the bishops' national conference in Washington, dioceses across the country were also shifting institutional priorities in ways that crowded out the church's historic social justice emphasis. In 2011, Catholic bishops in Ohio announced a statewide ban on church and parochial school donations to the Susan G. Komen for the Cure because the national breast cancer charity provided a portion of its funding for breast cancer screenings at Planned Parenthood clinics.[73] Komen had been a generous funder of Catholic universities and other Catholic institutions, which received $7.4 million from the charity in 2011 alone, compared to $684,000 for Planned Parenthood.

At the same time that Ohio bishops prohibited Catholic institutions from helping the breast cancer charity, they were conspicuously silent as the state's workers faced the most significant threat to labor rights in a century. While other religious leaders in the state mobilized an interfaith coalition to fight anti-union legislation that would have restricted collective bargaining rights for more than 360,000 public employees, the Ohio Catholic Conference, the bishops' public policy arm in the state, sat on the sidelines and took a "neutral" stance.[74]

More than a century of Catholic social teaching defending living wages, labor rights, and what the Vatican's *Compendium of the Social*

Doctrine of the Church calls the "indispensible" role of unions was not enough to spur Ohio bishops to act. "A voter's position on Issue 2 involves a prudential judgment where people of good will may differ on the specifics of this proposal," Ohio bishops explained in general language that sounded a lot different from the detailed policy arguments staffers at the U.S. bishops' conference were making just a year earlier when disputes broke out over whether health care reform legislation would result in the funding of abortions. "It was a failure to lead and a failure to embrace the history of the church's commitment to collective bargaining," said Thomas Allio Jr., who directed social justice efforts for the Cleveland diocese for two decades at a time when the Catholic Church in that struggling postindustrial city was at the forefront of interfaith efforts to address urban poverty, inclusive economic development, and affordable housing. The diocese's "Church in the City" initiative, launched by then Bishop Anthony Pilla in 1993, became a national model for faith-based advocacy.

After the 2006 appointment of Bishop Richard Lennon to Cleveland, Allio said a "calculated diminishment of justice and peace efforts" began in earnest. During the height of the Great Recession in 2008, Allio's office led a major initiative on economic justice that included reflections, prayer resources, and ways for Catholics to connect the church's long history of social teachings to current debates. The bishop, he said, showed no interest. When the social action office in the Cleveland diocese became the first in the country to lead a campaign against payday lenders whose exorbitant interest rates were devastating low-income communities and the working poor, Allio said the bishop questioned why he was spending so much time on the effort. When more than two thousand religious leaders and social justice activists representing congregations from across Cleveland met in 2011 to launch the faith-based advocacy network Greater Cleveland Congregations, Bishop Lennon prohibited Catholic pastors and parish administrators from participating.

Dick Dowling retired in 2010 after nearly two-and-a-half decades as the executive director of the Maryland Catholic Conference, the public policy arm of bishops in Baltimore, Maryland; Washington, DC; and Wilmington, Delaware. While Catholic bishops still advocate for living wages and immigrants, Dowling noted, in his experience too many church leaders are now so focused on fundraising and suspicious of liberals that wealthy conservatives who don't have much fire in the belly for addressing systemic injustices dominate their inner circles. When Maryland passed the nation's first living wage law in 2007 with help from the Maryland Catholic Conference, Dowling recalls some church leaders openly expressing alarm that deep-pocketed donors helping to restore Baltimore's historic basilica would be put off by the law. The insularity came with an ideological accent.

"I began to see lay Catholics like George Weigel and past U.S. ambassadors to the Holy See from Republican administrations invited to have a seat at the table while liberal Catholic voices were denied access to those tables," Dowling said. "You had a one-note song being heard by the hierarchy." Dowling worked to defeat a same-sex marriage bill that ultimately passed the Maryland legislature and was signed into law by the state's Catholic governor in 2012. It's not something he seems to relish discussing, and he thinks the church is at a pivotal turning point. "I'm saddened by the drift of the church toward a conservatism that seems to have forgotten the least among us and toward a righteous conservatism whose focus is almost exclusively on the life issues and sexuality," he said. Dowling is cautiously hopeful that Pope Francis will inspire the American hierarchy to broaden its focus. "There are so many Catholics hungering for the kind of compassion and commitment this pope is bringing to the poor and marginalized," he said.

Whether U.S. Catholic leaders will embrace the pope's call for a "new balance" in the church and reclaim a broader moral agenda in the public square will depend in part on how sharp divisions over Catholic identity play out in the years ahead.

5

THE BATTLE FOR CATHOLIC IDENTITY

The red brick building on a quiet street a few miles outside of the nation's capital doesn't appear to be the kind of place that would rouse suspicion from the Vatican office that once directed the Roman Inquisition. On the second floor, Catholic sisters gather for meetings wearing sensible shoes. Walls showcase vibrant religious art—a Salvadoran cross, a print of Jesus washing the feet of an African man, and a stained-glass image of Our Lady of Guadalupe. A poster of the late Brazilian bishop Dom Hélder Câmara reads, "If we are not deaf, we hear the cries of the oppressed. The cries are the voice of God." Every Friday morning, the sisters take Communion together as a group. Here at the national headquarters of the Leadership Conference of Women Religious—an umbrella group that represents more than 80 percent of U.S. nuns—sisters who embraced the call of Vatican II to read the "signs of the times" advocate for immigrants, speak out against water privatization, and lobby to protect social safety nets. For these women religious, the work is not a checklist of disparate political causes but a ministry rooted in the radical call to solidarity with the marginalized that is at the heart of the Gospel.

On an April morning in 2012, Catholics woke up to headlines that for many seemed like a punch in the gut. The Vatican's Congregation for the Doctrine of the Faith reprimanded the nuns for espousing "radical feminist themes incompatible with the Catholic faith" and criticized them for not doing enough to publicly defend the church's traditional teachings on abortion and marriage.[1] The report, the product of a two-year investigation, described the doctrinal situation as "grave." While noting "the great deal of work . . . promoting issues of social justice," the assessment said LCWR had been "silent on the right to life from conception to natural death." It added that "crucial" issues, like "the church's biblical view of family life and human sexuality, are not part of the LCWR agenda in a way that promotes church teaching. Moreover, occasional public statements by the LCWR that disagree with or challenge positions taken by the bishops, who are the church's authentic teachers of faith and morals, are not compatible with its purpose." The Vatican tasked Seattle bishop Peter Sartain with overseeing the process of reforming LCWR. It was a stinging rebuke handed down just two years after the conference joined Sister Carol Keehan of the Catholic Health Association and NETWORK, a national Catholic social justice lobby led by Catholic sisters, in supporting President Obama's health care reform law.

The nuns' enthusiastic endorsement of the Affordable Care Act, a defining moment that helped push the bill across the legislative finish line, shaped an irresistible, if at times simplistic, story line for national media: nuns versus bishops. The U.S. Conference of Catholic Bishops, which for decades advocated for health care reform, opposed the final Senate bill citing an expansion of "federal funding and the role of the federal government in the provision of abortion services." The bill, Cardinal Francis George said in a statement, "forces all of us to become involved in an act that profoundly violates the conscience of many, the deliberate destruction of unwanted members of the human family still waiting to be born."[2]

For Catholics who view sisters as the backbone of the church for their ministry in hospitals, schools, and homeless shelters, the Vatican crackdown provided the most recent evidence of the church's rightward drift, and it signaled how tone deaf the hierarchy had become. News began to surface in Catholic media that felt like vinegar poured over open wounds. Americans in Rome, including the former Boston cardinal Bernard Law, were the most forceful proponents of reining in the nuns long before the health care showdown.[3] Cardinal Raymond Burke—sent from St. Louis to Rome in 2008 to lead the Vatican's highest court—reportedly supported the probe along with Cardinal James Stafford, a former Denver archbishop. Vatican analyst John Allen reported that bishops in the United States, including Bishop William E. Lori, then of Bridgeport, Connecticut, pushed the investigation from his perch as the chair of the U.S. bishops' doctrine committee.[4] Lori had replaced Cardinal William Levada in that role after the archbishop of San Francisco was appointed by Pope Benedict XVI to lead the Vatican's chief doctrine office (a first for an American).

For some, the hypocrisy was as rich as it was outrageous. "American Catholics have not forgotten how long it took for bishops to wake up to the sexual-abuse crisis they created. And now they see that the Vatican took just three years to determine that it had no other option but to put 80 percent of U.S. nuns—whose average age is 74—into receivership," wrote Grant Gallicho, an associate editor of the liberal Catholic magazine *Commonweal*. "That decision has unified a good deal of Catholics all right—against Rome."[5]

Some U.S. Catholic bishops saw the nuns' public support of health care legislation they opposed as an unacceptable challenge to their authority. At a time of dwindling religious vocations, Bishop Lawrence Brandt of Greensburg, Pennsylvania, prohibited women religious who signed a public letter from NETWORK supporting the health care bill from promoting their recruitment events in parishes or in the diocese's newspaper. A spokesman for the diocese sniffed that "an environment of dissent and public opposition does not provide an appropriate seedbed for vocations."[6] Providence, Rhode Island, bishop Thomas J. Tobin simply could not stomach that Sister Carol Keehan, president and CEO of the Catholic Health Association, one of the church's foremost experts on health care issues, came to a different policy conclusion than bishops after reading the final Senate bill. Sr. Carol, as everyone from CEOs to custodial staff in hospitals call her, is widely respected for her more than three decades of experience and leadership in health care administration. Pope Benedict XVI awarded her the prestigious *Pro Ecclesia et Pontifice* (For the Church and Pontiff) honor. The Catholic Health Association includes 600 hospitals and 1,400 long-term care facilities across the country. "Your enthusiastic support of the legislation, in contradiction to the position of the Bishops of the United States, provided an excuse for members of Congress, misled the public and caused serious scandal for many members of the Church," Tobin wrote in a pointed letter to Keehan.[7] Tobin asked CHA to remove St. Joseph's Health Services of Rhode Island, sponsored by his diocese, from CHA membership rolls. "Even the association with CHA is now embarrassing," the bishop added with a haughty jab.

Eight months later, Bishop Thomas J. Olmsted of Phoenix revoked the Catholic status of a hospital in Phoenix and excommunicated a nun who served on its medical ethics board after a pregnant woman with severe pulmonary hypertension had a lifesaving surgery that resulted in the termination of her pregnancy. Doctors had reached a consensus that there was no way to save both the life of the mother and the fetus. The hospital's medical ethics team, which included Mercy Sister Margaret Mary McBride, agreed. The surgery was performed, and the mother survived. The fetus died. Olmsted stripped the hospital of its Catholic status and prohibited Mass from being celebrated at the hospital. The Blessed Sacrament was promptly removed from the chapel. [8]

"The Catholic faithful are free to seek care or to offer care at St. Joseph's Hospital but I cannot guarantee that the care provided will be in full accord with the teachings of the Church," the bishop warned at a news conference. Olmsted requested a formal analysis of the case, but he rejected the findings of a moral theologian who teaches seminars at a Catholic medical school. The outside evaluation concluded the hospital's actions were morally and medically sound. "The act, per its moral object, must accurately be described as saving the life of the mother," the analysis found. "The death of the fetus was, at maximum, non-direct." The Catholic Health Association agreed in its own analysis, noting the hospital faced a "heartbreaking situation" and "correctly applied the Ethical and Religious Directives for Catholic Health Care Services to it, saving the only life that was possible to save." [9]

Sister McBride still sounds stunned when she talks about the bishop's certainty in the face of a painful and complex health care decision. "When I asked him what we should have done," McBride recalled, "he told me we should have let the mother and fetus die. I received the notice of my excommunication on the day after Easter. He must have signed the paperwork on Holy Thursday and put it in the mail. I took the symbolism of that very seriously. It was vindictive and so out of sync with the church I love. When you have been a part of the church for so long and suddenly you can't go to Mass, and that's where you get your strength, it's difficult." In order to clear the excommunication, McBride agreed to go to confession and leave her position on the hospital's ethics team. While her case is dramatic, she sees a frequent disconnect between a hierarchy that refers to its own authority in a juridical sense and Catholics in the field whose lived experience and expertise confer another kind of authority.

It's there in the trenches where ideal and theory meets the practical reality that decisions are not always neatly packaged in the certainties of black and white. "Women religious are out there serving people, and we're often at the bleeding edge of issues," she said. "Sometimes church leaders are cloistered in what they experience on a daily basis. I think they can become isolated."

The roiling tensions between the hierarchy and women religious are emblematic of a larger struggle over the nature of Catholic identity and religious authority. Who speaks for the church? What does it mean to be a "good Catholic"? What distinguishes healthy debate from disloyal dissent? These questions raise hard and essential issues that Catholics have wrestled with for two millennia. As the "pray-pay-and-obey" Catholicism of the 1950s gave way to a more educated laity willing to question authority, debates over Catholic identity only grew sharper. In different ways, they play out today at Catholic universities, in politics, in the hierarchy's relationship with theologians, at Catholic hospitals, and in heated disputes over whether Catholic institutions should partner with social justice coalitions that hold some views that are at odds with church teaching.

Sister Pat Farrell, a past president of the Leadership Conference of Women Religious, chooses her words carefully as she reflects on Catholic identity and the nature of authority. A soft-spoken Franciscan from Iowa, Farrell is no stranger to turmoil. Vatican authorities do not easily rattle a woman who once stared down gun-toting paramilitaries in Latin America. Her experiences living beside the poor and marginalized in Peru, then under the Chilean military dictator Augusto Pinochet, and in civil-war-ravaged El Salvador in the 1980s, deepened her faith and honed her skills in dialogue that served her well as she sat through tense meetings in the Vatican's doctrine office. Women religious put a premium on "listening from the bottom up," she explains, and recognize that discernment and diversity of views can nourish a faith community.

"We have developed over time a style of participatory, decentralized leadership that focuses on discerning the voice of God that is being expressed not through a single person, but the entire community," Farrell said. "We live a style of leadership, obedience and authority that has been the fruit of a fifty-year process responding to the call of Vatican II. I think this is our gift to the church." The courageous sisters who founded the earliest religious communities and hospitals, she notes, brought fresh insights that often made the hierarchy uncomfortable. This spirit still animates women religious today.

"As a person committed to the church, I feel bound by my conscience to address public issues that have moral content, and I'm compelled to do that by my baptism," Farrell said. "It seems narrow to me to say what is *the* Catholic voice. There is a broad Catholic voice because the Catholic Church is big. If there are millions of people who now have access to health care who didn't have access before, that certainly is a value. The bishops have particularly authority as a teaching voice, but when on earth can that be considered infallible when it comes to public policy? Are they listening to the *sensus fidelium* when it comes to issues that affect a wide population?"

"LOYALTY OATHS" AND CONSCIENCE

As a fifth-generation Catholic, Kathleen Riley wanted to serve the church. When her parish in Arlington, Virginia, asked for volunteers to teach Sunday school, she jumped at the chance. The fifty-two-year-old computer scientist has her disagreements with the church's prohibition on women clergy, and, like many in the pews, she thinks the church's teaching about birth control is flawed. But, as a graduate of Catholic schools who went on to teach in a parochial school, Riley is deeply rooted in a faith tradition she values as a gift to be passed on to others. The enthusiasm she felt about teaching Sunday school at St. Ann's parish quickly fizzled after a letter arrived in the mail from Bishop Paul Loverde. It required her—and all teachers in the Arlington diocese—to make a submission "of will and intellect" to the teaching authority of the pope and bishops.

In the presence of a priest, Riley would be asked to pledge her loyalty to the church by promising to "firmly accept and hold each and every thing definitely proposed by the church regarding the teaching of faith and morals." Riley couldn't square the all-encompassing language with a Catholic moral and intellectual tradition she knew valued discernment, the role of conscience, and moral reasoning. "The bishops are human, and sometimes their judgment is not God's judgment," Riley told the *Washington Post*. "We always have to be vigilant about that. The Holy Spirit gives us the responsibility to look into our own consciences."[10]

Rosemarie Zagarri, a history professor at George Mason University in Virginia, also refused to take the oath. Zagarri says she would have signed a statement of her commitment to the church's core dogma—belief in the Incarnation and the Resurrection, for example—but an oath that asked Catholics to explicitly agree with the church's teaching on contraception and other hot-button issues at a time when the bishops were sparring with the Obama administration over contraception coverage and the 2012 presidential campaign was in full swing was a step too far. "It felt like a way of ferreting out Catholics who didn't support the conservative line," Zagarri said. "It was just another attempt to impose a certain political view on the Catholic laity. I found it absolutely appalling. It was all so ill conceived and tone deaf."

The controversy was not limited to Arlington. An oath of fidelity in the Diocese of Baker, Oregon, established by then Bishop Robert Vasa in 2004, required all lay Catholics who served in schools or parishes to agree to a detailed *Affirmation of Personal Faith*.[11] The list included the "sinfulness of contraception," the "evil of extra-marital sexual relationships," the "unacceptability of homosexual relationships," "the legitimacy of Marian devotions," "the existence of hell and purgatory," and the "legitimacy of the Holy Father's claim to infallibility." The language on abortion was particularly strict. "I do not recognize the legitimacy of anyone's claim to a moral right to form their own conscience in this matter," the oath read. Vasa, who has criticized the "heresy" of pro-choice Catholic politicians and called the health care reform law "positively evil," said Catholics in the diocese would have no legitimate conscience claims for not agreeing to the oath.[12]

> No one can claim a legitimate right to follow a conscience which is clearly not formed in a fashion consistent with the very clear teachings of the Catholic Church. The following of one's own conscience is a strict moral obligation but that obligation is preceded by the obligation to assure that the conscience one is following is properly formed. When that conscience leads to judgments which are diametrically opposed to the clear and consistent teachings of the Catholic Church then the conscience has established itself as a new and individual, infallible personal magisterium which far exceeds the definition of conscience.[13]

Rev. John Langan, the Cardinal Bernardin Chair in Catholic Social Thought and a professor in the department of philosophy at Georgetown

University, says this assertion of episcopal authority has old roots. "During the Counter-Reformation the church modeled a top-down leadership style," Langan said. "The social context is different now. The church is not dealing with communities of European peasants anymore so the form of governance has to be challenging but also persuasive." Discomfort with the reforms of the Second Vatican Council, he noted, sparked a countermovement. "For many conservatives Vatican II was an ominous event. In the restoration project visible in the papacy of John Paul II, and embraced by conservatives in the United States, you begin to see a very deductive, legalistic notion of what is morally right rather than an understanding of the lived experience of the faithful. One thing that particularly bothered some conservatives was the appeal to conscience. These loyalty oaths are the work of lawyers, not pastors. The notion that you can by ecclesiastical fiat forbid people to consult their conscience is an appalling and untraditional idea."

Indeed, the role of conscience in the church's moral tradition is clear. For St. Thomas Aquinas, every conscience is binding, even an erring one. In his 1969 commentary on the Second Vatican Council's "Pastoral Constitution on the Church in the Modern World," the future pope Cardinal Joseph Ratzinger observed:

> Over the pope as the expression of the binding claim of ecclesiastical authority there still stands one's own conscience, which must be obeyed before all else, if necessary even against the requirement of ecclesiastical authority. The conscience of the individual confronts him with a supreme and ultimate tribunal, which in the last resort is beyond the claim of external social groups, even of the official church. [14]

When Bishop Salvatore Cordileone, then of Oakland and now the archbishop of San Francisco, demanded that the Catholic Association for Lesbian and Gay Ministry declare an "oath of personal integrity" that would require the group to affirm church teaching on marriage, hell, and chastity or risk being deemed "not authentically Catholic," the board refused. The national organization provides pastoral care for gay Catholics and their families in twenty-five states, and it includes almost two dozen diocesan and parish ministries. The association and its members interact regularly with bishops nationwide, and several bishops have spoken or celebrated the Eucharist at its national conventions. "In good faith, we have done most everything required of us to maintain a legitimate space within the boundaries of the institutional church," president Sheila Nelson wrote to board members. "Yet, this has not seemed to be adequate or satisfactory to the office of the bishop. We have repeatedly, abundantly and humbly submitted that our work is pastoral in nature and not political or primarily doctrinal." [15]

Rev. John Coleman, an associate pastor at St. Ignatius Church in San Francisco who has taught social ethics at Loyola Marymount University and lectured around the world, is no stranger to loyalty oaths. When he was preparing to be ordained in 1967, the Jesuit was expected to sign the infamous "Oath Against Modernism" initiated by Pius X in 1910. Along with another classmate, Coleman refused. "I had read enough about the anti-modernist movement to know that it had done great harm to innocent people and the church," he said. "It blackballed good people." His superior grumbled but conceded. (The oaths were dropped as a requirement the following year.) "We should care about the Catholic identity of our institutions," Coleman says, "but how we do that is important."

Fidelity oaths, he says, are a deeply flawed way of keeping tabs on Catholic identity, and they underscore larger problems with the way some church leaders and conservative activists have discarded classic Catholic moral reasoning. Aquinas stressed that applying universal moral principles requires the virtue of prudence in evaluating context and the particulars of a situation. "This kind of careful reasoning is getting lost," Coleman said.

LGBT CATHOLICS UNDER SCRUTINY

Molly Shumate, a first-grade teacher in the Cincinnati Catholic school system, felt she had no choice. A new "teacher-minister" contract she and other teachers were required to sign in 2014 included a vow to not publicly support what it described as the "homosexual lifestyle." It hit close to home. Shumate, a Catholic, thought of her twenty-three-year-old son Zachary, and she refused to sign. It broke her heart to leave after fourteen years in the classroom, but turning her back on her own son was unthinkable. "In my eyes there is nothing wrong with my son," she told the *Cincinnati Enquirer*. "This is what God gave me and what God created and someone I should never be asked not to support." [16]

Cincinnati's new six-page contract, which nearly doubled in size from previous ones that consisted of a general morals clause, for the first time proscribed a detailed list of prohibitions. Among other things, it asks teachers to agree to avoid "public support of or publicly living together outside marriage, public support of or sexual activity out of wedlock, public support of or homosexual lifestyle, public support of or use of abortion and public support of in vitro insemination and public membership in organizations whose mission and message are incompatible with Catholic doctrine or morals."[17] Hyperfocused on issues of sexuality, the contract makes no mention of the church's teachings on a spectrum of other issues like divorce, poverty, war, racism, or the death penalty. It also applies to non-Catholics working in the schools, and it defines teachers and support staff as "ministerial" employees. The revised language was designed in part to protect the archdiocese, which oversees the school system in the greater Cincinnati area, from lawsuits filed by terminated teachers. In recent years, the archdiocese has faced a number of high-profile lawsuits, including one from an unmarried teacher fired after becoming pregnant by artificial insemination. Designating teachers as ministers puts them in the same category as clergy and gives Catholic school systems legal room to claim exemptions from antidiscrimination statues and prohibit collective bargaining efforts.

The controversial contract became a national story. "Would Pope Francis Sign the New Catholic Teacher Contract?" a dozen billboards, sponsored by Cincinnati Voice of the Faithful, asked. Online petitions generated more than twenty thousand signatures in protest. CNN aired a lengthy segment. National Public Radio covered rallies of teachers and students voicing opposition. Richard Hague taught literature and writing at a Catholic high school in Cincinnati for forty-five years. Chairman of the English department and a noted author nominated for the National Book Award, Hague planned to teach until he reached his fiftieth anniversary in the classroom. Instead, he could not bring himself to sign the contract and resigned. "The explicit spelling out of this list of mostly sexual 'thou-shalt-nots,' coming from an institution whose former Cincinnati leader has pleaded guilty to covering up the sexual abuse of children, is so hypocritical as to beggar belief," Hague wrote in his resignation letter. He also criticized efforts by the archdiocese in the early 1970s to prevent teachers from unionizing. "That legal maneuvering to avoid the Catholic Church's own teaching on social justice and the rights of workers to organize was only the first example of the archdiocese's cold abortion of what should have been warm and loving negotiations," Hague wrote. "And now we have this contract, which could never have been thrust upon us had we been able to organize to protect our own dignity as workers back then."[18]

The superintendent of the Cincinnati Catholic schools defended the contract in a *Cincinnati Enquirer* op-ed. "Our culture is changing quickly in this area, and many of our school employees, including me, have family members who are lesbian, gay, bisexual or transgender," he wrote. "The contract does not stipulate that relationships of love for LGBT relatives should be severed. As Christians, we are called to love and serve all people, particularly those who have been victims of abuse or bullying. . . . We cannot control a person's inner beliefs. We cannot, nor should we, peek through the windows of our employee's homes to see whether they are living a moral lifestyle. The contract is not an excuse for some type of witch hunt, but merely a clearer verbalization of what it means to be a Catholic schoolteacher."[19]

As fights over Catholic identity and morality clauses roiled Cincinnati, Mark Zmuda, the vice principal at Eastside Catholic High School in Seattle, was fired in 2014 after archdiocesan officials learned he had married his gay partner. Students rallied behind the popular teacher and swim coach. An online campaign in support of "Mr. Z" went viral. "I was asked by the school to break my wedding vows to keep my job," Zmuda said at a news conference. "I was told I could either divorce or be fired. How could anyone ask anyone else to make that choice?"[20] The controversies in Cincinnati and Seattle are not isolated cases. Since 2008, there have been nearly fifty cases of employees at Catholic institutions who have been fired or had offers rescinded because of issues involving sexuality. At least five dioceses have instituted new teacher contracts that require employees to promise they will not professionally or personally support same-sex relationships. After Florida legalized same-sex marriage at the end of 2014, Archbishop Thomas Wenski of Miami sent a memo to all church employees reiterating that any expression of support for gay marriage—even a tweet or Facebook post—could be a cause for termination.[21] Cardinal Sean O'Malley of Boston is the only bishop to date who has publicly expressed concern over the wave of firings of legally married gays and lesbians working in Catholic institutions. The trend, he said, "needs to be rectified."[22]

It's not just Catholic schoolteachers who have faced pressure. Nicholas Coppola was an active parishioner at St. Anthony Catholic Church in Oceanside, New York, for a decade. He visited homebound seniors, fed hungry families, taught religious education classes, and served in a consolation ministry that comforted those grieving the death of a loved one. Nearly everyone in the parish knew Coppola was gay. No one seemed to care, including priests who occasionally socialized with him and his longtime partner, David. When New York State legalized same-sex marriage in 2011, the couple was civilly married. Several of his fellow parishioners were at the ceremony. On Martin Luther King Jr. Day, Coppola attended Mass at St. Anthony's, a time to reflect on justice and equality. After the service, he was called into the office of his pastor, who informed him that an anonymous letter complaining about his sexuality and marriage had been sent to Bishop William Murphy of the Rockville Centre Diocese. Coppola was told that he would no longer be able to serve in any official parish capacity.

"What they did to me really hurt," Coppola said. "I was never bullied growing up. The first time I faced prejudice because of my sexuality was from my church. I was forty-eight-years old so I could handle it, but if I was a teenager I'm not sure what I would have done. The church is sending dangerous messages to young people," he said, noting the high suicide rate for LGBT teens. Bishop Murphy refused to meet with Coppola. The news of Coppola's banishment from any official duties at the parish he served so faithfully over the years went public just a few days after Cardinal Timothy Dolan of New York acknowledged in an Easter Sunday interview with ABC News that the church had work to do when it came to welcoming gays and lesbians. "We've got to do better to see that our defense of marriage is not reduced to an attack on gay people," Dolan said. "And I admit, we haven't been too good about that. We try our darnedest to make sure we're not anti-anybody."[23]

When Colleen Simon saw the advertisement for a social ministries job at St. Francis Xavier Catholic Church in Kansas City, she considered it a dream position but worried that being a lesbian would disqualify her. Simon had worked for three years in the Catholic diocese in Richmond, Virginia, and thought she was a qualified candidate. After getting reassurance from the church that her sexual orientation was not an issue, Simon also informed staff that she was married to a Lutheran pastor and that their marriage was well known in the community. No concerns were raised. Simon got the job. She threw herself into social justice work with a passion, managing a food pantry that served seventy families each month and helping the working poor in need of emergency assistance. When an article in the *Kansas City Star* described her work as part of a story about economic revival in a once blighted section of the city, the reporter made a passing reference to her same-sex marriage.[24]

The pastor who hired Simon at St. Francis Xavier had moved on, and the new pastor was not pleased with the public disclosure of her relationship. When the pastor called Simon into his office, she was told that someone had mailed a copy of the newspaper article to Bishop Robert Finn. The pastor received a phone call and a letter from the diocese about the situation. Simon was eventually asked to resign.

"This was more to me than losing a job," she said. "This felt like I had lost a loved one because I had grown to love the clients I served and the people of the parish. My journey since has reflected the stages of grief. It is a horrible loss for me. I find it ironic that in an age when young and very old people are bypassing the sacrament of marriage altogether, we who are LGBTQ and desiring marriage are persecuted. We could be the best allies the defense of marriage groups have in promoting the beauty and sacredness of marriage, and yet we are the ones persecuted."

The firing of Colleen Simon was the last straw for Benjamin Brenkert, who was preparing to become a Jesuit priest. In the fall of 2014, he left the religious order discouraged and began pursuing a possible religious life in the Episcopal Church. "I can't be an openly gay Jesuit discerning priesthood in the Catholic Church if LGBT employees are being fired from Catholic institutions," he told the *National Catholic Reporter*. He even wrote an open letter to Pope Francis encouraging him to "speak out against laws that criminalize and oppress LGBTQ people around the world."[25]

Brenkert described coming out to Jesuit priests as he was discerning a call to the priesthood. The initial welcoming embrace did not hold. "Instead, over time, I felt more and more alienated and ostracized by the institutional church," he wrote in the *Washington Post*. "Some of my Jesuit classmates refused to talk to me . . . I worked alongside my classmates in silence—they were silent to me over meals and in our home. My Novice Master even told me I made a fundamental mistake in coming out—that I, by fully embracing who I was, not shying away from God's love of and for me, nor by retreating into the closet, that I had caused them to reject me. I immediately spiraled into the dark night of the soul."[26]

Frank DeBernardo, executive director of New Ways Ministry, has spent decades offering pastoral support for LGBT Catholics. Something of a "don't ask, don't tell philosophy," he said, once guided leaders of Catholic institutions who probably knew they had gay colleagues but saw it as irrelevant because most people were closeted and no legal, public recognition of their relationships existed. In the last five years, the rapid advance of same-sex marriage under the law and in cultural acceptance means that LGBT Catholics are now marrying and are far less likely to feel the need to tiptoe around. In response to this shift, he said, church leaders have been more assertive in speaking out.

"The bishops have made opposition to same-sex marriage the litmus test for orthodox Catholicism," said DeBernardo, noting that teachers who use contraception, are divorced, or are out of step with Catholic teaching on non-sexual issues are not singled out for firing as gays and lesbians have been. "This has become the *sin qua non* of Catholic identity. The hierarchy realizes that one of the few areas they might have left for influence are in matters of personal morality," DeBernardo added. "Marriage equality is like a perfect storm for them because it involves questions about gender, sexuality and reproduction. If this piece falls, if they fail on this issue, then it calls into question other issues involving gender and sexuality. It's the lynchpin."

The Catechism of the Catholic Church insists that gays and lesbians must be treated with "respect, sensitivity and compassion." In 1997, the U.S. Conference of Catholic Bishops released a pastoral letter, "Always Our Children," that struck a welcoming tone. "God does not love someone any less simply because he or she is a homosexual," the bishops wrote. "God's love is always and everywhere offered to those who are open to receiving it." The letter also encouraged pastors in the church to "welcome homosexual persons into the faith community, and seek out those on the margins. Avoid stereotyping and condemning. Strive first to listen."[27] There are Catholic churches and institutions that take up this call quite well. A few brave priests and pastors have even declined to join their bishops' ramped-up lobbying against civil same-sex marriage. And when Archbishop Peter Sartain of Seattle encouraged pastors to collect signatures as part of a mobilization effort to defeat a same-sex marriage ballot referendum in his state that passed in 2012, several prominent churches refused. Fr. Michael Ryan of St. James Cathedral said the signature drive would "prove hurtful and seriously divisive in our community."[28]

In most cases, however, the message the Catholic Church sends to gays and lesbians is one of exclusion. A 1986 *Letter to the Bishops of the Catholic Church on the Pastoral Care of Homosexual Persons*, drafted by Cardinal Joseph Ratzinger in his prepapal role as the prefect of the Vatican's doctrine office, didn't exactly extend an inviting hand. "Although the particular inclination of the homosexual person is not a sin, it is a more or less strong tendency ordered toward an intrinsic moral evil; and thus the inclination itself must be seen as an objective disorder," Ratzinger wrote. Writing seventeen years later, in 2003, Ratzinger and the doctrine office responded sternly to the growing recognition of civil same-sex unions in countries around the world: "Legal recognition of homosexual unions or placing them on the same level as marriage would mean not only the approval of deviant behavior, with the consequence of making it a model in present-day society, but would also obscure basic values which belong to the common inheritance of humanity."[29]

When the Boy Scouts of America changed its policy of refusing membership to openly gay scouts in 2013, Bishop Loverde of Arlington, Virginia, quickly blasted off a public statement that excoriated the Scouts for caving to "political causes at the cost of its moral integrity."[30] The organization's long history of denying openly gay young men the same opportunities as their fathers and brothers, the bishop thought, demonstrated "principled and steadfast resolve." Loverde warned, "The result of this policy change will likely not bring harmony, but rather continuing controversy, policy fights and discord."

It was a disproportionate and alarmist response given that the new policy did not endorse same-sex marriage, gay sex, or any activity the church teaches is sinful. In fact, the decision was not about *sex* at all, as the National Catholic Committee on Scouting underscored in a more sober reaction. "We should be encouraged that the change in BSA's youth membership standard is not in conflict with Catholic teaching," wrote Edward Martin, the organization's national chairman. "Any sexual conduct, whether homosexual or heterosexual, by youth of Scouting age is contrary to the virtues of Scouting. The Boy Scouts of America does not have an agenda on the matter of sexual orientation, and resolving this complex issue is not the role of the organization, nor may any member use Scouting to promote or advance any social or political position or agenda."[31] The national committee includes a bishop who is a liaison from the U.S. Conference of Catholic Bishops, and the statement cited a church canon lawyer popular with conservatives who wrote that while he disagreed with the Scouts' decision, it did not violate church doctrine.

Rev. James Martin, a Jesuit priest and prominent author, is consistently eloquent in calling the church to be more inclusive and respectful of gays and lesbians. In a 2014 *America* magazine essay, "Simply Loving," Martin used the firing of gay teachers at Catholic schools to offer an extended reflection on the topic.

> The language surrounding gay and lesbian Catholics is framed primarily, sometimes exclusively, in terms of sin. For example, "We love our gay brothers and sisters—but they must not engage in sexual activity." Is any other group of Catholics addressed in this fashion? Imagine someone beginning a parish talk on married life by saying, "We love married Catholics—but adultery is a mortal sin." With no other group does the church so reflexively link the group's identity to sin. The language of "hate the sin, love the sinner" is difficult for many gay people to believe when the tepid expression of love is accompanied by strident condemnation.[32]
>
> What might it mean for the church to love gays and lesbians more deeply? First, it would mean listening to their experiences—all their experiences, what their lives are like as a whole. Second, it would mean valuing their contributions to the church. Where would our church be without gays and lesbians—as music ministers, pastoral ministers, teachers, clergy and religious, hospital chaplains and directors of religious education? Infinitely poorer. Finally, it would mean publicly acknowledging their individual contributions: that is, saying that a particular gay Catholic has made a difference in our parish, our school, our diocese. This would help remind people that they are an important part of the body of Christ. Love means listening and respecting, but before that it means admitting that the person exists.

SECULARISM AND THE "NEW INTOLERANCE"

Over the clinking of polished silverware at the Washington Golf and Country Club, Mary Eberstadt delivers a grim assessment to a crowd of lawyers, policymakers, and journalists. Christians in the United States may not be facing the kind of violent persecution tearing apart Christian religious communities in the Middle East, she concedes, but Americans must face up to "the non-stop, slow-motion marginalizing and penalizing of believers on the very doorsteps of churches of North America, Europe and elsewhere." For many Christian in the affluent West, she says, a "new intolerance" has "unmistakably made their world darker and more punitive than it used to be." A senior fellow at the Ethics and Public Policy Center in Washington, and author of *How the West Really Lost God: A New Theory of Secularization*, Eberstadt looks out at a country where religious Americans are threatened by "intimidation, humiliation, censorship, and self-censorship." "There is no mercy in putting butchers and bakers and candlestick makers in the legal dock for refusing to renounce their religious beliefs," she says. "There is no mercy in stalking and threatening Christian pastors for *being* Christian pastors or in casting out social scientists who turn up unwanted facts." The cause of this silent persecution? The church's "single most deadly enemy in our time, the one with which it is locked in mortal combat," she says, "is not the stuff of the philosophy common room. It is instead the sexual revolution. The new intolerance is a wholly owned subsidiary of that revolution. No revolution, no new intolerance."[33]

Sexuality is a common theme for Catholics like Eberstadt, who see traditional views on gender and marriage as "under siege," says Boston College theologian Lisa Sowle Cahill. "The mainstreaming of women in the United States happened faster here than other countries and part of that was a feminist movement in which the flag waving issues became women's reproductive rights and self-determination in the areas of sex and family," Cahill remarked. "This ran directly into the teachings of the church, which many understandably saw as not having a particularly egalitarian agenda for women."

Along with Catholic leaders reacting with unease to broader cultural shifts in society, Cahill noted that internal church divisions over contraception—specifically after Pope Paul VI reaffirmed the ban on birth control in 1968—fueled a strain of Catholic identity that often became hyperfocused on sexuality. "You see this marking of boundaries where the church's teaching on sexuality becomes a primary way of assessing who is in or out," Cahill says. As the clergy abuse scandals came to national attention with the *Boston Globe*'s groundbreaking reporting in 2002, Cahill began to see a beleaguered church narrowing the scope of its public moral claims. "The Catholic Church in the United States begins to lose some of its political clout and instead of looking outward and speaking broadly the focus becomes more internal."

In many ways, the muscular affirmation of a distinct Catholic and Christian identity is a predictable response to secularism. The United States remains by several measures a highly religious society compared to other industrial nations. More than a third of Americans identify as "born again" Christians, and more than nine in ten profess belief in God. Nearly 80 percent of evangelicals, a 2014 survey from Public Religion Research Institute found, believe that climate change and extreme weather are signs of the "end times" and the Apocalypse rather than human behavior.[34] A 2014 Pew Research study found that most Americans think religion is losing its influence, and most see this as a negative trend.[35] More citizens also say that churches and other religious institutions should express views on social and political issues, up to 49 percent in 2014 from 43 percent in 2010. The steady growth in the number of Americans who no longer identify with a religious denomination and the dizzying pace of cultural change, as seen in the rapid acceptance of same-sex marriage, all present formidable challenges for institutional Catholicism and Christianity writ large.

"Radical secularism" is gaining ground in America and poses a "grave threat" to the church's freedom, Pope Benedict XVI told American bishops in 2012. Catholics must be on guard to confront a "reductive secularism," he said, which tries to "delegitimize the church's participation in public debate."[36] Explaining why cardinals rejected an interim report to strike a more welcoming tone toward homosexuals and divorced Catholics at an Extraordinary Synod on the Family at the Vatican in 2014, Cardinal George Pell, a powerful Australian prelate whom Pope Francis tasked with leading the Vatican's financial reform, was clear. "We're not giving in to the secular agenda," he said. "We're not collapsing in a heap."[37] Carl Anderson of the Knights of Columbus warned more than eight hundred Christians at the annual National Catholic Prayer Breakfast in 2012 that they faced an unprecedented challenge. "Never in the lifetime of any of us here present has the religious liberty of the American people been as threatened as it is today," he proclaimed at a time when the Catholic makeup of the U.S. Congress has reached a historic high and six out of nine U.S. Supreme Court justices are Catholic.[38]

Brad Gregory, a professor of early modern European history at the University of Notre Dame, says even if some of these reactions are unduly alarmist, they reflect "genuine concerns" over the trend toward privatizing religion and the unease about the shifting definitions of bedrock institutions such as marriage and family. "The underlying concerns are not mere hype and hysteria, but the way the issue gets framed and the rhetoric are a reflection of the political culture we find ourselves in now," Gregory said. "It's a symptom of a broader problem in American public life. The meta-problem is the ferociously polarized and poisonous character of our public discourse. The attitude becomes either you're with us or against us. It's black and white. There is a reluctance to make distinctions. There is a sense that if the other side is hammering and propagandizing, then unless we meet them with the same blunt rhetorical force we have no chance."

While some conservatives in the church and in politics act like a secular menace was unleashed the day Barack Obama took the oath of office or when same-sex marriage gained traction, Gregory cautions against simplifying what is a complex historical narrative. "We can't really understand the character of the problems today unless we see they are the product of the long-term, unintended consequences that came out of the doctrinal disputes among Christians in the sixteenth and seventeenth centuries," he said. If the Catholic worldview insists that religion has a vital role to play in public life—informing debates over economic decisions, international relations, and how to serve the common good—the impulse to privatize religion as a matter of merely personal belief is a legacy of the Reformation era that informs our culture today. Unless we are "precise and specific" about what we mean by secularization, Gregory says, the idea gets sucked into what he calls the "vortex" of political polarization. "The most persuasive case the church can make is not only to model a more civil discourse, but to be a profound witness for the service to the marginalized and the common good in ways that draw the admiration and support from a wide range of Americans," he said. "The kind of hunkered down, anti-secularism line that is taken by some bishops is too closely associated with one political party. The extraordinary emphasis Pope Francis has put on service to the poor is a huge opportunity for the church."

Meanwhile, the hardliners press on and the rhetoric of victimization intensifies. In a 2014 lecture titled "Strangers in a Strange Land," Archbishop Chaput of Philadelphia argued that traditional religious Americans now face a cultural exile similar to that of the ancient Israelites in Babylon. The U.S. Supreme Court's decision not to review appeals against gay marriage laws in several states was a "tipping point," Chaput said, and he chastised gay rights activists for being "dishonest and evil" in depicting opponents of same-sex marriage as homophobic. He urged bishops to consider refusing to sign civil marriage licenses for all couples in response to what he called the "new marriage regime" of same-sex civil marriage. The archbishop did see opportunity in this picture of crisis. "We also need to thank God for the gift of this present, difficult moment," the archbishop reassured his audience. "Because conflict always does two things: It purifies the church, and it clarifies the character of the enemies who hate her."[39]

CATHOLIC CAMPAIGN FOR HUMAN DEVELOPMENT: PURITY OR PARTNERSHIPS?

While those enemies at the gate that Archbishop Chaput eyes vigilantly are viewed as relatively new threats from outside the church, some Catholics have long claimed the hierarchy is also complicit in compromising orthodoxy. When Catholic bishops launched a national anti-poverty campaign in 1969 to fund local social justice efforts, the initiative had ambitions far beyond the church's traditional charitable services. The resolution creating the Catholic Campaign for Human Development (CCHD) called for the church to help people living in poverty "develop economic strengths and political power . . . through specific projects aimed at the very causes of poverty."[40]

Since 1970, according to the U.S. bishops' conference, the campaign has "contributed over $280 million to more than 7,800 low-income led, community-based projects that strengthen families, create jobs, build affordable housing, fight crime, and improve schools and neighborhoods." In 2014 alone, CCHD approved over $14 million in grants to support more than two hundred organizations. The campaign is rooted in several core pillars of Catholic social teaching, including solidarity and subsidiarity. When Pope John Paul II visited the United States in 1979, he praised the campaign for being "a witness to the church's living presence in the world among the most needy, and to her commitment to continuing the mission of Christ, who was sent to 'bring glad tidings to the poor, to proclaim liberty to captives and release to the prisoners.'"

Conservative Catholic activists and their ideological allies on the political right have organized against CCHD for decades. Thomas Pauken, while serving as a Reagan administration official in 1984, circulated a document that denounced the bishops' campaign as funding "leftist political activists plotting to destroy our economic system." William E. Simon, a Catholic who served as Treasury secretary in the Nixon administration, sent a copy of Pauken's document to every U.S. member of the Knights of Malta, an influential network of Catholic benefactors. Rev. Richard John Neuhaus of *First Things* said the bishops' campaign had "nothing to do with Catholicism."

In recent years, efforts to defund and delegitimize CCHD have grown more sustained, well funded, and effective. The American Life League, a Stafford, Virginia–based organization with a $6 million budget, launched a "Reform CCHD Now" coalition in 2009 made up of more than two dozen supporting groups, including Human Life International, Church-Militant.TV, and the Catholic Advocate. The coalition exists, in its words, "to document cases of Catholic funding going to groups that promote abortion, birth control, homosexuality, and even Marxism."

Using guilt-by-association and other tactics from the McCarthy-era playbook, these activists are part of an increasingly aggressive movement of Catholic activists who view themselves fighting for a smaller, "purer" church. The American Life League produces detailed reports that are sent to every bishop in the country, and it calls for boycotts of parish collections that fund the campaign. One report claimed that more than seventy CCHD-funded organizations are violating Catholic moral teaching. The stepped-up activism against CCHD is having an impact. A Portland-based group that advocates for immigrant day laborers was disqualified for a grant from the bishops' campaign in 2014 because of its association with the National Council of La Raza, the nation's preeminent Hispanic civil rights organization. La Raza primarily focuses on immigration reform, economic justice initiatives, and a host of other issues supported by Catholic bishops. It also has a stated position in support of marriage equality for gays and lesbians. The Voz Workers' Rights Education Project, which received church funding since 1994, was declared ineligible for a $75,000 grant from the bishops because it would not cut ties with La Raza. The predominately Hispanic men that Voz serves every day are not activists on the front lines of LGBT rights. They are poor immigrants, many of them undocumented, who are struggling to find jobs, put food on the table, get decent health care for their kids, and learn English. "Marriage equality is not the focus of our work," the group's director Romeo Sosa told the Associated Press. "We focus on immigrant rights."[41]

The Land Stewardship Project, a Minnesota nonprofit that for five consecutive years received church funds, abruptly lost a $48,000 CCHD grant in 2012 to help immigrant farmers because of its association with the Minnesota Council of Nonprofits and TakeAction Minnesota. While the issue of gay marriage is not fundamental to the mission of either organization, both opposed a ballot initiative that year that would have amended the state's constitution to exclusively define marriage as between a man and a woman. The state's Catholic bishops made the ballot initiative a central focus of their policy work, as they did in 2010 when the Archdiocese of St. Paul and Minneapolis sent more than four hundred thousand DVDs to Catholics in the state with an "urgent message" from Archbishop John Nienstedt that called civil marriage for gays and lesbians a "dangerous risk."[42] "We're being penalized not because of anything we did, but because of who we were associated with," said Mark Shultz, a Catholic who is the policy and organizing director of the Land Stewardship Project. "We just felt like we could not be bullied," Shultz said. "We're actually a stronger organization because of all this. We have coalesced around values of Catholic social teaching like solidarity."

In some cases, church leaders are not just pulling funding from organizations that have associations with secular groups; they have also distanced themselves from ecumenical partnerships. North Carolina's two Catholic dioceses withdrew from the North Carolina Council of Churches, an ecumenical organization whose members include seventeen denominations representing more than six thousand congregations across the state. After membership dating back to the 1970s, the dioceses of Raleigh and Charlotte split with the council in 2013 after growing divisions over a state constitutional amendment prohibiting same-sex marriage. "This is a step back for ecumenism," said Rev. Steve Hickle, president-elect of the council and a United Methodist minister for forty years. "It takes us away from the constant conversations we've been able to have around a broad variety of issues such as workers' rights, peace and climate change."[43]

CATHOLIC ON CAMPUS

On a rainy fall night in the nation's capital, the lobbyists and lawyers on K Street rush out of offices to beat the rat race home or head for an expense-account steak dinner at the Palm. The Catholic Information Center, a bookstore and spiritual oasis complete with a chapel where daily Mass is celebrated, seems out of place on this famed street where hard-charging power brokers ply their trade. Led by an Opus Dei priest, the store and prayer space is a popular spot for conservative Catholics who take their faith and politics seriously.

The guest lecturer tonight, a lanky, Australian priest with a quick wit, grows animated as he talks about what he sees as a crisis in American Catholicism. "Some Catholic institutions," says Rev. Wilson Miscamble, a professor of American history at the University of Notre Dame, "are Catholic in name only!" It's a theme he explores at length in his book *For Notre Dame: Battling for the Heart and Soul of a Catholic University*, a series of critical essays that argue the nation's flagship Catholic institution is abandoning its religious character in a "quest for prestige." Tonight he warns about the "temptations of the secular model," laments that the cause is already lost on "certain Jesuit campuses," and holds up a network of small Catholic schools—Christendom College, Franciscan University of Steubenville, the University of Dallas—as models.

"The false gods attract powerful attention to the unwary and to those who fail to appreciate what matters. But if a Catholic university bows down before them, it will assuredly lose its heart and its soul," Miscamble tells the crowd of more than two dozen, a number of whom are Notre Dame alums. Miscamble and other critics like the Sycamore Trust, a Notre Dame alumni network dedicated to fighting what it calls "the tide of secularization" washing over Notre Dame, see plenty of reasons to question Notre Dame's Catholic identity. The university's staging of the *Vagina Monologues*, its invitation to President Obama to deliver the 2009 commencement address, and a 2014 decision to extend benefits and housing to legally married same-sex couples have provoked the ire of conservative Catholic activists and some bishops. After Notre Dame's decision on benefits and housing, which followed a move by the U.S. Supreme Court not to hear challenges to same-sex marriage in Indiana and several other states, Fort Wayne–South Bend bishop Kevin Rhoades called for the university to "affirm its fidelity to Catholic teaching on the true nature of marriage."[44]

Battles over Catholic identity have a long history at Notre Dame. In 1967, less than two years after the close of Vatican II, the university's charismatic president at the time, Rev. Theodore Hesburgh, convened several of the most influential leaders in American Catholic higher education for a meeting imbued with the same reforming spirit as the historic church council in Rome. Meeting in Land O'Lakes, Wisconsin, at a conference center owned by Notre Dame, the group consisted of presidents of universities, leaders of religious orders, a few lay leaders, and some bishops, including Archbishop Paul Hallinan, a young U.S. historian. The *New York Times* religion reporter was also there. Notably missing was William Joseph McDonald, rector of the Catholic University of America, the only American university chartered by the Vatican. A suspicious McDonald sent a dean instead. The meeting led to a bold statement, "The Idea of the Catholic University," which served as a clarion call for academic freedom, intellectual inquiry, and the necessary independence from church interference the leaders viewed as essential for an American Catholic university to thrive in a pluralistic society. The document's opening words quickly set the tone:

> The Catholic university today must be a university in the full modern sense of the word, with a strong commitment to and concern for academic excellence. To perform its teaching and research functions effectively the Catholic university must have a true autonomy and academic freedom in the face of authority of whatever kind, lay or clerical, external to the academic community itself. To say this is simply to assert that institutional autonomy and academic freedom are essential conditions of life and growth and indeed of survival for Catholic universities as for all universities.[45]

Phil Gleason, the distinguished historian of American Catholic higher education, described the document as "a declaration of independence from the hierarchy and a symbolic turning point," which made clear that the church's "cold war with modernity" was over.[46] Nearly four decades later, the campus was still at the center of controversy, and a then retired Hesburgh continued to fight for a vision of Catholic identity that did not barricade the university off from the rest of society. The "real test of a great university," he said in 2006 as debates flared over the university's decision not to prohibit the staging of the *Vagina Monologues*, "is that you are fair to the opposition and that you get their point of view out there. You engage them. You want to get students' minds working. You don't want mindless Catholics. You want intelligent, successful Catholics."[47]

As noted earlier in this book, few clashes over Catholic identity in recent years have been as stark as the one that broke out after the University of Notre Dame invited President Obama to deliver the 2009 commencement address. "So quite apart from the president's own positions, which are well known, the problem is in that you have a Catholic university—the flagship Catholic university—do something that brought extreme embarrassment to many, many people who are Catholic," Cardinal Francis George of Chicago told a conference hosted by the archdiocese's Respect Life Office and Office for Evangelization. "Whatever else is clear, it is clear that Notre Dame didn't understand what it means to be Catholic when they issued this invitation."[48]

Rev. John Jenkins, president of Notre Dame, says he was surprised by the backlash over the invitation to President Obama. "The U.S. bishops statement, *Catholics in Political Life*, did not give clear directives on whether non-Catholic politicians should be invited and honored, and so I see no basis for the claim that Notre Dame was defying the bishops," he said. "In retrospect, I should have done more to speak with bishops, express my views and listen to theirs, before announcing this decision. The lack of discussion prior to the announcement contributed to the controversy, and I take responsibility for that. I continue to believe that the intensity of the conflict had a lot to do with political currents and anxieties in our nation at the time." He stressed that honoring Catholic identity, academic freedom, and civil debate are not contradictory pursuits: "Serious and balanced discussion of any issue is not only not incompatible with Catholic identity, but essential to a genuinely Catholic love of truth. Universities, Catholic and secular, are places that debate what activities should go on in their communities. There is nothing wrong with that. It's not surprising that the very important values of the Catholic faith should stimulate vigorous debate."

Notre Dame is a visible target because of its prominent stature, but it's just one of many Catholic universities that often come under scrutiny from the Cardinal Newman Society. Depending on your perspective, the organization is either a courageous voice that defends Catholic identity or a rabid watchdog that needs to be reined in. Founded in 1993 by a Fordham University graduate alarmed that the Jesuit school was considering student groups for gays and lesbians and those who favored abortion rights, the organization's mission is to "promote and defend faithful Catholic education." In 2005, the group sent out fundraising letters targeting several Boston College professors it accused of being part of a "culture of death" for supporting the decision to remove a feeding tube from Terry Shiavo, a brain-damaged woman whose case sparked a national debate over end-of-life issues. The letter pledged that donations would "finance a major effort to expose the heretics within our Catholic colleges." At the time, Rev. John Beal, a canon law professor at the Catholic University of America, described the campaign as "red-baiting in ecclesiastical garb."[49]

Mary Lyons, president of the University of San Diego, has been both praised and prodded by the Cardinal Newman Society over the years. "They rarely ask questions, make assumptions and use heavy-handed tactics," Lyons observed. "The vileness and obscenity of the communication from some of those who consider themselves to be the soldiers of righteousness is very telling to me." At the same time, Lyons has received pressure and derision from the left, and says, "Zealots from either end of the spectrum are to be avoided if possible."[50] Rev. Jenkins of Notre Dame says groups like the Cardinal Newman Society "are without ecclesiastical or academic standing, and their tendentious and inflamed rhetoric may serve fundraising activities, but they undermine the church by sabotaging understanding and healing."

The Cardinal Newman Society beefed up its operations in 2011, launching what it called an "Investigative Task Force" to monitor campuses. It took credit that year for sparking the resignation of a University of Notre Dame trustee over her donations to a pro-choice organization and, after an intense lobbying campaign, for convincing St. Francis University in Loretto, Pennsylvania, to cancel an invitation to then *Boston Globe* columnist Ellen Goodman, a Pulitzer Prize winner, to deliver a lecture about civility on campus because of her support of abortion rights.[51]

Two years later, the Newman Society touted its role in pushing Anna Maria College in Massachusetts to rescind its invitation to the widow of Sen. Ted Kennedy, who was scheduled to give a commencement address. Victoria Kennedy, a pro-choice Catholic, has long been active in Catholic social justice causes, spoke at the centennial gathering of Catholic Charities USA, and served on the board of the National Leadership Round-table on Church Management. The group's campaign to cancel her appearance caught the attention of Bishop Robert J. McManus of Worcester, who put his own pressure on the college. Kennedy responded with a lament about the culture of fear and blacklisting evident in some sectors of the church.

> I am a lifelong Catholic and my faith is very important to me. I am not a public official. I hold no public office, nor am I a candidate for public office. I have not met Bishop McManus nor has he been willing to meet with me to discuss his objections. He has not consulted with my pastor to learn more about me or my faith. Yet by objecting to my appearance at Anna Maria College, he has made a judgment about my worthiness as a Catholic. This is a sad day for me and an even sadder one for the church I love. [52]

"UNIQUE AMONG CATHOLIC COLLEGES"

Christendom College in Front Royal, Virginia, is nestled on the idyllic banks of the Shenandoah River and framed by the Blue Ridge Mountains. If traditionalists lament the steady erosion of Catholic identity on campuses, and some even fear that Pope Francis is watering down the church's pro-life voice, Christendom is regarded as a bulwark. Crucifixes hang in every classroom. Confessions are available twice a day. The college's president leads students and faculty in the rosary. Students fill the pews during evening Holy Hours and all-night adoration of the Blessed Sacrament. Outside the John Paul the Great Student Center, a life-sized statue of the late pope keeps watch over campus with a steady gaze and shepherd's staff in hand. Less than a half-mile down the road is the headquarters of Human Life International, an anti-abortion organization, and the Seton Home Study School, the nation's largest Catholic homeschool network, started by the wife of Christendom's founder. Rick Santorum, the former Catholic senator from Pennsylvania and GOP presidential candidate, is an adviser to the college's board of directors. American Cardinal Raymond Burke, a vocal critic of Pope Francis's efforts to build a more inclusive church, chaired the college's thirty-fifth anniversary dinner in 2012. "Unique among Catholic colleges," Archbishop Chaput has described a school where the pre–Vatican II Latin

Mass is common and all professors take an oath of fidelity to the Magisterium, the teaching authority of the pope and bishops.[53] In its college guide, the Cardinal Newman Society applauds Christendom for setting "a standard for fidelity and traditional education." Founded in 1977 as a response to what its promotional materials describe as "the devastating blow inflicted on Catholic higher education by the cultural revolution which swept across America in the 1960s," Christendom proudly touts its "authentic" Catholic identity.

Students on this campus known for its pro-life activism and traditional liturgy are closely watching what Pope Francis says and does. Mary Townsend, a twenty-one-year-old philosophy major, is a certified nursing assistant and wants a career in medicine. Homeschooled in high school, as were many students here, Townsend says Christendom fosters "intellectual curiosity in a place that won't let you go astray." When asked about Pope Francis, she smiles. "I think there has been some slight concern about him being misunderstood. Some people follow the news and think he is saying he is pro-homosexual. I always say, 'did you read his whole statement or just a headline?'" Above all, she thinks the pope has done a good job speaking to young people and is sparking conversation about the church. "There are times when he could say things better so he is not so easily misinterpreted, but it's good he is encouraging dialogue."

Matthew Marcolini grew up in a Catholic family, but "I didn't know the difference between a venial and a mortal sin," the senior says with a laugh inside Regina Coeli Hall, the college's administration building. When he first visited Christendom for a summer program while attending a public high school, he was awestruck. "The pursuit of truth and the freedom to ask why was incredible. I went to Latin Mass and was like 'wow, what is this awesome language no one ever told me about?' I was so attracted to the beauty of the learning and that allowed me to go deeper in my faith. I had a second conversion."

Marcolini, the president of the college's debate society, insists Christendom is not just teaching students to spout Catholic teaching mindlessly. Along with Aquinas and G. K. Chesterton, he says, they read the *Communist Manifesto* and Martin Luther on the Reformation. In debate, he explains, students who were homeschooled and may not have been exposed to some aspects of the wider culture learn from playing "Devil's Advocate Games" (DAG, for short), where one side is assigned to argue for what he calls a "heterodox position"—in favor of ordaining women in the Catholic Church, for example. "We're taught to put on the armor of God and defend and elucidate our faith." This has implications, he says, for politics and public policy. He has attended the Conservative Political Action Conference (CPAC), an annual meeting in Washington that features activists, public officials, and Republican presidential candidates like Rick Santorum, who also happens to be his girlfriend's father. "I'm a fiscal conservative, but I also believe in Catholic social teaching and that families deserve a living wage," he says.

When it comes to what is going on at the Vatican these days, he sits up in his chair and grows animated. "I get really frustrated with how people talk about Pope Francis. He can't ever change objective truth. The church gets painted as a bigot sometimes, but as Archbishop Fulton Sheen once said, people don't hate the Catholic faith, they hate what they think Catholicism is. Pope Francis's biggest point is if you want people to listen, you don't yell at them and shove it down their throat."

Christendom's student body president, Katie Brizek, agrees. She sees Francis building on the "new evangelization" that Pope John Paul II called for and is encouraged that the pope is persuading people to take a second look at the church. "It's wonderful he is getting so much attention and is admired even by people outside the church," Brizek says. "There was some unrest and questions because if you're a traditionalist, you worry about change, but people have to remember the church does not change and doctrine doesn't change. At the same time, the church does change in a way because she helps us to interpret doctrine so we can practically apply the same truth we have always known since the Resurrection." Brizek describes her political outlook as "not very well formed" but said some basics guide her views and help shape her Catholic identity. "You can't be a Catholic and vote for a politician who is pro-abortion," she says. "That's a deal breaker. There are other issues that are more nuanced and that involve personal conscience like how you think about our immigration laws or welfare or Obamacare. If a politician is pro-abortion, that's a deal breaker. Abortion is black and white."

THEOLOGIANS UNDER FIRE

If the 1967 Land O'Lakes statement signaled a desire on the part of Catholic universities to carve out a sphere of independence from church authority, Pope John Paul II saw this kind of posture as part of a troubling drift away from authentic Catholic identity, and a misinterpretation of the Second Vatican Council. His 1990 apostolic constitution, *Ex Corde Ecclesiae* (From the Heart of the Church), called for a renewal of Catholic identity more closely aligned with the hierarchy. The document implemented church canon law that theologians at Catholic universities must have a "mandatum," a license to teach, from a local bishop. The controversial requirement, widely ignored in the 1980s after it was first prescribed in canon law, mandates that a professor of theology commit to teaching "authentic Catholic doctrine." *Ex Corde Ecclesiae* sparked another round in an old debate over the nature of church authority, Catholic identity, and the proper role of theological inquiry. These tensions all surfaced in the cases of several prominent U.S. theologians publicly rebuked by Catholic bishops and the Vatican in recent years.

Sister Elizabeth Johnson, a feminist theologian at Fordham University, has produced acclaimed works that are standard texts in many undergraduate theology classes. Her *Quest for the Living God: Mapping Frontiers in the Theology of God* has sold more than twenty thousand copies and is translated into six languages. The book examines how God is understood differently through the experiences of women, the poor, Holocaust victims, and non-Catholics. In 2011, the doctrine committee at the U.S. bishops' conference flagged the book for failing to faithfully articulate Catholic teaching. "The book does not take the faith of the Church as its starting point," the doctrine commitment wrote in a twenty-one-page statement. "Instead, the author employs standards from outside the faith to criticize and to revise in a radical fashion the conception of God revealed in Scripture and taught by the Magisterium."[54]

Johnson said bishops never raised concerns with her or requested a meeting before the public critique. In her response, the theologian said the doctrine committee "thoroughly misunderstood and consistently misrepresented" the book. Noting that *Quest for the Living God* is "a work of theology" and "not a catechism, nor a compendium of doctrine," Johnson described her inquiry as "presenting areas of Christian life and study where the mystery of the living God is being glimpsed anew in contemporary situations."[55]

> Theological research does not simply reiterate received doctrinal formulas but probes and interprets them in order to deepen understanding.

To do this well, theology throughout history has articulated faith in different thought forms, images, and linguistic expressions. Its work employs all manner of methods and ideas taken from other disciplines in order to shed light on the meaning of faith.

When the Leadership Conference for Women Religious gave Johnson its 2014 Outstanding Leadership Award, Cardinal Gerhard Müller, the prefect of the Vatican's doctrine office, described it as a "rather open provocation against the Holy See and the Doctrinal Assessment" that "further alienates the LCWR from bishops as well."[56] During her acceptance speech at the LCWR national assembly, Johnson addressed the criticism head on:

> This kind of institutionalized negativity sheds some light on how the critique of my book and criticism of LCWR are intertwined. For the doctrinal investigation of LCWR gives evidence of a similar generalized negative pattern that has been building over recent decades. While reluctant to examine the context in scholarship and in light of statements made at LCWR Assemblies, the investigation's statements express more of a vague overall dissatisfaction or mistrust on certain topics. Judgments are rendered in a way that cannot be satisfactorily addressed. In the absence of careful analysis, negativity spreads. Both of us are caught in an adverse situation not of our own making.
>
> It would be a blessing for the church if [Müller] could find a creative way to bring this investigation to an end in a productive manner. When the needs of the suffering world are so vast; when the moral authority of the hierarchy is hemorrhaging due to financial scandals and to many bishops' horrific dereliction of duty in covering up sexual abuse of children, a cover-up which continues in some quarters to this day; when thousands are drifting away from the church; when the liberating gospel of God's abounding kindness needs to be heard and enacted everywhere: the waste of time and energy on this investigation is unconscionable.[57]

A year after Johnson's book was flagged for criticism in 2011, another Catholic sister and noted theologian came under scrutiny. Margaret Farley, a professor emerita at Yale University who has taught Christian ethics for fifty years, received a five-page "Notification" from the Vatican's doctrine office that took issue with her award-winning book *Just Love: A Framework for Christian Sexual Ethics.* A wide-ranging study of human sexuality in different cultures over time that explores the subject of Christian sexual ethics through Scripture, tradition, secular disciplines, and contemporary experience, *Just Love* won the prestigious Louisville Grawemeyer Award in Religion and received praise for its scholarship from several Catholic publications, including *Catholic Books Review* and *America* magazine. "Among the many errors and ambiguities in this book are its positions on masturbation, homosexual acts, homosexual unions, the indissolubility of marriage and the problem of divorce and remarriage," the Vatican doctrine office said. In her official response, Farley— the first woman appointed full time to the Yale Divinity School—clarified that her work was "not intended to be an expression of current official Catholic teaching, nor was it aimed specifically against this teaching. It is of a different genre altogether." Farley explained that her lens of observation included "both traditional and present-day scientific, philosophical, theological and biblical resources." She acknowledged that her responses to "some sexual ethical questions do depart from some traditional Christian responses," but affirmed that she "tried to show that they nonetheless reflect a deep coherence with the central aims and insights of these theological and moral traditions."[58]

Tension between theologians and church authorities is nothing new. Catholic priests and theologians once disciplined by the Vatican became key figures at the Second Vatican Council. Along with the American Jesuit John Courtney Murray, who was silenced for his writings about church-state issues, the French Dominican priest Yves Congar faced relentless pressure from the Vatican for his writings on ecumenism and church reform. Banned from teaching and even confined to house arrest at the Dominican house of studies at Oxford University in 1955, Congar found his career dramatically rehabilitated only a few years later with the election of John XXIII and the convening of Vatican II. His writings on divine revelation, ecumenism, missionary activity, and religious freedom were visible in almost every major document that came out of the council.

During the twenty-seven-year papacy of John Paul II, when the future pope Cardinal Joseph Ratzinger led the Vatican doctrine office, theologians and even some progressive-minded bishops were under frequent scrutiny. In 1989, the Vatican mandated that new presidents, rectors, and professors of theology and philosophy at Catholic universities and seminaries sign an oath of loyalty and make a profession of faith. "The move was shocking for several reasons, not least because it was done with

virtually no consultation and came as a surprise to other curial depart-
ments that would be affected by the new policy," wrote David Gibson,
author of *The Rule of Benedict: Pope Benedict XVI and His Battle with
the Modern World*. "The oath also smacked of the McCarthyist paranoia
of the anti-Modernist purge of the early twentieth century, when all
priests and seminary teachers were required to take an oath against Modernism. That oath had been dropped in 1967 as an embarrassing anachro-
nism. The new oath was not much better, and in fact it had so many
imprecise wordings and irregularities in its promulgation that it was
widely ignored."[59]

CATHOLIC IDENTITY AND FALSE CHOICES

In some respects, the contours of debate over Catholic identity are un-
helpfully framed. Either you're viewed as a "big tent" Catholic—think of
James Joyce's quip that the church means "Here Comes Everybody"—or,
at the other extreme, you identify with what the Christian writer Rod
Dreher has called the "Benedict Option," a countercultural identity that
has attracted some conservative Catholics and evangelicals who define
themselves in stark opposition to the secular world. In his 1981 book
After Virtue, Alasdair MacIntyre argued that amid the ruins of modern
civilization, traditional believers should embrace the model of St. Benedict, the sixth-century founder of Western monasticism, and create small,
intentional communities of faith distinct from the corrupted mainstream
culture. The cultural critic Peter Leithart has urged fellow believers to
accept that "Christian America" is over and "it's past time to issue a death
certificate." Christians, he writes, should not "slink back to our
churches," but develop a grassroots Christian culture that creates what he
calls "micro-Christendoms."[60] Cardinal Joseph Ratzinger gave credence
to this position before he became Pope Benedict XVI when he spoke of
Christendom entering a new epoch "characterized more by the mustard
seed, where it will exist in small, insignificant groups that nonetheless
live an intensive struggle against evil."[61]

The image of a smaller, "purer" church—where Catholics huddle together to form what Pope Benedict once termed a "creative minority"—in
contrast to an open church where the faithful engage the broader culture
with less suspicion, might provide a certain shorthand for distinct types of

religious identity. However, most faithful, perhaps in a typically Catholic fashion, know these either/or categories miss the fact that religious identity is often not easily pigeonholed. Most "big tent" liberal Catholics agree that faith includes a countercultural dimension. Rejecting the crass materialism and radical individualism of contemporary culture, for example, can be understood as an act of authentic Christian discipleship. At the same time, plenty of Catholics whose references to the Magisterium role easily off the tongue—and who strike an oppositional stance toward mainstream culture—are not all hunkering down in separatist enclaves and still see the value of engagement and dialogue.

At its best, different visions of Catholic identity and a multiplicity of perspectives in the church can be a sign of a healthy faith. "Open and fraternal debate makes theological and pastoral thought grow," Pope Francis has said. "That doesn't frighten me. What's more, I look for it."[62]

If some policing Catholic identity play the part of border guards quick to draw boundaries between the righteous and the reviled, Francis challenges this comfortable certainty. "If a Christian is a restorationist, a legalist, if he wants everything clear and safe," he says, "then he will find nothing. . . . Those who today always look for disciplinarian solutions, those who long for an exaggerated doctrinal 'security,' those who stubbornly try to recover a past that no longer exists—they have a static and inward-directed view of things." Speaking to the Vatican's doctrine office in 2014, the pope warned of the "temptation to understand doctrine in an ideological sense or to reduce it to an ensemble of abstract and crystalized theories." Instead, the pope clarified, "Doctrine has the sole purpose of serving the life of the People of God."[63]

This vision, as ancient as the Gospel and refreshingly new in tone, has emboldened a cadre of new "Francis bishops," even as it threatens some Catholics who see the very soul of the church at risk.

6

THE FRANCIS ERA IN AMERICA

It began with a phone call from the apostolic nuncio, the Vatican's envoy to the United States. The unassuming bishop of Spokane, Washington, a small diocese far removed from the nation's most influential Catholic urban centers, knew he was now on the short list. Bishop Blase Cupich met friends for dinner and kept tight-lipped. Media and church pundits had speculated for months about whom Pope Francis would tap to lead the Archdiocese of Chicago, a powerhouse of American Catholicism with a storied history and more than two million faithful spread across a sprawling network of churches, schools, and hospitals.

Visibly ailing from a battle with cancer, a seventy-seven-year-old Cardinal Francis George had commanded the Chicago archdiocese for seventeen years, served a term as president of the U.S. bishops' conference, and became one of the most consequential figures in the church over the past half-century. Well respected as an intellectual leader among conservatives in the hierarchy, the sometimes pugnacious prelate didn't shy away from controversy. He once compared organizers of a Chicago gay pride parade to the Ku Klux Klan and declared liberal Catholicism an "exhausted project." George had submitted his resignation a few years earlier, and his illness now sped up the search process. The high-profile pick would send a decisive message. How did a pope eager to shake up old structures, build a "poor church for the poor," and broaden the Catholic narrative beyond flash points of sexual morality intend to put his imprint on a U.S. hierarchy seemingly unable or unwilling to escape bruising cultural fights? If the "Francis effect" was about more than a change of tone, Chicago came to be viewed as a test of whether the pope's ambitious reform and renewal agenda would have legs in one of the most important dioceses in the United States.

BISHOP CUPICH TO CHICAGO: "THE 'FRANCIS ERA' STARTS TODAY"

In Rapid City, South Dakota, and then Spokane, Washington, Cupich earned a reputation as a pastoral leader uncomfortable with the sharp elbows preferred by some of his brother bishops. Even as some in the hierarchy depicted President Obama as something of an anti-Catholic tyrant, Bishop Cupich took to *America* magazine with a measured call for a "return to civility" and warned that "in the long run threats and condemnations have a limited impact."[1]

Cupich didn't want the integrity of the church's pro-life witness to begin with confrontation or get hijacked by some fringe elements in the anti-abortion movement, so in Spokane he discouraged priests and seminarians from protesting outside abortion clinics.[2] As an equality referendum in Washington State heated up in 2012, he opposed efforts to grant same-sex couples legal recognition as married couples, but, in a rare acknowledgment from the hierarchy, he stressed in a letter read at all Masses that many of the church's adversaries on the issue were "motivated by compassion for those who have shown courage in refusing to live in the fear of being rejected for their sexual orientation." Cupich highlighted what he called "the tragic national stories of violence against homosexuals, of verbal attacks that demean their human dignity, and of suicides by teens who have struggled with their sexual identity or have been bullied because of it." The message was consistent with traditional Catholic teaching that insists on respect for gays and lesbians, but the letter stood out as a moment of sanity in a charged environment in which some bishops viewed the growing acceptance of same-sex civil marriage as an existential threat that had to be defeated at all costs.

Even with his focus on social justice and engaging style, Bishop Cupich was likely not well known in Rome when Pope Francis was elected. Spokane is not exactly New York, Los Angeles, or Boston, where cardinals and archbishops are public figures in the spotlight of major media markets. His reluctance to hurl rhetorical grenades and understated demeanor garnered respect, but it also kept Cupich's profile relatively low. When Cupich delivered an address at the Catholic University of America in Washington in the summer of 2014, he caught the eye of Honduran cardinal Óscar Rodríguez Maradiaga, one of the pope's key advisers. Maradiaga gave an impassioned speech denouncing "the structural causes of poverty and injustice," and he challenged libertarian economics as incompatible with Catholic social teaching. [3]

Organizers of the conference asked Cupich to offer a response to the cardinal. Quoting Pope Francis extensively, Cupich warned about the dangers of excessive individualism and materialism. Inequality, he said, is a "powder keg that is as dangerous as the environmental crisis the world is facing today." A smiling Cardinal Maradiaga looked on, impressed. Whether Cupich was already on the short list for Chicago or not, his stock was clearly rising. Less than four months later, the pope bypassed more prominent bishops in larger dioceses and named him the next archbishop of Chicago. Even before formally beginning his tenure, Cupich took a page from the austere-minded pope and announced that he would not live in the $14 million mansion known as the "House of 19 Chimneys" that the city's archbishops have called home since the 1890s. Instead, Cupich, who lived in a seminary in Spokane, would take up residence in a rectory. [4]

"The 'Francis Era' in America Starts Today in Chicago," declared one headline that typified the exuberant coverage. The Catholic analyst John Allen crystallized the outsized expectations that the new bishop faced before he even unpacked his bags. "By virtue of Chicago's history, and because from here on in Cupich will be known as Francis' man—his first major appointment in America—the success or failure of the Francis revolution on these shores will rest to some extent on Cupich's shoulders," Allen wrote. [5] If he felt daunted by his unofficial coronation as the American Francis, Cupich didn't shy away from embracing the pope's inclusive and engaging style. As he walked down the aisle at his formal installation Mass, the hymn "All Are Welcome" filled Holy Name Cathedral. "We as a church should not fear leaving the security of familiar shores, the peacefulness of the mountaintop of our self-assuredness and walk into the mess," the bishop said in a homily that echoed Pope Francis's call for the church to be "bruised, hurting and dirty because it has been out on the streets." In the first minute of his homily, Cupich praised "the extraordinary contribution women religious have made and continue to make to the church and society."

The simple appreciation sent a signal of solidarity to American nuns then still facing oversight from the Vatican and U.S. bishops.[6]

Speaking before an audience that included more than a dozen archbishops and cardinals, Cupich reminded those who feared change to consider the Gospel: "Jesus invites us, not only to take the risk of leaving our comfort zone, but also to deal with the tension involved in change, not dismissively but in a creative way, and to challenge each other to do so." Careful observers noted that Cupich had invited the retired Archbishop Emeritus John Quinn of San Francisco, a well-regarded intellectual beloved by Catholic liberals, to celebrate Mass with him. A leading church figure in the late 1970s and early 1980s, Quinn served as president of the U.S. Conference of Catholic Bishops before being eclipsed by a generation of more conservative bishops. His 1999 book, *The Reform of the Papacy: The Costly Call to Christian Unity*, was a civil yet unambiguous challenge to the governance style of Pope John Paul II. It called for the decentralization of power away from the Vatican, and more collegiality and flexibility for local churches. "I've read your book," Cardinal Jorge Mario Bergoglio of Buenos Aires told Quinn just days before being elected pope, "and I'm hoping it will be implemented."[7]

"Today's clear albeit unspoken message: Chicago's back in business in its traditional role—the seat of progressive Catholicism in the US," tweeted the prolific Catholic blogger and respected clerical chronicler Rocco Palmo. Political pundits were also taking notice. E. J. Dionne Jr., a *Washington Post* columnist and liberal Catholic, observed that far more than internal church matters were at stake. Cupich's appointment "will have an impact beyond the Catholic Church," Dionne predicted, "because it tells us a great deal about the role Pope Francis wants the church to play in American life."[8] Cupich told me that the pope has "exploded the narrative," and that is what has caused disquiet among those few vocal commentators "who thought they owned the church." "I think the pope looks around and sees so much human suffering and is convinced that the church can't turn itself into a bastion of defending the few, the pure, the elect," he said. "His metaphor of the church as field hospital is wonderful." The archbishop sees the church entering "a period of adapting and growth. . . . We can't be afraid to stretch."

If Catholic moderates and liberals celebrated the changing of the guard, those who had enjoyed favor under previous papacies found themselves increasingly whiplashed by strong winds blowing from Rome. Just ten days before the Cupich era began in Chicago, Pope Francis removed Cardinal Raymond Burke—an American best known for his penchant for extravagant liturgical vestments and arguing that Catholic politicians should be denied Communion—from his post as the leader of the Vatican's highest court. A few days before his demotion, the cardinal gave an exclusive interview to the right-wing Brietbart.com and warned of "a risk of schism" if bishops were perceived by the faithful to be moving against "unchanging and unchangeable truths."[9] It was the second demotion in short order for the former archbishop of St. Louis brought to the Vatican by Pope Benedict XVI in 2008 to become prefect of the Supreme Tribunal of the Apostolic Signatura, the highest judicial authority in the church outside of the pope. Pope Francis had earlier removed him from the powerful Congregation of Bishops, which advises the pope on candidates for the episcopate. One of the most outspoken prelates in the church, Burke became a startling, blunt public critic of Pope Francis's reform agenda in the runup and aftermath of the first session of an Extraordinary Synod on the Family held at the Vatican in the fall of 2014.

"A PASTORAL EARTHQUAKE": SHOWDOWN AT THE SYNOD

The pope convened the unexpected meeting in part to consider more pastoral ways for responding to divorced and remarried Catholics barred from the sacraments, couples who live together before marriage, and gay and lesbian Catholics. Some two hundred bishops, along with a handful of married couples picked to make presentations, met for two weeks of discussion. "Speak clearly," Francis told the participants at the start of the meeting. "No one must say, 'this can't be said.'" The pope got what he asked for in spades. The synod pulled back the curtain on sharp divisions inside the church, which naturally sparked widespread coverage in mainstream media, an extraordinary event itself given that the last synod in 1980 under Pope John Paul II seemed little more than a staged event, with conclusions already written before anyone opened their mouths. The bishops' preliminary report, drafted by a committee handpicked by the pope and issued midway through the meeting, signaled a stunning shift in tone from the church on a host of contentious issues. Pastors should recognize that there are "positive aspects of civil unions and cohabitation," the report said, and that some gay couples provide each other with "precious support in the life of the partners." Gays and lesbians have "gifts and qualities to offer to the Christian community." While bishops were divided over the reception of Communion for divorced and remarried Catholics, the draft report urged church leaders to avoid "any language or behavior that might make them feel discriminated against."[10]

One longtime Vatican reporter called it a pastoral "earthquake . . . the 'big one' that hit after months of smaller tremors."[11] Rev. James Martin of *America* magazine described the interim report as a "revolution in the way the church speaks about our gay and lesbian brothers and sisters."[12] Conservatives pounced before the ink was dry. Cardinal Burke warned of "worrying tendencies" coming out of the synod. "A large number of bishops do not accept the ideas of openness," he told an Italian newspaper.[13]

While the synod's final report walked back much of the eye-catching language because controversial passages did not receive the two-thirds majority needed for approval, strong majorities did support them. Some reform-minded bishops even publicly acknowledged they voted no because the language didn't go far enough in emphasizing that the church should welcome, respect, and value gays and lesbians. "I didn't think it was a good text because it didn't include those words strongly enough," said British cardinal Vincent Nichols. Predictable reaction came in waves: "Catholic Bishops Scrap Welcome to Gays," the *Huffington Post* harrumphed in a headline. "For Francis, a Resounding Defeat," cheered *Rorate Caeli*, a traditionalist Catholic blog.

Liberals and conservatives were still missing the real story about a transformational, unpredictable moment in the life of the church. Pope Francis is calling the church to experience a deep spiritual renewal. His foes are clericalism, a narrow religious legalism, and anything that obscures the joy of the Gospel. "We must always consider the person," Francis says in what could be considered a distillation of his pastoral focus. Reform, of course, is in the eye of the beholder. For some on the right, Pope Francis is playing with fire that threatens to burn down the house. Some liberals will never be happy until the church ordains women, marries gays and lesbians, and endorses birth control. These are all legitimate debates to have, and Francis is clearly not afraid of discussion. The pope has his eye on something more fundamental. "We always need time to lay the foundations for real, effective change," he told the Jesuit editor Antonio Spadaro. "The structural and organizational reforms are secondary. . . . The first reform must be the attitude." Francis stands in a long tradition of reformers and spiritual troublemakers. When Francis of Assisi came along in the twelfth century, his embrace of poverty, personal holiness, and peacemaking were a walking rebuke to an institutional church mired in worldly corruption. The Franciscans, and later religious orders like Pope Francis's own Jesuit order, sparked spiritual movements that still inspire people in ways that the fine print of the church's Catechism never will.

The pope's closing address at the synod cautioned against triumphalism from the left or right. Speaking to those he called "traditionalists," Francis warned of a tendency toward "hostile inflexibility" and of being "closed" in the letter of the law. Turning his attention to "so-called progressives and liberals," the pope warned of a "deceptive mercy" that "binds wounds without first curing them and treating them."[14] The synod's fractious opening act only served as a preview for a concluding meeting in October 2015. "So the drama continues," a smiling Cardinal Luis Tagle of the Philippines told the media.[15]

In some quarters, the synod prompted what can only be accurately described without much exaggeration as a first-class fit of hysteria. The often insightful Ross Douthat, a *New York Times* columnist who is a conservative Catholic, sounded an alarm that the church could soon be "on the brink of a precipice." Allowing remarried Catholics to receive Communion, he warned, "would leave many of the church's bishops and theologians in an untenable position, and it would sow confusion among the church's orthodox adherents—encouraging doubt and defections, apocalypticism and paranoia (remember there is another pope still living!) and eventually even a real schism." Those orthodox faithful, who Douthat argued "have done the most to keep the church vital in an age of institutional decline," did not "deserve a theological betrayal."[16] Several American bishops were also not holding their tongues. "Pope Francis is fond of 'creating a mess.' Mission accomplished," Bishop Thomas Tobin of Providence, Rhode Island, wrote on his diocesan website. If the pope has warned that the church becomes sick by being too self-referential, Tobin instead feared that in the name of openness the church "risks the danger of losing its courageous, counter-cultural, prophetic voice, a voice that the world needs to hear." As for the synod's deliberate and collegial discussions that many praised for their refreshing transparency, Tobin remained unconvinced. "The concept of having a representative body of the church voting on doctrinal applications and pastoral solutions strikes me as being rather Protestant," he wrote in blunt language. Praising Cardinal Burke as "a fearless spokesman for the teachings of the church," Tobin reassured his flock that amid all the uncertainty "God's still in charge."[17]

Whether fearless or just plain reckless, Burke's demotion only seemed to embolden him. Insisting he was not speaking against the pope, Burke compared the church to "a ship without a rudder" in an interview with a Spanish Catholic weekly newspaper.[18] And in response to a question after a lecture in New York, Archbishop Chaput of Philadelphia had a less than glowing assessment of the synod. "I think confusion is of the devil," the archbishop said, "and I think the public image that came across was one of confusion." Chaput denied he was criticizing the meeting and blasted the media for willfully misinterpreting his remarks.[19] When Walter Kasper addressed a standing-room-only crowd at the Catholic University of America in Washington just weeks after the synod, the German cardinal often dubbed "the pope's theologian" quipped that while the Francis papacy marked "the beginning of a new spring," for many it's "a temporary cold spell." Kasper called Francis "a pope of surprises" who "within a short period of time succeeded in brightening the gloomy atmosphere that had settled like mildew on the church." Addressing an audience filled with priests, theologians, and seminarians, Kasper was direct in describing the tensions. "There are a lot of you, even among the episcopate and the younger clergy, who do not really trust this new style or new enthusiasm," he said.[20]

"WHAT DOES HE WANT US TO DO?"

At the annual bishops' meeting in Baltimore, just a few days after Cardinal Kasper's lecture in Washington, confusion about the pope's intent and message was in evidence. Cardinal George of Chicago, just days before his retirement and five months before his death, acknowledged in an interview with the *New York Times* that the Francis papacy had left him

disoriented. "He says wonderful things but he doesn't put them all together all the time, so you're left at times puzzling over what his intention is,"
George said. "What he says is clear enough, but what does he want us to
do?"[21] In a separate interview with *Crux*, the *Boston Globe*'s Catholic
publication, George wondered aloud about whether the pope knew how
he was being interpreted. "Does he not realize the consequences of some
of his statements, or even some of his actions? Does he not realize the
repercussions? Perhaps he doesn't. I don't know whether he's conscious
of all the consequences of some of the things he's said and done that raise
these doubts in people's minds."

A columnist at the liberal *National Catholic Reporter*, Michael Sean
Winters, assessed the cardinal's angst as emblematic of a hierarchy struggling to make sense of a maverick pope. "As many as half of the bishops
are those who simply do not understand what Pope Francis is trying to
achieve," Winters wrote. "Whether you like the pope or fear the pope,
this pontificate is something of a roller-coaster ride, and very few bishops
could be characterized as 'thrill-seekers.' They are conservative by nature
and training, and in the past 30 years they have seen issue after issue go
from the 'debated' category to the 'decided' category. They value the
security of knowing contentious matters are settled and are not sure why
Pope Francis seems hell-bent on unsettling those matters." John Thavis, a
former Rome bureau chief for *Catholic News Service*, agreed. "Many of
the U.S. bishops have been disoriented by what this new pope is saying
and I don't see them really as embracing the pope's agenda," he said. "To
a large degree, the U.S. bishops have lost their bearings. I think up until
now, they felt Rome had their back, and what they were saying—especially politically—would eventually be supported in Rome. They can't
count on that now."[22]

"THE ENGAGE AND PERSUADE CAUCUS": FRANCIS BUILDS HIS AMERICAN BASE

Even with the obvious tensions, there are signs that more bishops are
taking a page from the Francis playbook. Some moderate prelates over-
shadowed in recent years by a vocal chorus of combative conservatives
are finding their voice. When Archbishop Joseph Kurtz was elected president of the U.S. Conference of Catholic Bishops in 2013, he quickly

aligned himself with the pope's priorities. "One of the major challenges is what, really, our Holy Father has said over and over again: How can we warm hearts and heal wounds?" he told reporters. In his first presidential address a year later, Kurtz seemed to channel Francis when he reflected on his own pastoral approach. "When I'd come to someone's home, I wouldn't start by telling them how I'd rearrange their furniture. In the same way I wouldn't begin by giving them a list of rules to follow. I would then invite them to follow Christ, and I'd offer to accompany them as we, together, follow the Gospel invitation to turn from sin and journey along the way. Such an approach isn't in opposition to Church teachings; it's an affirmation of them."

The official agenda for the bishops' national meeting that year inspired less hope than the more welcoming tone. Key issues at the forefront of the Francis papacy—poverty and economic justice—were once again missing from the action items filling the bishops' binders. The bishops did find time to approve the first English-language version of the ancient rite "Of Exorcisms and Certain Supplications." Archbishop William Lori of Baltimore, the point person for the bishops' religious liberty campaign, vowed the conference would continue to fight laws dealing with "so-called sexual orientation and gender identity."[23] But, in a sign that the levers of institutional bureaucracy were at least starting to churn, Archbishop Peter Sartain of Seattle reported that his committee was discussing specific ways to incorporate Pope Francis's priorities and "work them into our strategic planning."[24]

John Carr spent more than two decades at the U.S. Conference of Catholic Bishops advising bishops on social justice issues and navigating the often fraught drafting process of "Faithful Citizenship," the conference's statement on political responsibility that church insiders and some Catholic politicians pore over with a magnifying glass every presidential election year. He sees the pope's challenge to the American hierarchy and all Catholics as both simple and profound.

"Pope Francis has gone back to the fundamentals and that comes with a mandate to lift up what's at the core of the Gospel," said Carr, who now leads the Initiative on Catholic Social Thought and Public Life at Georgetown University. "He is reminding us of why we believe and why we belong to the church." For those who think that the Vatican has simply orchestrated a public relations coup, he has a dry retort: "Can you name the last successful Vatican P.R. campaign? Pre-Crusades, I think." The challenge now is one of leadership and vision. "If you think as Catholics, we've lost and the culture is overwhelming us, you are tempted to hunker down and throw thunderbolts," he said. "If you think we can make our case and prevail, then you reach out to engage and persuade. There is a battle not between left and right, but between the hunker down caucus and the engage and persuade caucus." Carr quoted the longtime journalist, Catholic, and PBS commentator Mark Shields: "You can tell the health of an organization by whether they are looking for heretics or converts."

Two of the most influential voices in the American hierarchy—Cardinal Sean O'Malley of Boston and Cardinal Donald Wuerl of Washington—are card-carrying members of the engage and persuade caucus. Pastoral leaders who have long frowned upon culture-war antics, O'Malley and Wuerl have emerged as heavyweights in the Francis papacy. A Franciscan known for his focus on the poor and widely lauded for reviving the Archdiocese of Boston in the wake of horrific clergy abuse scandals, O'Malley is the only American on the pope's elite nine-cardinal committee tasked with helping to reform the church's governance. Pope Francis also appointed O'Malley to a new Pontifical Commission for the Protection of Minors, an effort to strengthen measures to prevent clergy sexual abuse. During a freewheeling interview with *60 Minutes* in 2014, O'Malley called the Vatican investigation of American nuns "a disaster" and said if he were founding a church, "I'd love to have women priests," but "Christ founded it and he has given us something different."[25] O'Malley, who wears a simple brown tunic and has been spotted mowing his own lawn, acknowledged after the interview that he was commenting on "provocative issues that are seldom addressed by members of the hierarchy." It's hard to imagine that level of openness and candor during previous papacies.[26]

Cardinal Wuerl of Washington sits on the powerful thirty-member Vatican body that helps the pope select new bishops. In that role, he is positioned to play a key role in shaping the direction of the hierarchy in the United States and around the world. A skilled administrator adept at defusing tensions, Wuerl has led an archdiocese at the center of American political debates with a careful hand. When Nancy Pelosi, a pro-choice Catholic reviled by the right, was the Speaker of the House, he faced pressure to deny her Communion and take a harder stance against other pro-choice Catholic politicians. He refused to turn a holy sacrament into a political weapon. "That's the new way now to make your point. We never—the church just didn't use Communion this way," he said in a 2009 interview. "It wasn't a part of the way we did things, and it wasn't a way we convinced Catholic politicians to appropriate the faith and live it and apply it; the challenge has always been to *convince* people . . . I have yet to see where the canonical approach has changed anyone's heart."[27] As insider accounts trickled out after the papal conclave, reporters learned that the cardinal from Washington had played a key role in rallying his fellow American cardinals behind Bergoglio. After Francis's election, Wuerl praised him as "the perfect choice for this moment in time."[28] Writing from Rome during the synod in 2014, Wuerl demonstrated his moderate instincts when he updated his flock on the meeting in his archdiocesan newspaper by noting that "the church's teaching on human sexuality is not up for debate," while at the same time acknowledging "it is important that we examine the language we use and our pastoral approach toward individuals with same-sex attraction."

Robert McElroy is a rising star in the hierarchy. A graduate of both Stanford and Harvard, the auxiliary bishop in San Francisco was tapped by Pope Francis in 2015 to lead the diocese of San Diego. He is widely respected for his incisive writing and intellectual chops. While some across the ideological spectrum argue the Francis papacy is merely an image makeover, McElroy thinks that the pope is "signaling important changes in the life of the church on many levels."

"The most promising thing in my mind is a shift to a framework of pastoral theology as the primary entry point for the church," McElroy said. "The pope is showing us that pastoral outreach must proceed from Jesus and the way he approaches people in the Gospel. He embraces them with the love of God, heals them of their wounds and then asks them to reform their lives. The overarching pastoral framework that Francis is demonstrating himself and calling us to return to is embracing, healing and then reforming and renewing. It's always done in this order. He embodies a principle of pastoral theology, the principle of gradualism. Jesus begins where people are, not where they fall short. It is accompaniment of a person, which is really a beautiful theology."

McElroy is not surprised by the pushback Francis is facing from some commentators and clerics. "There is a difference in tone and emphasis that is not merely symbolic. It calls for a change in heart and mind. We're being called to live a different life and that's not easy for any of us." He expresses frustration that bishops over the last few years have been "consumed with a religious liberty push," largely focused on same-sex marriage and battles with the Obama administration over contraception coverage. "I do think there will be a movement out of a preoccupation with those issues, and an effort to bring poverty front and center. The bishops have the memo from Pope Francis, and we are trying to integrate this into our work in dioceses. It's like a big ship adjusting course. It can't be done all at once."

Pope Francis appointed Christopher Coyne as bishop of Burlington, Vermont, at the end of 2014. Coyne, fifty-six, leads a small diocese and won't likely make as many headlines as bishops in Chicago or Los Angeles. Even so, institutional shifts in the church are not just about the five-star changes. Reform builds with steady momentum, almost imperceptibly, one diocese at a time. The pope has emboldened Coyne, who acknowledges at times feeling uneasy with the direction of the U.S. hierarchy in recent years. "Francis has a pastor's heart, and he changes the conversation because we're now talking about what we are for rather than what we're against," he said. "I've been a back bencher in the bishops' conference for years. It often felt like the agenda was set without an opportunity to say, 'wait, is this the way we should go?' Some bishops didn't speak up because there really was no signal that there was a push to move in a contrary direction. Now with Pope Francis there is more freedom to be outspoken than some of us would have been in the past."

Coyne sees a pope with a fresh vision for the future drawing on the wisdom of the past. "We have to return to our roots," he said. "Early Christianity became attractive to so many people because Christians were people known for their good acts. They emphasized community and ministered to those in need. These were people who had a profound encounter with Jesus." Coyne acknowledges that at times bishops don't help themselves. "The culture wars are a non-starter. We have to shift from being a mainstream church to being a missionary church. We can no longer assume people are listening to us," he insists. "If you're a missionary church, you don't start by attacking people and challenging laws; you convert hearts and minds and then you can talk about how someone orders their life. The U.S. bishops have been too overtly focused on culture war issues. There are bishops who feel like the priority needs to be religious freedom, same-sex marriage and the right to life. They are not guided by politics or a GOP agenda. They really believe these are the primary issues. So when Pope Francis says let's set out our priorities in a different direction that does lead to a certain dissonance in our conference about what we're going to do. This is healthy. I don't see it as a matter of one side winning or losing." Coyne describes a "wrestling going on among bishops" as they try to make sense of an unconventional pope. "I was talking to one of my bishop friends and he says to me, 'Francis needs to know he is making our job harder.' I looked at him and said, 'This is probably a good thing!'"

Young Catholics, he senses, are looking for an active church that reaches out rather than a stuffy institution that simply scolds them. He began blogging as a pastor back in 2007, and has been on Twitter and Facebook for several years. Coyne's blog, *Let us Walk Together: Thoughts of a Catholic Bishop*, is written in a conversational style and is updated frequently with videos. He posts on Facebook every morning. In many ways, this kind of engagement comes naturally to Coyne, who as a priest once worked for Boston's Catholic television station and even received an Emmy nomination. "Social media is where communication is taking place today so we have to be there," says Coyne, who had the unenviable task of serving as a spokesperson for the Archdiocese of Boston during the height of the clergy abuse scandals and now chairs the U.S. bishops' communications committee. "I take my lead from St. Augustine, who said the teacher must teach and persuade. We need to offer something attractive to people."

A DÉTENTE IN THE CULTURE WARS?

When organizers of the New York City St. Patrick's Day parade announced in 2014 that they were ending the ban on openly gay groups marching under their own banner, Cardinal Timothy Dolan had a decision to make. The city's powerful Cardinal John O'Connor once dismissed calls from gay and lesbian groups to open up the parade as "political correctness" not worth "one comma in the Apostles' Creed." Dolan—an affable conservative who has sparred with the *New York Times* and liberal critics of the church—perhaps recognized that in the Francis era that haughty attitude wouldn't cut it. "I have no trouble with the decision at all. I think the decision is a wise one," Dolan said at a news conference that prompted a firestorm from conservative Catholics.[29] A writer at the

National Catholic Register blasted the cardinal for affirming "gay identity" and showing himself "unequal to his responsibility as a successor to the Apostles."[30]

A priest who blogs for the Archdiocese of Washington wrote that the St. Patrick's Day parade and other Catholic traditions such as the Al Smith Dinner—which features the New York archbishop yukking it up with the two presidential nominees from both political parties every four years—have "been hijacked by the world." The priest called on Catholics "to pray in reparation for the foolishness." The archdiocese quickly removed the commentary, but it made the rounds on right-wing blogs.[31] A month before Dolan's welcoming stance toward LGBT groups at the parade, he sent another message that some Catholic leaders in the United States were responding to the Francis moment. In a lengthy interview with the *Boston Globe*, Dolan said efforts to withhold Communion from pro-choice Catholic politicians were "in the past" and emphasized that Pope Francis wanted bishops "who would not be associated with any one ideological camp." If this wasn't an end to the culture wars, it hinted perhaps at the prospect of a détente.[32]

Sister Jeannine Gramick, a hero to many gay and lesbian Catholics for her ministry to those in the church who have often felt like outcasts, also senses an important shift. Back in 1999, when Pope Benedict XVI was a cardinal and led the Vatican's doctrine office, he ordered Gramick and the late Rev. Robert Nugent of New Ways Ministry to end all of their pastoral work with LGBT Catholics, citing "ambiguities and errors" in their approach that "caused confusion among the Catholic people and have harmed the community of the church."[33]

After a period of reflection, Gramick continued her ministry. "I chose not to participate in my own oppression," she said. In recent years, Gramick has noticed a more welcoming attitude in many dioceses and churches. She and other staff from New Ways Ministry were even given VIP seats at Pope Francis's weekly audience in the spring of 2015, a first for the group.

Some bishops well known for their vocal opposition to gay marriage, she says, are reaching out and starting to modulate their tone. When Pope Benedict XVI named Salvatore Cordileone as the archbishop of San Francisco in 2012, a diocese known for its gay-friendly Catholic parishes and a history of moderate bishops at the helm, many saw it as a smack in the face to the local gay Catholic community. Before his appointment to

San Francisco, Cordileone became a key figure in pushing Proposition 8, which banned same-sex marriage in 2008. During his time in Oakland, he tussled frequently with a Catholic LGBT ministry, and his stormy tenure in San Francisco has included a high-profile clash over morality clauses in teachers' contracts.

More than one hundred Catholics in San Francisco—including the retired director of the city's Catholic Charities agency—took out a full-page advertisement in the *San Francisco Chronicle* calling for Pope Francis to remove him. The signatories charged that the archbishop "sets a pastoral tone that is closer to persecution than evangelization."[34] When the archbishop made plans in 2014 to attend the March for Marriage in Washington, an event that critics say has ties to groups known for hateful rhetoric toward gays and lesbians, Gramick's organization joined others in asking the archbishop not to attend. He did go but promised to meet with any people who had objections.

When Gramick and staff sat down with Cordileone for a dialogue session in their offices, the Catholic sister said the vibe was relaxed and the conversation genuine. "I was surprised that he took us up on the offer to meet but looking back on it I think this is part of the Francis effect," she said. No major breakthroughs happened, but the conversation helped establish a better context for civil conversation and broke down some stereotypes on both sides.[35] During the meeting, the archbishop quoted Pope Francis on the need for "encounter" and meeting people where they are with love. The following year, Cordileone took a pass on going to the March for Marriage, tweeting that his "priority" was "dialogue" with teachers in his city. In the face of growing criticism against the morality clause, the archbishop issued a conciliatory press release vowing "there will be no witch hunts," pledging to "heal any rifts" and opening the door to "adjustments" to secure the rights of teachers.

Gramick is under no illusion that Pope Francis supports same-sex marriage or that years of suspicion and animosity will dissolve easily. Even after being given VIP seating at the pope's general audience and meeting with Archbishop Cordileone, the bishop of Charlotte, North Carolina, prohibited her from giving a scheduled talk at a church in the diocese that was to focus on how to make faith communities more welcoming for gays and lesbians. But the Catholic sister is still buoyed by the new tone and small openings in the Francis era. "The culture warriors in the church are trying to be more pastoral and part of that is sitting down face to face with people," she says. "There is a new atmosphere in the church."

REFORM IN THE EYE OF THE BEHOLDER

Pope Francis has a shepherd's staff, not a magic wand. Even the spiritual leader of more than a billion Catholics can't turn the ocean liner that is the global Catholic Church on his own. At seventy-eight, Francis is unlikely to have the nearly three decades to make his mark on the church in the way that Pope John Paul II did when he was elected at the age of fifty-eight. It should not have been a surprise when the Pew Forum on Religion & Public Life Project, only a year into his papacy, found no measurable rise in the percentage of Americans who identify as Catholic (22 percent) or any statistically significant change in how often Catholics say they attend Mass. These numbers have remained relatively unchanged for years. Pew did report that about a quarter of Catholics said they had become "more excited" about their Catholic faith, and four in ten said they had been praying more. There was broad consensus among Catholics polled that Francis "represents a major change in direction for the church, and that this is a change for the better."

There are some signs that Pope Francis has been good for vocations to the priesthood, or at least to the Jesuits, the largest male religious order in the Catholic Church. Jesuit vocation directors have reported a spike in interest since the pope's election. Rev. Chuck Frederico, SJ, a vocations director for the Jesuits, told *America* magazine that he has been "flooded with inquiries" from men discerning a vocation. "From the day that Pope Francis was elected through the present our website has been constant with people filling out the form," he said. "I'm psyched. This is good. I'm busy."[36]

The Archdiocese of Washington welcomed 1,306 new Catholics during Easter of 2014, the highest number it has ever recorded. While it's unclear how much Pope Francis had to do with that increase, it's hard not to think that a pope who has generated so much positive media coverage for the church and seems to appear on a new magazine cover every week didn't play some role in attracting people to the faith. Mark Gray of the Center for Applied Research in the Apostolate at Georgetown University analyzed data from the 2014 General Social Survey, a leading resource for sociologists, and found that 34 percent of Catholics described their religious affiliation as "strong," up from 27 percent in 2012, the year before Pope Francis was elected. The increase, while not at all dramatic, represented a "significant bounce," Gray noted.[37] A 2013 survey released by Foundations and Donors Interested in Catholic Activities (FADICA), a network of private philanthropists supporting Catholic-sponsored programs, found that one in four Catholics had increased their giving from the year before. Seventy-seven percent cited Pope Francis as an influence in doing so.[38]

Statistics, of course, can't adequately capture the reality of how Francis is reaching people inside and outside the church. Mass attendance is not the only, or even (perhaps) the most essential, barometer of the church's vitality. Religion journalist Daniel Burke of CNN found in his reporting in Boston, a heavily Catholic city that became the epicenter of the clergy abuse crisis, signs of shifting attitudes:

> Start asking around—here in Boston and beyond, Catholics and atheists alike—and it's easy to find people eager to share how one man, in just one year, has changed their lives. There's the gay man who finally feels welcome in his church. The woman who weeps when headlines deliver good news at last. The former priest who no longer clenches his fist during Mass. The Latinos who waited forever for a Pope who speaks their language. "I'm telling you, brother, if you focus on the numbers, you're missing the story," says the Rev. John Unni, a Boston pastor with an accent as thick as clam chowda. "There's an energy, a feeling, a spirit here. It's like a healing balm."[39]

Not everyone is so bullish on the potential of this pope. Paul Baumann, the editor of *Commonweal*, a liberal journal edited by lay Catholics for the past ninety years, raises an important note of caution for those investing outsized hopes in Francis. "The truth is that the more the world flatters the Catholic Church by fixating on the papacy—and the more the internal Catholic conversation is monopolized by speculation about the intentions of one man—the less likely it is that the church will succeed in moving beyond the confusions and conflicts that have preoccupied it since the Second Vatican Council," he wrote in *Slate*. "The church desperately needs to reclaim its cultural and spiritual equilibrium; it must find a density and richness of worship and mission and a renewed public presence, which far transcend mere loyalty to the pope. Lacking such equilibrium and self-possession, the church cannot find its true voice. But to find this voice, Catholics will have to turn not to Rome but toward one another, which is where both the problems and the solutions lie." Francis, "despite his evident charm and pastoral style," Baumann argues, "won't have much more luck than his more theologically anxious predecessors in ameliorating the church's ideological conflicts."[40]

Other Catholic progressives find different reasons for skepticism. Jamie Manson, an award-winning journalist at the *National Catholic Reporter* who writes frequently about LGBT issues and the church, praises Francis for his "authentic warmth" and "deep passion for the poor and marginalized." However, she warns that the pope is more similar than not to his predecessors. "Francis is changing the tone in the hope that the church will be perceived in a better light, but there is little evidence to suggest he will or wants to make doctrinal changes on women's equality, same-sex relationships or contraception," Manson wrote. "Have we gotten to the point where our desire to realize the church of our dreams and our insistence that Francis will be the man to make our dreams come true is clouding our perception of what Francis is really saying?" "Why do Catholics," she asks, "especially many progressive Catholics, continue to give him a pass?"[41]

Manson is an eloquent voice for inclusion in the church, and her essential writing should prick the conscience of Catholic leaders. Nevertheless, her assessment of Francis—along with the broader disillusionment of some progressives who will only be satisfied by swift doctrinal changes—risks a similarly reductive approach preferred by conservatives. If the right wing often distorts the fullness of Catholicity with a fixation on zealously guarding the church's doctrine on sexuality, some Catholic liberals can also appear preoccupied with a pelvic theology by creating their own personal litmus tests for reform. This is not to dismiss deeply felt aspirations for a church that lives up to its own calls for human dignity, but simply to propose a different starting point for evaluating the Francis era. If you're grading Pope Francis primarily on whether he will end the church's ban on birth control, ordain women priests, and allow gays and lesbians to marry in the Catholic Church, you're likely to walk away disappointed. This doesn't mean the pope isn't a genuine reformer. It means his paradigm for renewal is different and unlikely to fit easily into secular categories of left and right. Above all, Francis is proposing a both old and new way of *being* church that is as simple as it is challenging. "He does not represent a liberal position, but a radical position, understood in the original sense of the word as going back to the roots, the *radix*," explained German cardinal Walter Kasper, whose book, *Mercy: The Essence of the Gospel and the Key to Christian Life*, has been publicly praised by Pope Francis.

The pope wants a church that seeks out the marginalized, heals what is broken, and gets dirty because it's out in the streets taking risks. His vision for the church jolted cardinals to attention during meetings held in the days just before the papal election. Cardinals are allotted five minutes to speak in these general congregations. When Cardinal Bergoglio stood up, he spoke for just over three minutes. The Argentine's reflection left the room hanging on his every word. The archbishop of Havana was so stunned by Bergoglio's wisdom he asked the cardinal for his notes. After the election, he released them publicly. The world now had a glimpse of the brief reflection that helped persuade the College of Cardinals that Bergoglio was the man of the hour.

"The church is called to come out of herself and to go to the peripheries, not only geographically, but also the existential peripheries: the mystery of sin, of pain, of injustice, of ignorance and indifference to religion, of intellectual currents, and of all misery," Bergoglio told his fellow cardinals in Italian. "When the church does not come out of herself to evangelize, she becomes self-referential and then gets sick." While many church leaders point to secularism and relativism as the primary threats faced by Christianity, the soon-to-be pope warned of "theological narcissism" and "spiritual worldliness." He contrasted "two images of the church": one that "evangelizes and comes out of herself," and "the worldly church, living within herself, of herself, for herself. This should shed light on the possible changes and reforms."[42]

While commentators debate whether Pope Francis is going too far or not far enough in his reform efforts, those conversations typically play out far from the reality of daily life in parishes. It's here where the Francis agenda will either take root or fail to find fertile soil. At Immaculate Conception Church outside of Dayton, Ohio, Fr. Satish Joseph, forty-eight, can't get enough of the pope. "I'm feeling more emboldened, affirmed and validated in the church's ministry to the poor and marginalized," he said. "In the past, if I preached about 'the preferential option for the poor,' you had the stigma of being a liberal, a socialist or even a Marxist! Now I don't have to justify the poor and marginalized taking center stage in my preaching and parish ministry because that is exactly what Pope Francis has done." The pope has also made Joseph bolder when it comes to welcoming LGBT people in his parish. He recalls a recent homily he gave about a young woman at his church who prayed for her same-sex attraction to go away. When it didn't, she left the church. "I told the church we have to figure out what to do. Francis wants the church to be a missionary disciple who takes care of people wherever they are struggling."

Joseph found the Synod on the Family, which sparked sharp disagreement among cardinals over the church's posture toward gay couples and divorced Catholics, a healthy development. "Apart from the hotly debated topics, it was the methodology adopted for the discussion that was truly interesting," Joseph wrote in the church's parish bulletin. He contrasted a "theology from above"—anchored in the clarity of doctrine—with a "theology from below," where doctrine is still important but the "starting point is the context within which people and families find themselves, either because of their own choices or simply because life and relationships are complex realities."[43]

Other priests are more anxious as the Francis era upends old certainties. Fr. Dwight Longenecker of Our Lady of the Rosary Parish in Greenville, South Carolina, felt so uncomfortable that he wrote an open letter to the pope published in *Crux*, the *Boston Globe*'s Catholic publication. Under the eye-catching headline, "Dear Pope Francis: Please Defend the Faith," Longenecker praised the pope for his desire to "open the doors of the Church to all with a warmhearted and affirming form of evangelization by attraction" but said the pope was also sending troubling messages. "This is teamwork, Holy Father," the priest wrote. "I can only do the job you want me to do if you do the job you have been called to do. With the greatest respect and love, please don't feel that it is your job to tinker with the timeless truths. If my job is to be the compassionate pastor for those in the pew and beyond, then your job is to be the primary definer and defender of the faith. I can't do my job if you don't do yours."[44]

FRANCIS AND MISSIONARY DISCIPLESHIP

William Skylstad, a retired bishop from Spokane, Washington, who served as president of the U.S. Conference of Catholic Bishops from

2004 to 2007, believes that the pope's pastoral emphasis and focus on poverty is a wakeup call for lay Catholics and the American hierarchy. "The tone has changed dramatically and that is very significant," Skylstad said. "Francis has not set himself up as different from the last two popes, but in many ways he is laying the foundations differently. Pope Benedict and John Paul II wanted to make sure Catholic orthodoxy and identity was strengthened. Both were deeply committed to the church. But we're at a new moment now. We have been strong on the dogmatic side of things, but the pope is taking Catholic identity to a much deeper level by focusing on the Gospel." Over the last several decades, he said, there has been a drift away from a broad "consistent ethic of life" focus that animated the U.S. church's posture during the time when Cardinal Joseph Bernardin and others connected issues of war, poverty, and abortion. "The reaction against Bernardin was one of fear that we would weaken our stance on the pro-life issue," Skylstad said. "It was a very narrow vision. Pope Francis is trying to change that approach. We're not a single-issue church. In the conclave, the cardinals saw the writing on the wall. We needed to change some things. We have come to a watershed moment in the church, and a new course has been set."

Richard Gaillardetz, a past president of the Catholic Theological Society of America and a Boston College professor, sees Pope Francis ushering in a "new kairos for Catholic ecclesiology." In doing so, the pope is reclaiming and building on earlier themes of collegiality and pastoral leadership developed by Pope John XXIII and Pope Paul VI during the Second Vatican Council. The "root metaphor" of the Francis papacy, Gaillardetz observes, is an embrace of Vatican II's image of the church not simply as the hierarchy but also as "the pilgrim people of God."[45] "This is a different modality of papal leadership that teaches by leading a conversation," he said. "Francis says doctrine is important, but the Gospel is more important. People say 'he is not changing church teaching.' This misunderstands what's going on. He is doing something more profound. He is saying that doctrines are not abstract and have to be grounded in the real experiences of people. Francis is reading the doctrinal tradition with an ear to the ground. This creates the conditions for development."

Gaillardetz notes that in recent decades prominent U.S. church leaders have challenged "the so-called liberal Catholic agenda for church reform because, in their view, it is susceptible of a too-easy accommodation with secular modernity." He recalls Cardinal Francis George of Chicago dismissing liberal Catholicism and its emphasis on structural reform as "an exhausted project." In contrast, Gaillardetz says, Pope Francis "does not see the church's mission and structural reform as mutually exclusive." He cites the pope's 2013 address in Brazil to the coordinating committee of the Conference of Latin American Bishops (CELAM). In that speech, Francis said that "the change of structures (from obsolete ones to new ones) will not be the result of reviewing an organizational flow chart, which would lead to a static reorganization; rather it will result from the very dynamics of mission. What makes obsolete structures pass away, what leads to a change of heart in Christians, is precisely missionary spirit."[46]

The blueprint for the Francis papacy is found in *Evangelii Gaudium* (The Joy of the Gospel), perhaps the only papal exhortation in the history of the church to achieve breakout coverage in the mainstream media. Francis develops his image of a missionary church in the exhortation. "I dream of a 'missionary option,' that is, a missionary impulse capable of transforming everything, so that the Church's customs, ways of doing things, times and schedules, languages and structures can be suitably channeled for the evangelization of today's world rather than for her self-preservation," the pope writes. Indeed, for Francis the church must always be in a state of continual reform and renewal or risk becoming stagnant and unhealthy. The pope's desire for a restless church that emphasizes a "culture of encounter" as an antidote to a "globalization of indifference" can't be understood apart from his Latin American roots.

When hundreds of bishops met in Aparecida, Brazil, in 2007 for a meeting of the Latin American Bishops' Conference, the future pope played a key role in shaping the church's vision for a continent riven by poverty, inequality, and violence. His brother bishops elected Francis to chair a key committee responsible for drafting the final document. The church must "rid itself from all expired structures that do not favor the transmission of the faith," the bishops (led by Francis) wrote.[47] The document spoke of "the joy of being disciples and missionaries," and it insisted that the church is "called to a deep and profound rethinking of its mission." Turning their attention to social inequalities, the bishops warned of "concentration of power and wealth in the hands of the few." Six years later, the first pope from Latin America appointed key leaders from Aparecida, Honduran cardinal Óscar Rodríquez Maradiaga and Javier Errázuriz (then co-president of the Latin American bishops' conference), to be on his nine-cardinal commission tasked with reforming the church's governance structures. "It could be said that the election of the Pope 'from the other side of the world' actually started in Aparecida," wrote Andrea Tornielli, a prominent church analyst for the Italian daily *La Stampa*.[48]

Bishop Ricardo Ramírez of Las Cruces, New Mexico, remembers Aparecida well. He was there as part of a delegation representing the U.S. bishops' conference. "It really was a remarkable ecclesial event," said Ramírez, who was named the first bishop of Las Cruces in 1982 and retired in 2013. "Liberation theologians were simultaneously meeting at the same site and some bishops consulted with them. The main theme was all of us who are baptized are called to be missionary disciples. Now you see Pope Francis is always talking about a missionary church that goes out to the margins." The seventy-nine-year-old represents a generation of bishops shaped by the experience of the Great Depression as children and later the civil rights movement. Social justice is in Ramírez's blood. When Cesar Chavez led a grape boycott in 1969 to call attention to the dehumanizing conditions of farmworkers, Ramírez was still a young seminarian, one of the few Latinos at his seminary in Michigan. He stood in front of supermarkets urging people not to buy grapes and later marched with farmworkers in San Antonio. He cites the legendary Gustavo Gutiérrez, a Peruvian theologian and Dominican priest regarded as the father of liberation theology, as an influence. Bishops today, he believes, are less familiar with the church's social teachings and often lack the experience of living in poverty or walking with those who do.

Ramírez worries that the church has prioritized religious freedom campaigns in a way that "is very close to becoming too partisan." Some in the hierarchy, he said, "are very outspoken and practically tell people how to vote. That is not the way to go." He is hoping the pope will provide the opportunity for a course correction. "Francis is asking us to look at the poor from the perspective of structural sin and is talking about the life issues in a broader way," Ramírez said. "Some people pay more attention to the unborn than those who are born. Immigration is a life issue. Poverty is a life issue." Pope Francis, he emphasizes, brings the struggles of Latin America to the Chair of St. Peter. "John Paul II was shaped by the experiences of Communism and Nazism. Francis is informed by the martyrs like Archbishop Oscar Romero, those killed for the cause of the poor, all of the horrible atrocities, *los desaparecidos.* He comes from that history. He will bring his own theology of liberation."

"SMELL OF THE SHEEP"

Pope Francis wants bishops and priests so involved in the grit of daily life that they should have, in his now famous description, "the smell of the sheep." In a 2014 speech to the Vatican congregation that is tasked with helping select future bishops, Francis said church leaders should "be shepherds, close to the people. They should not have 'the mindset of princes.'"[49] His insistent challenges to clericalism—an inwardly looking mind-set that views the clergy as superior and separate from the laity—is a reoccurring theme in the pope's speeches and homilies. Church leaders, Francis says, are to reject the "habits and ways of acting typical of a court." He cautions against "spiritual worldliness" and a "self-absorbed vanity" that he compares to a peacock: "It's beautiful if you look at it from the front but if you look at it from behind you discover the truth."[50]

In a Christmas message to the Curia in 2014, Francis delivered a bracing warning to cardinals and archbishops who hold senior positions in the Vatican's bureaucracy. Church officials, the pope said, should avoid the "pathology of power" and the temptation to "narcissism." He listed fifteen "spiritual diseases" that Vatican leaders must guard against, including what he called "spiritual Alzheimer's" or the "progressive decline in spiritual faculties." Russell Shaw, a former spokesperson for the U.S. bishops' conference and author of several books on the Catholic Church, says the "evils of clericalism" represent a formidable challenge to the pope's reform agenda taking hold. "Clericalism is so deeply embedded in the Catholic psyche," he said. "Bishops need to recognize that reality and root it out."

A wealthy American church will likely find itself especially challenged by Francis's call to radical spiritual renewal and personal simplicity. A CNN investigation found that at least ten active archbishops in the United States live in residences worth more than $1 million.[51] When Archbishop John Myers of Newark, New Jersey, decided that a 4,500-square-foot home with five bedrooms, a three-car garage, and an outdoor pool was not suitable for his retirement, he made plans for an expansion that included an indoor pool, three fireplaces, and a hot tub.[52] Archbishop

Wilton Gregory abandoned plans to move into a $2.2 million mansion after outcries from parishioners in his Atlanta archdiocese. Gregory offered a lengthy and heartfelt apology, acknowledging that under Pope Francis "the world and the church have changed." Gregory's decision to scrap those plans came just a few days after Pope Francis removed a German bishop dubbed the "Bishop of Bling" for his ostentatious tastes in upgrading his $43 million residence.[53]

"The example of the Holy Father, and the way people of every sector of our society have responded to his message of gentle joy and compassion without pretense, has set the bar for every Catholic and even for many who don't share our communion," Archbishop Gregory wrote in his diocesan newspaper.[54]

THE NEXT GENERATION OF CLERGY

The seminarians sip beer as bluesy lyrics ease into a brisk fall night. "Give me one reason to stay here . . . and I'll turn right back around," Tracy Chapman sings from a laptop as a handful of future priests at Mount St. Mary's Seminary in rural Maryland sit sprawled around a table outside their dorm. It's after 10 p.m., and the mountain air is crisp. One lanky student strums a guitar. A young priest visiting for the day chews meditatively on a pipe. The vibe is friendly and relaxed—a brief respite from the rigorous studies of Ratzinger, Aquinas, and systematic theology.

If a generation of priests has been shaped by the personal charisma of Pope John Paul II and the theological brilliance of Pope Benedict XVI, assessing the "Francis factor" here at the second largest seminary in the country offers a glimpse into the mind-set of those men who will soon be tasked with leading the church from the ground up. Often called the "Cradle of Bishops" for the number of graduates who have risen through the clerical ranks, Mount St. Mary's is focused on training diocesan priests. During a six-year formation period, the 161 students here, whose average age is twenty-five, will immerse themselves in church history, dogma, liturgy, theology, and philosophy. They will also spend time in schools, hospitals, and prisons, where doctrinal certitudes bump up against the messy complexity of life.

Daniel Shine, twenty-seven, grew up in a traditional Catholic family, and the altar boy sometimes followed the monsignor around at his church imagining life as a priest. At Purdue University in Indiana, he delved deeper into his faith with a steady diet of Bible study classes and Eucharistic adoration. By sophomore year, he felt the tug of vocation and left to enter the seminary. "The priesthood is not a job," he says. "When you feel called you are called to be who God wants you to be." The day Pope Francis was elected, Shine raced back to the seminary still sweaty from a racquetball game. He knelt in front of the television with his classmates as a new, unknown pope bowed his head in quiet prayer. Benedict's resignation left him "shocked and sad," Shine recalls. "I was saying, Dad can't resign!"

"We're still early in Pope Francis's papacy, so we're really just learning his language," says Shine, who describes himself as one of "Benedict's Boys" and cited the acclaimed "Jesus of Nazareth" book trilogy that Benedict wrote as a major influence. "The genius of Francis is how he interacts so freely with everyone. There is no pretense to him. I love the images of him in the crowds. He is so accessible and that teaches us to be more involved in the real life of our parishioners. We're not supposed to be functionaries. We are called to be fathers. He is applying the doctrine of the church in a very tangible way by being present in people's lives. People are perking up and listening. There is definitely something happening with Francis." He waves off questions about whether Francis is helping to revive the image of the church and what the challenges the pope has faced to his reform agenda mean for the future. "The church is rescued by Jesus Christ," he says. "She is guided by the Holy Spirit." Even at a time when a growing number of Americans no longer identify with a religious denomination, Shine still sees hope.

"People today are cut off from a sense of the divine," he says as the night grows late and a few of his classmates head off to bed. "You hit a button on your key and your car starts. You drive down paved roads and into the comfort of your office. All of this is a controlled environment. It's why people get excited about a good storm and the electricity goes out. We have a great chance in this environment to reach people with the new evangelization because people have less preconceived notions about faith. Jesus is such a stark contradiction to our society, and we can help people meet him and fall in love with him."

Fr. Chris Schocklee, thirty-four, a Mount graduate and a priest in the Diocese of Lafayette, Indiana, is older and more experienced than others at the table. He is visiting to lead a workshop intended to help priests better understand financial management. It's the kind of practical skill that doesn't hit home until the more mundane aspects of priestly life set in. Pope Francis is "getting people to take a second look at the Catholic Church," Schocklee thinks, even if those perceptions are filtered through what he views as distorting lenses. "So much of it gets positioned as you're either in this camp or in that camp. We hear things from our own perspectives. The pope is trying to bring different camps together. The people I associate with are probably more right leaning, and we don't see Francis doing things that are dramatically different from John Paul II or Benedict. Those on the left see him as very different. The left camp used to have this attitude of 'don't listen to the pope.' Now they're listening to the pope, which draws people in who felt disenfranchised from John Paul and Benedict." Schocklee describes himself as "a moderate conservative," but, he adds, "mainly I just call myself Catholic." Asked whether seminary education will need to consider beefing up its focus on the church's social teachings in light of Pope Francis's priorities, he isn't sure. "Social justice got overemphasized in the past because of the culture of the sixties and seventies. It was connected to political action," he said. "It was what the cultural moment was all about. My generation grew up hearing about social justice as a buzzword without a good articulation of what that really meant."

Early the next morning, it's still dark outside, and the Catoctin Mountains that frame the grotto shrine of Our Lady of Lourdes above campus are barely visible as seminarians file into pews for 7 a.m. Mass. Some finger rosary beads or read from well-worn breviaries. A few follow the daily prayers that make up the church's Liturgy of Hours on smartphones that give off a strange modern glow in a sacred space where candles, incense, and stained glass set the mind for ancient rituals. Seminary life, as might be expected, is a prayerful existence. Along with daily Mass, each student has a spiritual director he is expected to meet with at least once every three weeks. Frequent confession is encouraged. A daily Holy Hour is held so students can sit in quiet adoration of the Blessed Sacrament. Marian devotion has a special emphasis here, and the chime of bells on campus ring out the melody of "Ave Maria." Today, a sixth-year seminarian with an impossibly literary name—Dortimus Bigg—is at the pulpit giving a homily. He reflects on the Gospel story of Jesus calling a motley crew of fisherman and tax collectors as his first disciples. "The church is the bride of Christ, but she also has an imperfect side because she is made up of imperfect people who are struggling," he tells his classmates, professors, and a few locals from the community who stick out from the seminarians dressed in identical black. "We are entrusted with souls, but we all as seminarians and priests fail." Perhaps Bigg is feeling daring today or simply channeling his blunt pope. He brings up a T. S. Eliot poem that includes a less than flattering reference to the church's frailties. Eliot compares the church to a plodding hippopotamus. "I thought I married the bride of Christ," the seminarian says, pausing for effect, "but instead of marrying a beautiful bride I rolled over and I found a huge hippopotamus!" Laughter fills the sanctuary. "God can do so much with so little. Let us live lives of daily conversion. If we live this way, people will be able to see an image of Christ in all his splendor."

Msgr. Steven Rohlfs, the seminary rector here, and all those tasked with developing the next generation of Catholic priests, received some piercing words from Pope Francis when he warned that seminaries can sometimes produce "little monsters" if they are not careful.[55] "We must form their hearts," the pope told more than a hundred superiors of religious orders at a Vatican meeting in 2014. "Otherwise we are creating little monsters. And then these little monsters mold the people of God. This really gives me goose bumps." The training of priests, the pope emphasized, must "be a work of art, not a police action." Rohlfs laughs quietly when asked about that now famous sound bite from the pope. "Well, no one likes to be called a 'little monster,' but he has a point. You have to be able to educate seminarians and help form them in the context of the contemporary world in which they will minister. Seminarians like black and white. They don't like gray because gray is complicated. It takes some creative work to understand the gray areas instead of just memorizing something."

Rohlfs says his seminarians are just getting to know Pope Francis. John Paul II and Benedict XVI still loom larger because of their towering presence in the life of the church over more than four decades. "They grew up with those popes," says Rohlfs, who has been rector since 2005. "Both papacies were historic. Even if they never became popes, they were two of the greatest philosophers and theologians of the twentieth century. Students are immersed in their writing in class, and they gravitate toward them." In some ways, he thinks that the Francis impact won't be felt in full force until they are ordained. "They cheer him and always read his morning homilies and follow him on Twitter, but I don't think they get the whole import yet of what he is saying because they have not encountered the 'smell of the sheep' as parish priests do. What he is saying will not really get through until they are out in parishes."

After morning Mass, Danny McShane fills his plate with pancakes and sausage in the university cafeteria. The twenty-four-year-old from Peoria, Illinois, is paying close attention to Pope Francis. "He reminds us of our call to radical joy," McShane says. "He wants us to be captivated by the Gospel. The pope is challenging me to think. If I'm not willing to get my hands dirty, if I'm not comfortable with that, then I should not be a priest. He wants us to get out of our comfort zones. It's a good kind of uncomfortable." McShane recognizes that seminary can be something of a bubble where heady ideas are presented and debated in abstractions removed from the reality of daily life. "We can't argue with people about theology," he says. "The goal of conversion is to change hearts and minds. As Archbishop Fulton Sheen said, 'you can win an argument and lose a soul.'" If McShane is clearly energized by Francis, he also strikes a note from Pope Benedict XVI in his assessment of the world he will be entering as a priest: "It really is an exciting time to be a priest. There is a search for meaning in modern society and a lot of battles to be fought against the dictatorship of moral relativism. Flannery O'Connor said the truth does not change according to our ability to stomach it. We know the truth. We just have to get better at conveying it to people."

John Miravalle stands in front of his moral theology class, rubs his clean-shaven head, and sighs. "Halloween is coming up and it's a personal crisis for me, guys," the professor deadpans. "I want to dress up my kids like saints, but they are having none of it." With rolled-up sleeves and corduroys, Miravalle exudes a relaxed style that stands out in a place where buttoned-up formality and Roman collars are the norm. It's his first year teaching at the seminary. He left the School of Faith, a program that trains religious education teachers in the Archdiocese of Kansas City, when the Mount's rector saw him debating an atheist on YouTube and was impressed enough to invite him for an interview.

Miravalle's lecture today touches on celibacy, his in-laws, and marijuana legalization—an eclectic menu raised in the context of differing philosophical views about pleasure and emotions, and how to best use them in pursuit of virtue. "God gave us feelings, desires and drives for a reason," he says, pacing slowly in front of the room as the Madonna and Child gaze serenely from a picture on the wall. "The theology of celibacy isn't about desire elimination but desire redirection for a supernatural goal. Celibacy is not the same as mere virginity. It's not a denial. It's a reassignment and a reorientation." The class discusses the problems of Stoic philosophy and its surly antagonist, hedonism. "According to Aquinas, the goal is to harness the passions," he explains. "Our passions are like wild horses, but if you can get the bit in their mouth, they can take you where you need to go. How do you fight lust? Use your imagination. Sanctifying your imagination is a huge part of living a moral life. No one is imagining the goodness of heaven anymore, and that is a huge challenge for us." He tells the class that "there is a pretty direct connection between lust and abortion," which he calls an "unspeakable evil." A student asks about the prevalence of antidepressants. Miravalle nods his head. He wrote his doctoral dissertation on the topic, interviewing Catholic clinical psychiatrists as part of his research. "It's a huge pastoral issue now," he says.

During a short break in the class, I ask Miravalle what he wants the seminarians to take away at the end of the course and about the impact Pope Francis is having. "I want them to see the entire moral life as a call to grow in holiness, to become saints really. I give them an overview of the church's moral teachings in a way that I hope will be pastorally effective. I try and show them why what we are doing here is important. The world really needs the fullness of truth, and we should be generous with that. The pope has made it clear that there is a priority list, and the hot-button issues are not on it. The priority is leading people to Christ."

Fr. Brian Doerr, vice rector for human formation at the seminary, has a daunting job description. He is responsible for overseeing the seminarians' development as mature, holy, and prudent men capable of being "instruments of Christ's grace," as described in the *Program of Priestly Formation*, the U.S. bishops' detailed 137-page guidebook for seminary education. Celibacy and frequent reassignments pose significant challenges for priests. However, Doerr sees what he calls a "graver problem" in the vastly different ways older priests and younger clergy from the Millennial generation understand the church. Baby boomer priests, he said, are usually shaped by the epochal Second Vatican Council—a era characterized by dizzying liturgical changes, an emphasis on the church's social justice teachings, and the often bitter postconciliar divisions that pitted traditionalists against reformers. "There is not a lot of dialogue between the two generations," Doerr said. "I find Millennials want to be rooted in our heritage and tradition. They want to know why we do what we do as Catholics. They don't want a pre–Vatican II church because they don't know that church, but they do want beauty, substance and truth. The guys want to give themselves completely to the church of Jesus Christ and that is worth the challenges of celibacy, discernment and sacrifice." Doerr, who is fifty, describes himself as a "JP2 priest." It's a common moniker used to describe a generation of clergy most deeply inspired and influenced by the late Polish pope who guided the church for twenty-seven years. During that lengthy pontificate, approximately 14,432 priests in the United States were ordained. Doerr defines "JP2 clergy" as being "joyfully rooted in the tradition of the church." Pope John Paul II, he said, "was not afraid of the truth."

He seems less certain about the impact of Pope Francis. The pope's off-the-cuff style makes for good sound bites, Doerr observes, but he sees a less scripted papacy presenting complications. At times, he worries that the pope makes it too easy for the media to present a distorted picture of a church undergoing radical change, which causes unnecessary anxiety and doubt among seminarians, priests, and the lay faithful. "If someone is going to give their life to the church, he is not going to give his life to a question mark," Doerr says. He admiringly brings up Cardinal Raymond Burke, who drew attention during the first meeting of the Vatican's Synod on the Family for urging the pope to affirm church teaching that prohibits the reception of Communion for divorced and remarried Catholics.[56]

A pope who breaks tradition to wash the feet of women and once presided over the weddings of couples who lived together before marriage demonstrates a church of "charity," Doerr says, but also unintentionally sends a demoralizing message to priests tasked with upholding doctrine and creates unease for those faithful who have been most loyal to the church's often uncomfortable teachings. In the same way that politicians are reminded not to forget their "base" of most critical supporters, Doerr says, Pope Francis will need to spend time reassuring some in the pews. "We are Catholics because we pledge ourselves to a set of beliefs that have not always been easy to defend in our culture," he said. "There are people who have been faithful who are now wondering 'is the pope telling us we've been wrong?'"

Sister Katarina Schuth at the University of St. Thomas in Minnesota has studied seminaries for more than three decades. The Endowed Chair for the Social Scientific Study of Religion at the St. Paul Seminary School of Divinity, Schuth has found on her many site visits that priests who self-identify as part the "JP2 generation" are often unsettled by Pope Francis. In particular, the pope's repeated critique of clericalism, his challenge to authoritarian leadership styles, and his desire for open theological debates where hard questions are raised rather than definitive answers decreed can be discomforting for men who embrace a more certain model of a "heroic priesthood." These priests came to see themselves as a special class set apart from the laity in both dress and personal holiness to lead their flocks as unflinching defenders of doctrine. "There is a certain entitlement and clericalism that is rampant among younger priests over the last few decades," said Schuth, whose forthcoming book will examine trends in seminary education over the past thirty years. "You see an attitude that says 'I'm in charge,' and these are the rules. There is less appreciation for servant leadership. They are often more comfortable in the sanctuary than out in the world. I have visited plenty of seminaries where they are not always pleased with what Francis is doing. They are steeped in the culture of a different kind of church." This is not the case at those far fewer seminaries that specialize in preparing men entering religious orders—Franciscans, Dominicans, Jesuits—who have long emphasized a theology of the poor at the heart of Pope Francis's pontificate. "There is a very different attitude at religious order seminaries," she said. "They are readily picking up on what Francis is saying, and in many cases they have been saying similar thing for years even when that was often risky and criticized."

In the last few decades, there has been significant turnover in seminary faculty as aging professors, many of them priests of the Vatican II era, retired. "The number of teachers who are from religious orders like the Jesuits has dropped by half while the number who are in seminaries that teach future diocesan priests has grown. Many of these newer professors are lay men who are quite conservative," Schuth said. Lay faculty at seminaries now often come from places like the Pontifical John Paul II Institute for Studies on Marriage and Family at the Catholic University of America, where coursework and degrees primarily focus on the church's teachings on sexual morality, bioethics, family, and gender. While seminarians are exposed to the church's teaching on topics such as workers' rights and unions, living wages, the limits of markets, care for the environment, and the "social sin" of institutional injustices—all clearly presented in the Vatican's *Compendium of the Social Doctrine of the Church*—Schuth says those themes frequently receive less emphasis than abortion, contraception, marriage, and medical ethics. She doesn't expect major changes in how future priests are educated in the Francis era unless he has an unexpectedly long pontificate and perhaps writes his own lengthy treatment on the formation of priests, as Pope John Paul II did in *Pastores Dabos Vobis*, a 1992 document that has guided seminary preparation for decades. "Some have the feeling that Francis will die soon enough, and we will return to the good old days," Schuth said. "Between Benedict and John Paul they had 35 years in office. Change doesn't happen overnight."

CRACKS IN THE "STAINED GLASS CEILING"?

Many have been waiting a long time for changes in how the Catholic Church understands the role of women. Depending on who you ask, Pope Francis is either on the cusp of breaking new ground or simply putting a sunnier face on the status quo. Just like his predecessors, Francis has not entertained the idea of women priests, but he frequently emphasizes the importance of women in the church and the need to have more women in leadership roles.

The pope has named five women, a record number, to the International Theological Commission; praises the "feminine genius"; and, in a break with centuries of church tradition, washed the feet of women during Holy Thursday services. In one of his more headline-grabbing comments, Francis said at his weekly general audience that "the Christian seed of radical equality" means "supporting the right of equal compensation for equal work." The disparity in pay between men and women, Francis said with his typical bluntness, is "pure scandal." In discussing the challenge of declining marriage rates in Western countries, he objected to a common refrain from social conservatives that movements for women's rights are part of the problem. "Many consider that the change occurring in these last decades may have been set in motion by women's emancipation," Francis said, calling that "an insult! No, it is not true!"[57]

Francis is also a seventy-eight-year-old from Latin America, and he can sound like a man of his generation and culture. When he appointed several new women to the theological commission, he called them "strawberries on the cake." In a speech to the European Parliament, he compared the continent's low birth rate to a "grandmother, no longer fertile and vibrant," but instead "elderly and haggard." Writing in the *Los Angeles Times*, New Testament scholar Candida Moss of the University of Notre Dame and Yale University biblical professor Joel Baden panned those remarks as "nothing other than crass chauvinism."[58] After Pope Francis cautioned Catholic sisters not to become spiritual "old maids," *Washington Post* columnist Melinda Henneberger, a Catholic who has covered the Vatican, put words to what many Catholics were undoubtedly thinking: "I am at a loss to see how this could be other than insulting to women who've already given up having families of their own to serve God."

Kerry Robinson has a unique vantage point to evaluate the dissonance of how an ancient institution led by unmarried, celibate men relates to questions of women's identity and empowerment. The executive director of the National Leadership Roundtable on Church Management, Robinson is one of six women at the elite levels of Catholic philanthropy who since 2007 have met privately with cardinals at the Vatican to discuss the role of women in the church. Their annual trips to Rome are focused on building relationships with key church officials in an effort to find ways to elevate women to positions of leadership in the Roman Curia.

"A young Catholic woman in the West knows she can rise to the highest level of leadership, but when that same woman discerns a vocation of service to the church she loves, she is often met with roadblocks," Robinson says. "The more talented, driven and dedicated that woman is, the greater the frustration, so she often turns to the secular world. Pepsi or IBM benefits and the church misses out. We lose talent and the church is perceived as misogynistic. For the health of its mission, the church deserves to have women at the tables of decision making." There is data to back up Robinson's concern. A Pew Research Center poll found that 39 percent of young adults who leave the Catholic Church and are now unaffiliated with a religion said they were "unhappy with the way religion treated women."[59]

Robinson and her colleagues are an accomplished group—professional women with advanced degrees in theology, solidly grounded in canon law; mothers who have raised children in the faith; and savvy philanthropists with management acumen. Over the years, the women have met with the prefects and presidents at some of the most influential Vatican offices: the Secretary of State, the Congregation for the Doctrine of the Faith, the Congregation for Bishops, the Congregation for Divine Worship, and others. Robinson, forty-eight, acknowledges there were some nerves jangling on that first delegation to the Vatican in 2007. "I thought we would step off the plane and someone would say 'April Fools!'" Robinson joked. "It all seemed surreal that we would have this level of access and talk about this subject so passionately and candidly. The fear was that we would be perceived as angry women demanding justice."

The group doesn't push for women's ordination. Instead, they do their homework and come with practical suggestions carefully tailored for the particular official they are visiting. Recommendations have included expanding the number of women in professional roles in each office, increasing the number of women who serve on advisory councils to each pontifical congregation and council, and appointing women to the Vatican's diplomatic core. The group has also had discussions about the possibility of taking steps to allow women to become deacons and to ensure that in the selection of new bishops a candidate's ability to relate well to women is part of the criteria.

In one meeting, the group pushed for a review and updating of the Sunday lectionary, which maps out the readings for Mass, in an effort to include more readings where girls and women are the protagonists. The women also saw the need for a day care for the children of mothers working at the Vatican, many of whom live far from the center of Rome. The recommendation has been approved. There are bigger questions that could also be addressed, Robinson says. What are the obstacles that could be removed in order to appoint women to the College of Cardinals? Perhaps the pope could establish a Council for the Promotion of Women in the Church? Why couldn't the pope appoint a woman to serve on his council of nine advisers reforming the Curia?

Robinson acknowledges that access doesn't always mean changes follow quickly or even at all, but she believes awareness has been raised and questions are being asked that were not before. "We have a huge amount of work to do," she admits. "Women have to be at the tables of decision making. I can't imagine if mothers had been in those back rooms as the clergy sex abuse crisis was unfolding it would have ever reached the degree of horror it did."

While the Catholic Church can give the appearance of being a clerical boy's club (and for many that assessment is fact, not perception), women in the United States have been crucial to building and sustaining not only the church but also the wider society. Nuns, in particular, were in many ways the primary architects of the nation's Catholic health care and education systems. A 2011 traveling exhibit, "Women and Spirit: Catholic Sisters in America," chronicled the centuries-old history of how women religious in this country became the bulwarks of a vast infrastructure of educational, health, and social service institutions. "In the 19th century, Catholic nuns literally built the church in the American West, braving hardship and grueling circumstances to establish missions, set up classrooms and lead lives of calm in a chaotic world marked by corruption, criminality and illness," wrote Anne Butler, a professor emerita of history at Utah State University and author of *Across God's Frontiers: Catholic Sisters in the American West: 1815–1920.* "Their determination in the face of a male hierarchy that, then as now, frequently exploited and disdained them was a demonstration of their resilient faith in a church struggling to adapt itself to change."[60]

Today, women lead three of the largest and most effective social service and development organizations in the country: Sister Carol Keehan, CEO of the Catholic Health Association; Carolyn Woo, president and CEO of Catholic Relief Services; and Sister Donna Markham, the president of Catholic Charities USA. All three recognize opportunities and challenges when it comes to the role of women in the church. "The church thrived in this country because of women's leadership but sometimes we're poor students of history," said Sister Keehan. "We are poorer today in some ways as a church because as we have lost priests and sisters we are not replacing them with enough lay leaders. The church has become more clerical. A question to always ask is: Do women have a seat at the table? It doesn't always have to be the top spot. It's really foolish not to use fifty percent of the gifts God has given us and that's what happens when you exclude women."

Keehan, named "the most powerful person in health care" in 2007 by *Modern Healthcare* magazine, was such a key figure in helping push through national health care reform in 2010 that she has one of the few ceremonial gold pens handed out at President Obama's bill-signing ceremony. Her advocacy for that bill, opposed by the U.S. bishops' conference on grounds that it would fund abortion services, made her a lightning rod for some in the hierarchy who publicly criticized her and other Catholic sisters at the center of policy and advocacy work on Capitol Hill.

Keehan acknowledges some in the hierarchy have what she calls a "my way or the highway" approach, but she sees that as the exception, not the norm.

"I've been fortunate to know some incredible church leaders and lay men who have been supportive beyond words and who are dear friends. I've also borne the brunt of some really tough criticism, but my worldview is not the grouchy, archconservative bishop. Most bishops are incredibly appreciative, have a heart for the poor, and don't think they have all the answers," she said.

Carolyn Woo is used to breaking down barriers and being an outsider. Born in Hong Kong, she came to the United States to attend college at Purdue University, became the first female dean overseeing the accreditation body for business schools, and later went on to lead the University of Notre Dame's business school. In 2012, she was named the first female CEO of Catholic Relief Services, one of the world's largest and most respected international relief and development agencies that annually serves more than 130 million people in one hundred countries. Woo is amazed and energized by the excitement for Pope Francis. "Because of the clergy abuse scandals there was such cynicism about the church and now people want to know more about the church and social justice. Everywhere I go, whether it's the World Bank or a department of the federal government, people want to talk about the pope."

The former business school dean, who now manages an agency with a budget of more than $600 million, recognizes in Francis the qualities of a successful chief executive. "The pope lives by example and embodies a poor church for the poor," she observes. "He is a CEO who messages with his own behavior." Woo says her immigrant experience prepared her well for being a highly visible female leader in a church dominated by men. "The role of the outsider is something I'm used to and excel at now," she says, joking that being surrounded by so many men can at times make small talk difficult. "I'm not that really into sports!" The pope, she thinks, brings an unconventional approach in part because of his cultural background as the first pope from Latin America. "Pope Francis is an outsider. He brings a different perspective, and that's a benefit. I think he realizes that there is no longer any question as to whether women can make good leaders. Where we need to do a better job is making sure we promote the visibility of women and have them in those networks where major decisions and appointments are made. This takes work."

For more than a century, Catholic Charities USA has been on the front lines of serving the poor and working families in need of food, clothing, housing assistance, and other critical needs. Local agencies serve more than ten million people a year. Outside of the federal government, the church's flagship charitable arm is the largest social service provider in the country. Sister Donna Markham became the first woman president of the Alexandria, Virginia–based organization in June 2015. The Dominican sister, a clinical psychologist who was president of Behavioral Health Institute for Mercy Health, is inspired by a pope she says looks to the Gospel as his blueprint.

"As Jesus, he seems to be motivated by mercy, compassion and love more than by rigid adherence to the letter of the law," Markham said. "Such love is magnetic! What's exciting is there is such a visible and vocal leader who is preaching the Gospel of justice and love so persistently in our world." When it comes to women in the church, Markham already sees shining examples of women leading in vital ways, but she recognizes that there is a long way to go.

"Clearly, we have some work to do as a church in this regard," she says. "As women and men stand increasingly on equal footing in the board room, in business, medicine and the sciences, there is an ever more disconnect in our church where women often remain on the sidelines rather than the center of decision processes. I fear that if we don't address this issue and the gap widens between how women are regarded in the civic arena and how they are regarded in the church, we may stand to lose a number of very gifted and faith-filled women."

7

A "FRANCIS EFFECT" ON U.S. POLITICS?

A good Catholic meddles in politics.

—Pope Francis[1]

On the Monday morning after Thanksgiving, the halls of the Cannon House Office Building are strangely peaceful. Frenetic aides who escort their bosses to committee meetings and deftly navigate the underground corridor that connects this oldest of congressional buildings to the U.S. Capitol are hard to find. No reporters buzzing around in search of scoops or wide-eyed tourists staring up at marbled statues. Washington is slowly waking up from its holiday slumber. Rep. Jim McGovern of Massachusetts leans back at a desk in his fourth-floor office but can't seem to enjoy the brief respite from the legislative grind. He grows animated talking about billions cut from food stamps, rising income inequality, ballooning military budgets, the disproportionate power of corporations, and threats to workers' rights.

"What's happening here in Washington is we're creating a country without a conscience, and it's appalling," McGovern says. "Donald Trump doesn't need the government, but a poor, single mom from Worcester does. The U.S. is the richest country in the history of the world, and we still have 50 million people who are hungry even though it's a solvable crisis. Why aren't we ashamed about that?" It's the kind of hard question that the pope wants more public officials to ask. "I beg the Lord to grant us more politicians who are genuinely disturbed by the state of society, the people, the lives of the poor," Pope Francis has written.[2]

McGovern is a hero to Catholic progressives. His office walls are a tapestry of awards from national anti-hunger organizations and faith-based advocacy groups like the Ignatian Solidarity Network. A picture of the martyred Salvadoran archbishop Oscar Romero hangs near an honorary doctorate in human rights that the congressman received from the University of Central America, where in 1989 six Jesuit priests, their housekeeper, and her fifteen-year-old daughter were dragged outside by Salvadoran military in the middle of the night and shot dead. McGovern is just back from El Salvador, where he gave a speech commemorating the twenty-fifth anniversary of the Jesuit martyrs. He personally knew several of the slain priests from his work with Salvadoran refugees in the early 1980s, and he spent years helping to conduct an investigation that found the killers used U.S. weapons and received training at Fort Benning in Georgia. "I welcome a church that challenges all of us, and the Jesuits taught me that faith is about more than showing up for church on Sunday," he says. "The real question is: What are you doing after church? Faith requires action. Those priests were killed because they lived the Gospel. They stood up for the poor."

If McGovern is jaded by politics as usual in the nation's capital, he thinks the world's most famous Jesuit might help shake up the debate in Washington. "There is literally a war on the poor. The pope is in a unique position to be a moral voice. I appreciate that he is blunt and clear. He can help remind people the narrative on talk radio and Fox News that blames and demeans the poor is wrong."

It's not just idle chatter on a slow day at the Capitol to consider the impact Pope Francis might have on American political debates. Several leading Catholic politicians and presidential candidates are Catholic. While there is no monolithic "Catholic vote"—political preferences are shaped by various factors including ethnicity and frequency of Mass attendance—Catholics still remain a bellwether. Since 1972, only one presidential candidate, George W. Bush in 2000, has been elected president without winning a majority of Catholics. Congress has a high percentage of Catholic lawmakers, and a significant share of them, including House Speaker John Boehner, attended Jesuit colleges. Boehner and Rep. Nancy Pelosi, a Catholic Democrat, invited Pope Francis to speak before a joint session of Congress during his visit to the United States in the fall of 2015, the first pope to give such an address.

In recent years, Catholic political debates in the United States have focused disproportionately on a narrow range of issues. The church's broad social teachings on living wages for workers, the importance of unions, the prudent oversight of markets, the positive role of government, and care for the environment have been shortchanged. A pope who challenges an "economy of exclusion and inequality," raises the profile of climate change as a profound moral issue, and wants the most influential church in the world to be known for more than opposition to abortion and gay marriage offers a unique opportunity to rebalance and revitalize American values debates.

"Pope Francis' teachings on the rights of the poor have enormous implications for the culture and politics of the United States and for the church in this country," Bishop Robert McElroy of San Diego wrote in *America* magazine.[3] "Popular Voice in the Capitol? It's the Pope's," ran a 2014 headline in the *New York Times* that chronicled some lawmakers' efforts to highlight the pope's focus on poverty to rally support for increasing the minimum wage and extending unemployment assistance to jobless workers. President Obama has quoted from the pope's apostolic exhortation, *The Joy of the Gospel*, in a major speech in which the president called inequality the "defining challenge of our time."[4] In a sign of how some conservatives on Capitol Hill are worried that a spiritual leader 4,500 miles away might cause heartburn for the GOP, a simple bipartisan resolution praising the pope for his "inspirational statements and actions" stalled in a House committee. Only 19 of the 221 cosponsors were Republican. The lack of support may have been related to the fact that the pope is viewed as "too liberal," a Republican backer of the legislation told *The Hill*. Some conservatives think Pope Francis is "sounding like President Obama—the pope talks about equality. He actually used the term 'trickle-down-economics,' which is politically charged," the GOP official told the newspaper.[5] After Pope Francis played a role in helping the Obama administration and the Cuban government broker a historic deal restoring full diplomatic relations, Sen. Marco Rubio of Florida, a 2016 GOP presidential candidate who often worships at Catholic churches, blasted the deal and questioned the pope. "I would ask His Holiness to take up the cause of freedom and democracy," Rubio said.[6]

Catholic Republicans can't entirely brush off the pope as a typical liberal, and he is already having an impact on political rhetoric even if conservative policy proposals remain largely unchanged. "I think every

Republican should embrace the pope's core critique that you don't want to live on a planet with billionaires and people who don't have any food," Newt Gingrich, the former House speaker and convert to Catholicism who ran for president in 2012, said. "I think the pope may, in fact, be starting a conversation at the exact moment the Republican Party itself needs to have that conversation."[7] Paul Ryan not long ago warned "we could become a society where the net majority of Americans are takers, not makers." He derided the safety net as "a hammock which lulls able bodied people into lives of complacency and dependency." Ryan now seems more chastened and has since traveled the country on a national tour, visiting inner-city churches and homeless shelters before releasing a seventy-three-page anti-poverty report.[8] Most anti-poverty policy experts largely dismiss his plan as old ideas dressed up in new language. Ryan, however, credits Pope Francis with "breathing new life into the fight against poverty."[9]

Sister Simone Campbell is the executive director of NETWORK, a social justice lobbying group in Washington. The energetic Catholic sister spent years toiling in relative obscurity, urging lawmakers on Capitol Hill to pass moral budgets that help the working poor and marginalized. When the Vatican, under Pope Benedict XVI, flagged NETWORK in a scathing 2012 report that rebuked American nuns for not doing enough to oppose abortion and gay marriage, the family law attorney with the brain of a policy wonk and the heart of a poet found herself wrestling with unexpected notoriety as media beat down her door. When Campbell teamed up with other sisters to launch a nine-state "Nuns on the Bus" tour that challenged upside-down budget priorities and showcased the work of women religious serving the poor, it was an instant hit. Crowds greeted the nuns like rock stars as the bus pulled into cities and towns across the country. Subsequent tours focused on the moral imperative for immigration reform and the corrupting influence of money in politics. Along the way, Campbell became something of a minor celebrity, a talking head on cable news, and scored a primetime speaking slot at the 2012 Democratic National Convention, where she spoke about Medicaid expansion and poverty reduction as "pro-life" issues. Since Pope Francis's election, Campbell has hosted congressional briefings where she challenges lawmakers to take a cue from the pope. She hopes Francis can help break through Beltway gridlock and knee-jerk partisanship. "The pope has a heart for those who are most left out," Campbell says. "He reminds us that reality is more powerful than ideas, and he is staying grounded in the reality of the poor. The challenge is everyone wants to claim Francis as their own, but if we listen, he is really calling all of us and our society to a conversion. All economic decisions have moral dimensions, and it is the structural inequality that is at the heart of so much violence in our world."

FRANCIS AND THE ENVIRONMENT:
A WAKEUP CALL FOR CLIMATE CHANGE DENIERS

A pope who is rattling the American right with his searing critique of "trickle-down economics" and inequality is also diving head first into another highly charged issue that roils U.S. politics. It's hard to think of a papal communication in recent memory that garnered as much interest, commentary, and controversy as Pope Francis's encyclical on ecology and environmental justice released in the summer of 2015.

At a time when climate change is an urgent challenge—felt most acutely by the poor and those least responsible for carbon emissions—the pope's encyclical extensively noted the scientific consensus that human behavior is exacerbating global warming. He issued a bracing call for action. Asking for a "cultural revolution" to address what he described as "one of the principal challenges facing humanity in our day," Pope Francis wrote that "the same mindset which stands in the way of making radical decisions to reverse the trend of global warming also stands in the way of achieving the goal of eliminating poverty."

The first papal encyclical in history devoted specifically to environmental issues—timed for release before the high-stakes UN climate negotiations in Paris at the end of 2015—shines a spotlight on how global inequality and environmental degradation are deeply connected. It also asks for personal lifestyle changes not easily embraced in a country like the United States, where conspicuous consumption is celebrated as a sign of status. The pope faced a barrage of criticism from U.S. conservatives in the months before the encyclical was even released. Stephen Moore, a Catholic who is an economist at the Heritage Foundation in Washington, wrote in *Forbes* that the pope was aligning himself with "the radical green movement that is at its core anti-Christian, anti-people, and anti-progress." Moore called Pope Francis "a complete disaster when it comes to his public policy pronouncements" and charged that the pope had "allied himself with the far left and has embraced an ideology that would make people poorer and less free."[10]

In *First Things*, columnist Maureen Mullarkey easily took the prize for contemptuous snarling when she blasted Francis as "an ideologue and a meddlesome egoist" who "sullies his office by using demagogic formulations to bully the populace into reflexive climate action with no more substantive guide than theologized propaganda."[11] Robert George of Princeton University did his best to downplay the importance of the yet-to-be-released encyclical with the tired conservative trope that anything besides abortion and same-sex marriage was outside the realm of church competence. "Pope Francis does not know whether, or to what extent, the climate changes (in various directions) of the past several decades are anthropogenic—and God is not going to tell him," George wrote. When the Vatican convened a major climate summit in advance of the encyclical that featured economist Jeffrey Sachs of Columbia University and opening remarks from UN secretary general Ban Ki-moon, American climate change deniers held a news conference in Rome denouncing the effort. Opponents included the Heartland Institute, a Chicago-based libertarian group in part funded by the Charles G. Koch Foundation, led by the billionaire industrialists Charles and David Koch. The Koch brothers fund a constellation of organizations that oppose government action to address climate change. The preemptive strikes were so frequent that the pope's closest cardinal adviser directly called out "movements in the United States" as hostile to the encyclical. "The ideology surrounding environmental issues is too tied to a capitalism that doesn't want to stop ruining the environment because they don't want to give up their profits," said Cardinal Óscar Rodríguez Maradiaga.[12]

Prominent Catholic politicians who are climate change skeptics now find themselves in the unenviable position of not only disputing the overwhelming scientific consensus on this issue but also standing on the opposing side of the world's most influential moral leader. House Speaker John Boehner, who invited Pope Francis to address a joint session of Congress in September 2015, routinely slams the Obama administration for "job-killing" environmental policies. "The idea that carbon dioxide is a carcinogen that is harmful to our environment is almost comical," the graduate of Xavier University, a Jesuit college in Ohio, once scoffed.[13] GOP presidential candidate Sen. Marco Rubio has denied that human activity is driving climate change and insists measures to regulate emissions warming the planet will "destroy our economy."[14] Republican presidential contender Jeb Bush concedes global warming "may be real" and took some steps to protect the Everglades from offshore drilling, but he has described himself as a "skeptic."[15] A 2016 presidential candidate who frequently invokes his Catholic faith, Rick Santorum once dismissed human causes of climate change as "patently absurd." In the wake of the pope's encyclical, he scoffed that the church was better off "leaving science to scientists, and focusing on what we're really good at, which is theology and morality." He also strongly opposed a 2011 Environmental Protection Agency rule limiting mercury emissions from coal-fired plants that the U.S. Conference of Catholic Bishops hailed as "an important step forward to protect the health of all people, especially unborn babies and young children."[16]

Some critics of Pope Francis need a basic theology lesson when it comes to the environment. The pope isn't cribbing talking points from Greenpeace or sprinkling holy water on a progressive agenda. His views are rooted in a traditional religious commitment to protect the gift of God's creation, a biblical call to be good stewards, and respect for the sanctity of life and human dignity. Popes John Paul II and Benedict XVI both addressed care for the environment as a profound moral issue and called for action to tackle climate change. "The depletion of the ozone layer and the related 'greenhouse effect' has now reached crisis proportions," said Pope John Paul II back in 1990. He applauded "a new ecological awareness" that "ought to be encouraged to develop into concrete programs and initiatives."[17] Pope Benedict XVI, dubbed the "Green Pope" for taking steps to make the Vatican the first carbon-neutral state in the world, also warned against apathy. "Can we remain indifferent before the problems associated with such realities as climate change, desertification, the deterioration and loss of productivity in vast agricultural areas, the pollution of rivers and aquifers?" he asked in 2010.[18]

If anyone can help begin to break the political stalemate over climate change and reach an audience far beyond the progressive choir, it's a global leader with approval ratings most politicians crave and the moral gravitas they usually lack. "I think this moves the needle," Charles J. Reid Jr., a professor at the University of St. Thomas School of Law told the *New York Times.* "Benedict was an ivory-tower academic. He wrote books and hoped they would persuade by reason. But Pope Francis knows how to sell his ideas. He is engaged in the marketplace."[19]

A BETTER VALUES DEBATE IN AMERICAN POLITICS?

The pope's encyclical is another opportunity for Catholic leaders in the United States to put more institutional weight behind an urgent moral issue while at the same time sending a message that the church's voice in public life is not limited to issues of human sexuality and marriage. Every religion reporter has John Green on speed dial. A professor of political science at the University of Akron, and a senior fellow with the Pew Forum on Religion and Public Life, Green is one of the most respected analysts in the country when it comes to navigating the intersection of religion and politics. He thinks Pope Francis might help the American hierarchy find its way back from the wilderness. "The bishops as a whole don't have the same broad influence as they had three decades ago," Green says. As secular trends cut against many of the church's traditional teachings on sexuality and marriage, he noted, Catholic leaders find themselves in a similar corner as Southern Baptists and Mormon leaders.

"They are in a tough spot. I think emphasizing a broader, balanced agenda as Francis has done is their way back to a deeper influence many of these leaders enjoyed a generation ago. It's their best hope." After decades when the Religious Right dominated the debate over the role of faith in politics, Green senses the pope could be a catalyst for a deeper conversation. "People are really weary of the culture wars," Green said. "Pope Francis has a great capacity to influence the values debate."

Long before Rev. Jim Wallis became one of the most prominent evangelicals in the world, he was a wide-eyed twenty-year-old listening in awe to Dorothy Day. The founder of Sojourners met Day in the early 1970s in Chicago. Wallis drew inspiration from how the founder of the Catholic Worker movement put the radical call of the Gospel and Catholic social teaching into action by serving, learning from, and empowering the poor. The evangelical quickly became a student of Catholic social teaching. Over the years, Wallis marched, prayed, and organized with leading Catholic activists like Daniel Berrigan, the Jesuit priest who burned draft files as an act of civil disobedience during the Vietnam War. Wallis now works alongside Catholic bishops to prod Congress to pass comprehensive immigration reform and to protect government social safety nets as part of an ecumenical "Circle of Protection." Wallis is captivated by a pope who, like Dorothy Day, is doing something simple but transformative.

"Pope Francis is making faith credible again to a whole new generation of people because he is acting in ways people think a Christian
should act," Wallis said in his office in the Columbia Heights neighborhood of Washington, DC. "He is living out his job description as the
Vicar of Christ. Most of what he is doing and saying that draws admiration or controversy is what Jesus would be doing and saying." Wallis
points out that the "nones"—the research parlance for the rising number
of Americans who don't identify with any religious denomination—still
largely believe in God. Wallis thinks the problem is they rarely see faith
leaders living up to their own professed ideals. "Two things happen when
people see religious leaders actually speaking and acting in ways that are
authentic," he said. "First, they are surprised, and then they are attracted.
Even people who tell me they are agnostic on their best days love Pope
Francis."

Wallis sees a pope challenging the conventional politics of left and
right. "There are no political leaders in Washington of either party who
have made poverty and inequality an issue the way the pope has, so they
will all be made uncomfortable," he said. "It's not hyperbole any more to
say our system is bought and sold by the biggest corporate financial
interests in the country. Politicians will have to respond to what Pope
Francis is saying. Whether the pope will convert hearts and minds remains to be seen, but there is a real opportunity for people of faith to
build on his visit to the United States. It really depends on how effectively we can organize and mobilize around this prophetic moment." He
believes that the pope's "biblically rooted vision for justice and peace"
also offers a timely opportunity for Catholic leaders.

"I think Pope Francis is bringing Catholic bishops back to Catholic
social teaching, which is consistently pro-life but does not have an obses-
sion with abortion as a single issue. He has not changed doctrine, but he is
emphasizing the dignity of life in the context of how we treat the poor and
vulnerable. In that sense, his priorities are different from the priorities
we've seen from some bishops recently, but I think his priorities are more
faithful to Catholic teaching. When some bishops evaluate political candidates only on the basis of abortion or gay marriage and disregard what
they have done when it comes to war and the poor or the environment,
that is a politicization of Catholic teaching from the right." Creating the
space for a better values debate in the media and politics, he thinks, will
also require progressives to do some soul searching. "You had one politi-

cal party that totally embraced its religious allies," Wallis said. "The Republican Party gave them all kinds of attention and money and clout. They helped people like Jerry Falwell and Richard Viguerie. They literally said 'give us your mailing lists, and we will make you household names.' There is still real ambiguity or even animosity toward religion on the left and in the Democratic Party."

Alan Wolfe is one of the nation's preeminent scholars. The director of the Boisi Center for Religion and American Public Life at Boston College has watched students at his Catholic university perk up when Pope Francis speaks. "So many American Catholics have been hungering for the kind of things this pope is saying," observes Wolfe, the author and editor of more than twenty books, including *The Future of Liberalism*. "I see younger Catholics who have been alienated by the approach taken by some of his predecessors and other religious leaders, but they are still fiercely protective of their Catholicism even if they don't always know what that means theologically. They still have a strong Catholic identity. I see this pope filling a vacuum."

Pope Francis's focus on inequality and the poor, Wolfe thinks, provides an unexpected opening for the church in the United States. "The great story of our time is the unbelievable redistribution of income to the top. Where has the church been on this? One political party has been taken over by the radical right and the other party has failed to respond. We desperately need a moral language that challenges how much the Democratic Party and the Republican Party are tied to Wall Street. If Democrats and labor are too weak, the church can be the most important institution to raise these issues. A genuinely Catholic social vision of the common good is greatly helped by Pope Francis signaling that he is not going to fetishize the social issues. I don't expect the church to change its teaching on abortion, but it might reinterpret the commitment to life in a more consistent way where poverty is a life issue. This would help make a more communitarian liberalism possible again."

Lew Daly is skeptical. "I don't know that Pope Francis, or any pope, can inspire deep change in American politics, certainly not simply through his influence on the U.S. Catholic Church, which is a wounded institution on many levels," said Daly, who wrote a seminal essay on the Catholic roots of American liberalism and is the director of policy and research at Demos, a public policy organization in New York. "We have moved 180 degrees away from the common good liberalism articulated by Fr. John Ryan and other New Deal–inspiring architects of modern Catholic social ethics and social policy." Daly points to profound changes in both church and secular politics: "When some well-financed Catholic thought leaders broke with church's tradition to become apologists for liberal capitalism in the 1980s and 1990s, this was part of a larger ideological shift connected to the political mobilization of economic elites beginning in the mid-1970s, when inequality in the United States had reached an all-time low. This larger ideological shift has generated precious few gains except for the richest Americans. There is a compelling need to articulate an alternative vision that speaks to ordinary Americans in their daily struggles. Catholic social thought can provide a systematic frame for connecting values with action in a disciplined way. However, the cultural headwinds are strong, especially in the form of consumerism and technology."

Bill Ritter is a Catholic Democrat who takes his faith seriously. The former Colorado governor dislikes the "pro-life" label but opposes abortion and connects his policy work on environmental stewardship to Catholic teachings. At fourteen, he won a scholarship to attend a seminary in San Antonio, where the Oblate priests who taught him during his freshman and sophomore year left a lasting mark. As a rising star in the Denver District Attorney's office, Ritter became a lay Oblate missionary. He moved his wife and young son to western Zambia, where they worked alongside Catholic priests in schools and rural hospitals. Ritter now directs the Center for the New Energy Economy at Colorado State University, where he works to convince lawmakers to take practical steps to curb climate change.

"I see Pope Francis focusing on a different set of Gospel values that have not always been emphasized in recent years," Ritter said. "He is not undermining the primary importance of the ethic of life, but in a very modern way he is going back to Gospel basics by highlighting the experience of the world's poor and the economic conditions that create that reality. He is also reminding us as Catholics that we have a responsibility to be good stewards of our land, air and water. The pope is spending what you might call political capital on issues that some church leaders have not talked about as much but that have such an impact on the world's poor."

Unlike some Catholic Democrats, Ritter has maintained a mostly positive relationship with bishops over the years. This has not stopped him from speaking out when he sees some in the hierarchy veering close to partisan politicking. During the 2004 presidential election, Bishop Michael Sheridan of Colorado Springs, Colorado, made headlines for telling Catholics in his diocese they would exclude themselves from receiving Communion if they vote for certain politicians. "Any Catholic politician who advocates for abortion, for illicit stem cell research or any form of euthanasia *ipso facto* place themselves outside of full communion with the church and so jeopardize their salvation," Sheridan wrote in his diocesan newspaper. "Any Catholics who vote for candidates that stand for abortion, illicit stem cell research or euthanasia suffer the same fateful consequences." At the time, Ritter was Denver's attorney general. "What is disturbing is that he has broadened the field pretty significantly by saying anyone in an elected position, anyone who supports them or votes for them suffers the sanction of having Communion withheld," Ritter told the *Los Angeles Times*. "Receiving the sacrament of Communion is the most significant and sacred ritual available to Catholics, so to withhold it is an extremely punitive measure." Ritter pointed out that in the legislative district where he lived both candidates supported abortion rights. "If I abide by Sheridan, I am disenfranchised in that election," he said.[20]

As a Democrat who opposes abortion, Ritter felt pressure from those in his party who had "litmus tests" he didn't meet, and from some Catholic leaders who didn't see him as sufficiently "pro-life." "It was a tough place to be," he acknowledged. Ritter hopes that a pope who emphasizes that the global economy and the environment are also life issues will begin to push people out of the comfort of ideological boxes. "Pope Francis is the most important spiritual leader in the world, and we have the most divided Congress since before the Civil War," he said. "I think he is in a unique place to help bring together Democrats and Republicans around key moral issues in a way that is very significant."

Steve Driehaus is inspired by Pope Francis, but he is less confident that he can break through the partisan noise in Washington. The former House member from Cincinnati, who, along with other pro-life Democrats, lost his seat in 2010 after voting for health care reform legislation, seems far happier to be working alongside Catholic nuns and priests in Swaziland than fending off attacks from pro-life groups who targeted him for his health care vote. "If liberal and conservative Catholics are willing to open their ears and hearts to Pope Francis, we have some hope, but I'm a bit cynical," Driehaus said in an interview from Africa, where he is serving in the Peace Corps with his wife and children. "Those who want to hear a liberal message from the pope will hear that and those who don't will simply reject it. Politics has become a shouting match. People are not listening to each other."

The Susan B. Anthony List, a pro-life political action committee, ran billboard ads against Driehaus and other pro-life Democrats during the 2010 elections, claiming they voted for "taxpayer-funded abortion" by supporting federal health care reform legislation. Ten of the seventeen pro-life Democrats who voted for the health care bill lost their seats.[21] Driehaus grew up on the west side of Cincinnati, where a local obstetrician founded the National Right to Life. From an early age, he was no stranger to the sharp elbows of abortion politics. Even so, the battle lines that emerged during the debate over health care reform took him aback. "I'm pro-life, but the pro-life movement doesn't represent many of us," Driehaus said. "I've seen firsthand how nasty they can be and how willing they are to disparage good people. It's not about abortion. It's about electing Republicans. Many of the pro-life Democrats I worked with to pass health care reform believed in the seamless garment of life more than many of my Republican colleagues who never wanted to do anything about poverty or the death penalty. They only wanted to talk about abortion and call themselves 'pro-life.'" He is concerned with how some Catholic bishops enable partisan elements in the pro-life movement to claim the moral high ground. "The church allows these kinds of groups to politicize the issue," Driehaus said. "When Right to Life gets to distribute pamphlets in church, that's a problem. They are political and have an agenda. If there was any pretense that these groups are not political first, that façade was blown during the health care debate."

As a kid, Driehaus once served as an altar boy for Joseph Bernardin, then archbishop of Cincinnati. Pope Francis reminds him of the archbishop who defined pro-life values in a way that challenged both political parties. If that vision is going to take root again, he thinks, the priorities emphasized at the Vatican these days have to find a way into dioceses and local parishes. "The church should be engaged in public policy debates on issues of importance, but one would hope pastors and bishops are as engaged on issues of health care, poverty and the environment as they are on abortion. I don't see that happening. It's not what gets talked about on the west side of Cincinnati."

A CHALLENGE TO U.S. FREE-MARKET FUNDAMENTALISTS

When Pope Francis criticized "trickle-down" economics—a sacred ideology for many American conservatives who also tout minimal government and tax cuts for the wealthy—he stepped into one of the most contentious political debates of our time. Inequality, which the pope has described as "the root of social evil," is drawing increased scrutiny in the United States, where the gap between the wealthiest few and everyone else has reached its highest point since the 1920s.[22]

CEO pay is now nearly three hundred times that of an average worker.[23] Several companies—including Citigroup, Chevron, and JPMorgan Chase—spend more on compensating their chief executives than paying federal taxes.[24] Momentum is growing to address inequality. Fast food workers in cities around the country have led high-profile strikes. Several major companies, including Wal-Mart, have raised minimum wages. French economist Thomas Picketty sparked a new round of debate over inequality with a best-selling book, *Capital in the Twenty-First Century*, and his U.S. tour included top-level meetings with the U.S. Secretary of Treasury and a packed house at the International Monetary Fund. In his apostolic exhortation, *The Joy of the Gospel*, the pope had a global audience in mind when he said trickle-down theories have "never been confirmed by the facts" and "express a crude and naïve trust in the goodness of those wielding economic power." The pope is no stranger to the issue. He experienced firsthand the limits of neoliberal economic models during Argentina's debt crisis. "We live, apparently, in the most unequal part of the world, which has grown the most yet reduced misery the least," he said as archbishop of Buenos Aires. "The unjust distribution of goods persists, creating a situation of social sin that cries out to heaven and limits the possibilities of a fuller life for so many of our brothers."[25] The pope has good reason to speak up. An Oxfam International report found that eighty-five of the richest people in the world now control as much wealth as the 3.5 billion poorest.[26] When the pope called for "the legitimate redistribution of economic benefits by the state" in a speech to the heads of major UN agencies during a 2014 meeting in Rome, Americans surely had flashbacks to Barack Obama's 2008 run-in with "Joe the Plumber," who tangled with the candidate in a widely covered exchange over taxes.[27]

Pope Francis's understanding of wealth distribution and the moral dimensions of markets doesn't come from liberal think tanks or display a knee-jerk rejection of capitalism. It grows from traditional Catholic doctrine that is rooted in biblical values about human dignity and the shared gift of creation. As the Vatican's *Compendium of the Social Doctrine of the Church*, published during Pope John Paul II's pontificate, explains, "Goods, even when legitimately owned, always have a universal destination; any type of improper accumulation is immoral, because it openly contradicts the universal destination assigned to all goods by the Creator. . . . Evil is seen in the immoderate attachment to riches and the desire to hoard." The *Compendium* is clear that "wealth exists to be shared." The *Catechism of the Catholic Church* refers to "sinful inequalities" that are in "open contradiction to the Gospel." Unlike some liberals and conservatives, the pope does not reduce markets to a utilitarian framework of efficiency, GDP, and growth. The global financial crisis, he argues, is ultimately a moral crisis. "We have created new idols," Francis writes. "The worship of the ancient golden calf has returned in a new and ruthless guise in the idolatry of money and the dictatorship of an impersonal economy lacking a truly human purpose."[28]

While Rush Limbaugh's screed that the pope is preaching "Marxism" is an extreme view, his argument that the church should simply stay focused on providing "charity" is not uncommon. Many Americans, including more than a few Catholics, forget that the church is concerned not only with charity but also with justice. Some wealthy Catholics are scrambling to soften the pope's prophetic critique of the market, and they even look to baptize their anti-government ideology in Vatican holy water. When you think of Pope Francis, it's unlikely that Charles and David Koch come to mind. The billionaire libertarians, who helped bankroll the Tea Party movement, are the most influential funding source for a national network of conservative activists and Republican politicians denying climate change, attacking workers' rights, and targeting financial reform protections.[29] When a Koch foundation gave $1 million to the business school at the Catholic University of America in Washington, leading Catholic scholars and theologians warned that the brothers' opposition to unions, addressing climate change, and Medicaid expansion "contradict Catholic teaching on a range of moral issues."[30] Yet two Catholic philanthropists took to the op-ed pages of the *Washington Post* in 2014 to make the case that the Koch brothers and Pope Francis would get along splendidly.[31] "For us, promoting limited government alongside the Kochs is an important part of heeding Pope Francis's call to love and serve the poor," wrote John and Carol Saeman, financial contributors to the Koch-backed Freedom Partners Chamber of Commerce, which promotes the "benefits of free markets" and invests in energy companies, the Tea Party Patriots, firearm associations, and anti-union "right to work" groups.[32] The column gives a passing nod to the church's teachings about a "preferential option for the poor" before launching into the usual litany of right-wing talking points about Washington's "insatiable growth" and bloated welfare spending. The authors lament that all that wasted money would be better used by "philanthropists like us" who could "give to local charities" and to business that would "create the jobs the poor desperately need."

The idea that charity can make up for the damage caused by reckless politicians eviscerating social safety nets that help the elderly, the working poor, pregnant women, and children is a cruel myth. In fact, the nation's largest food bank announced that it's stretched so thin after federal cuts to food assistance that they have no choice but to turn some people away.[33] Anti-government ideologues also rarely acknowledge that many faith-based charities rely on government support. Catholic Charities USA, the largest social service provider outside of the federal government, helped more than seventeen million people in 2012 alone.[34] The charity receives more than half of its funding from the federal government. Pope Francis, rather than simply calling for more charity, is reading the signs of the times—extreme inequalities that cause preventable suffering and death—through the lens of traditional church teaching about the common good. He's not going rogue. "Charity is no substitute for justice withheld," St. Augustine observed long ago.

In order for Pope Francis's challenging perspective on the "absolute autonomy of markets" and growing inequality to have a chance of breaking through to an individualist American culture, the formidable obstacle of a well-financed network of Catholic libertarians and neoconservatives who drive an agenda more in line with the U.S. Chamber of Commerce than the Catholic Church must be faced. The Acton Institute, a think tank in Grand Rapids, Michigan, led by a Catholic priest and funded by wealthy conservatives, trumpets what it calls the "benefits of a limited government" and the "beneficent consequences of a free market."[35]

The institute, which raised more than $10 million in 2013, is powered by the DeVos family. These Christian conservatives have funded a host of Republican candidates, right-wing think tanks, and advocacy groups leading the charge for anti–tax ballot measures, financial deregulation, and anti-union campaigns since the 1970s. "Other than possibly the Koch brothers, few billionaires have a more established place in conservative America than the DeVos clan," according to *Forbes* magazine.[36] Dick DeVos Jr., now the public face of the Michigan family dynasty, played a key role in the successful passage of the state's 2012 anti-union "right to work" law in Michigan.[37] Acton Institute's cofounder and president, Rev. Robert Sirico, is the author of *Defending the Free Market: The Moral Case for a Free Economy.* A frequent Fox News commentator, Sirico echoed DeVos's talking points when he cheered the Michigan "right to work" law as "a landmark event that promises to accelerate the state's rebound from the near-collapse it suffered in the deep recession of 2008."[38] Bishop Thomas Gumbleton, a retired auxiliary bishop in Detroit, spoke to a more traditional religious commitment. "This legislation should not just offend Catholics, but all Christians and members of all faith traditions," he wrote. "At the core of Christianity, Judaism, Islam and all great religions are the values of dignity and respect, values from which economic justice and the right to organize can never be separated."[39] Gumbleton reminded anti-union activists that in the 1980s, the U.S. bishops' conference insisted "no one may deny the right to organize without attacking human dignity itself."[40]

Each year, the institute hosts "Acton University," which it bills as "a four-day exploration of the intellectual foundations of a free society."[41] More than eight hundred college and graduate students, priests, seminarians, and business leaders from over seventy countries gather for workshops, lectures, and networking at DeVos Place, a glistening modern glass and steel convention center in downtown Grand Rapids. Courses include "The Mystery of the Invisible Hand: From Adam to Adam Smith" and "Christian Vision of Government," where participants learn about what Acton describes as "Christianity's decisive moral and institutional contribution to limiting state power." "We're building a movement that is radically in favor of freedom," Rev. Sirico, a onetime 1960s liberal, says in a video promoting the conference. The institute also has a Rome office, Instituto Acton, and has cultivated an international presence with affiliations in several countries. Kishore Jayabalan, director of Acton's Rome headquarters, offered his interpretation of the pope's vision for a just economy. "When it comes to actually helping the poor, it involves much more than simply giving away our goods or, even worse, letting the State take from the rich and give to the poor," he wrote in a piece titled "Pope Francis and Truly Helping the Poor." "One thing we've learned with the help of economics is that wealth can be created, not just redistributed."[42] In the spring of 2014, Acton hosted an event in Rome, "Faith, State and the Economy: Perspectives from East to West," which connected the issue of religious freedom to limiting state intervention in the economy. One speaker, Fr. Martin Rhonheimer, a Swiss Opus Dei priest, told the conference that Catholics "should not be advocates of a social justice, which makes citizens more and more dependent on a state welfare."[43] Held at an independent conference center on the ground floor of the Pontifical Gregorian University, the gathering was the first of a five-part series Acton is hosting around the world on the relationship between religious and economic freedom.

In the fall of 2014, Acton hosted a conference—"The Relationship between Religious and Economic Liberty in an Age of Expanding Government"—at the Catholic University of America in Washington. Speakers included two cardinals, a bishop, and Samuel Gregg, Acton's research director. Gregg is the author of *Tea Party Catholic: The Catholic Case for Limited Government, a Free Economy, and Human Flourishing.* He argues that Pope Francis's analysis of markets and inequality "will strike many Catholics as less than convincing" and is built on assumptions that "are rather questionable." In no country does the market exist with "absolute autonomy," Gregg reasonably observes, before inveighing against government.[44] "How much more of the economy do we really want to put in the state's hands? Is there no upper limit?" he wrote in the *National Review.*

Another speaker at the Acton event at Catholic University, Michael Novak, is one of the most prominent Catholic voices of the past half-century. A liberal who once campaigned for Eugene McCarthy, Novak became a leading neoconservative whose writings in the 1980s and 1990s, including *The Spirit of Democratic Capitalism*, have been translated into multiple languages and read by influential leaders, including Pope John Paul II. The onetime informal adviser to the Reagan administration does not see a Catholic case for addressing inequality. "There is no way you can fight inequality without increasing government tyranny," Novak told me. "I don't see how knocking down the rich helps the poor. Which is better for the common good: a regime of collective control or a regime of private property, and its accompanying inequality? I'm glad Catholic bishops are not talking about inequality. It's the wrong issue. All it breeds is envy." He thinks Pope Francis has yet to develop a substantial economic analysis. "The pope did not use the term 'trickle down.' His translator did. This is not the first time English translators have shown a partisan spirit. Pope Francis is mostly off the cuff. I'm still waiting to hear what his economic thoughts are. Pope John Paul II and Pope Benedict XVI were much more detailed and more helpful. Out of his Polish experience, John Paul II saw the right to personal economic initiative and that nailed it. He was allergic to left-wing economic thoughts." Novak, a senior fellow with the American Enterprise Institute who wrote a 2010 commentary essay titled "God Bless the Tea Party," makes the case for limited government with a biblical reference.[45] "Jesus introduced the concept of limited government," Novak argues, "when he said not everything belongs to Caesar."

Charles Clark, an economics professor and senior fellow at the Vincentian Center for Church and Society at St. John's University in New York, sees the Acton Institute and free-market absolutists like Novak as offering false choices that are divorced from traditional Catholic teaching. "The whole idea that we either have freedom and capitalism or godless Communism is very Cold War," said Clark, a historian of economics. "It's like they didn't get the memo. Their framework is so narrow." Clark has debated Novak, whose main argument he describes as boiling down to the idea that capitalism has created more wealth than any other system. "My response is that's not the standard we are supposed to use as Catholics. You don't find the Gospel telling us do what makes you rich. The issue of inequality has become so obvious it's hard to explain away."

Clark is floored when Catholic conservatives claim the pope just doesn't understand American capitalism and is biased because of his Argentine experiences.

> This argument cracks me up. Wall Street is filled with crony capitalists. The Federal Reserve gave out billions to make sure rich financial institutions were bailed out while homeowners were left behind. We have this pure free market system but Argentina is corrupt? Underlying our financial crisis was a level of fraud and corruption that was

stunning. Pope Francis is reframing the issues of poverty and inequality around the idea of exclusion. It's the opposite of how Americans look at the economy from the perspective of productivity and how much value is created. The pope is challenging that by saying we've excluded so many from the entire process. Is our wealth created because we are excluding others? He forces you to think.

Clark is also troubled by the growing interest in libertarianism he sees among Catholic college students, a trend he says is in part due to the Acton Institute's successful efforts to reach young people with DVDs, conferences, and lectures on campuses. "I keep bumping into these young Catholics who love Friedrich Hayek, the Austrian economist. It's ironic because the early Austrian thinkers were hostile to the Catholic Church having an opinion on anything or even existing. Libertarianism has a flawed understanding of the human person. It's a view that is the furthest imaginable from the human person being made in the image of God."

Pope Francis's critique of global capitalism could present a particular challenge to the U.S. church, where wealthy corporate leaders and conservative politicians have built cozy ties with influential bishops. At the Napa Institute's summer retreat in 2014, held at the four-star Meritage Resort and Spa in Napa, Catholic CEOs and well-heeled philanthropists paid $1,700 to network with two cardinals and more than a dozen bishops and archbishops. Timothy Busch, a lawyer who owns Trinitas Cellars in Napa and a host of luxury hotels, resorts, and golf courses, cofounded the institute in 2010 as part of a call from Archbishop Charles Chaput for Catholics to prepare for what the archbishop dubbed the "next America"—a secular culture hostile to faith.

At the Napa conference, Archbishop Chaput spoke to the pope's statements about economic justice. "I should make a couple of obvious points about Francis," the archbishop said. "The first is that not everyone's happy with him. What Francis says about economic justice may be hard for some of us to hear. So we need to read the Holy Father's writings for ourselves, without the filter of the mass media."[46] At a lunch, former GOP senator and 2012 presidential contender Rick Santorum urged attendees to dedicate themselves to "the conservative movement." He received a standing ovation.

"The hierarchy, both U.S. bishops and Vatican officials, has always been solicitous of the wealthy who contribute significantly to their causes," said Daniel Finn, professor of economics and theology at the

College of St. Benedict and St. John's University in Minnesota. "Money certainly buys access, and by assumption influence. Wealthy groups from the Knights of Columbus to the Napa Institute get access that others don't." Finn points out that Catholic neoconservatives in the United States who trumpet market-friendly views and are often hostile to government have more in common with a new generation of bishops than in past decades. "There was a time when most bishops grew up in blue-collar families in the city with a father who was a union member," he said. "In recent decades, most bishops grew up in a white-collar family in the suburbs with a father who thought unions were a bad mistake. So rather than genuinely struggling with what the three millennia of Judeo-Christian teaching on economic life means for us today, some bishops have tended to jump on the misguided assumption that they should speak strongly only about 'intrinsic evils,' badly misunderstanding the term's meaning in traditional Catholic moral theology."

Finn notes that if Catholic conservatives are upset with Pope Francis's views on markets, their real problem is with church teaching. "Francis has used much sharper rhetoric than his predecessors, and he has put more emphasis on inequality than they did, but the substance of his message is in line with theirs," he said. "In their more intellectually responsible moments, Acton Institute authors like Samuel Gregg and others have said that what they're doing is making the best possible case for capitalism from the perspective of Catholic social thought. This at least implies that there are parts of Catholic teaching which are highly critical of capitalism and which they are ignoring. More frequently, they don't mention this caveat and simply claim that Catholic social thought supports free market capitalism. But this is an old tactic, begun by Michael Novak: cherry picking from Catholic social thought to prove a point. This is at the heart of the intellectual irresponsibility of the Catholic right on economic issues. They have not begun with Catholic belief and principles and asked what they imply for economic life today. They begin with an *a priori* commitment to free market capitalism and attempt to show how Catholic social thought supports their view."

R. Scott Appleby, a University of Notre Dame historian and dean of the university's school of global affairs, explains that this is because many neoconservatives in the church have a clear political agenda. "From the Reagan revolution to Karl Rove, these Catholics were part of a political movement that knew how to galvanize voters to vote against their economic interest by saying we are the party of 'family values,'" said Appleby, the coeditor of *Being Right: Conservative Catholics in America*. "Social issues were the barnacles on the ocean liner of their real ideology. Some conservative Catholics, like socially conservative Protestants, were sold a bill of goods by those who waved the flag of abortion and gay marriage, when the real concern was protecting their own economic self-interest. I'm a pro-life Catholic, but I don't buy into the seamless conservative garment that links anti-abortion activism with pro-capitalist, corporatist economic ideology that frequently ignores the poor. Pope Francis doesn't buy into that shotgun marriage and sees it as distorted. The right won the framing battle, and the narrative needs to be posed in a different way."

Despite the challenges, a new generation of Catholics in public life has the potential to rescue "family values" from the cheap seats of political theater to build a substantive "pro-family" policy agenda that cuts across partisan cleavages by drawing on our church's commitment to life and economic dignity.

8

THE SEARCH FOR COMMON GROUND

When Pope Francis canonized John Paul II and John XXIII a few weeks after Easter in 2014, he sent a message of unity by declaring as saints two men often deployed as symbols for competing Catholic camps. The pope consistently reminds the faithful, even if we find it tough to hear, that the Gospel leaves no room for ideology. He is inconveniently challenging the left and right to step outside our comfort zones. This is hard, essential work at a time of deep polarization in the church and American politics. Can progressive Catholics and conservative Catholics find fresh paths forward to heal the wounds in our church, and also forge common ground in the policy arena to address poverty and inequality, help struggling families, support pregnant women, and reduce the number of abortions? In many respects, the answer to that difficult question depends on how American Catholics choose to use the rare gift found in this unexpected moment of renewal and hope for the church.

It's no secret that the Catholic Church is diminished by the tribalism and litmus tests that often define the dysfunctional culture of secular politics. We are too often a church of MSNBC Catholics and Fox News Catholics who reinforce our own narratives and tune out opposing views. We can do better. Catholic Democrats and Catholic Republicans—or those who increasingly feel politically estranged from both parties—share a common faith that includes clear teachings about the sanctity of life, a preferential option for the poor, and a commitment to the common good. As the world watches the Catholic Church with new eyes, we must strive for something better than turf wars and dueling talking points. Pope Francis is challenging us to think bigger and build "a church of encounter" that goes to the margins where people are hurting and broken. A navel-gazing church obsessed with internal bickering and settling old scores will not meet that transcendent mission. Catholic liberals and conservatives have been locked in a fierce tug-of-war over Catholic identity for decades—or centuries, depending on how you read it. This conflict often has roots in legitimate disagreements between faithful Catholics who love our church in equal measure, even if we sometimes reach different conclusions. Pope Francis reminds us that diversity and debate is not to be feared, but is a sign of a healthy, vibrant church. "The church is like a grand orchestra, full of variety: we are not all the same and we don't all need to be the same . . . each of us brings something different to the church," the pope has said, adding that there should be "no dull uniformity" but the "richness of the gifts of the Holy Spirit."[1] A core challenge will be to move beyond confining labels and acknowledge the "cafeteria Catholicism" that both liberals and conservatives find comforting. In the Catholic tradition, defending life and fighting for social justice are not clashing political agendas, but rather part of the same moral framework for building a just society. When we unravel the strands that weave together the coherence of Catholic teaching, we always risk reducing faith to just another ideology in service of political ends. Instead, Pope Francis challenges our "throwaway culture" that tramples human dignity by treating life in the womb, migrants dying in the desert, and the homeless and forgotten elderly as disposable. It is challenging this "globalization of indifference"—as the pope describes a culture of comfort and extreme individualism—that should unite Catholics in service to the common good.

Charles Camosy kept thinking that it didn't have to be this way. As a doctoral student at the University of Notre Dame in 2009, Camosy found himself smack in the middle of a furor over the university's invitation to President Obama to give the commencement address. The bitter debate that ensued inflamed divisions in the church and fueled another round of nasty culture-war politics. Amid the shouting and finger pointing, there seemed little hope for civil dialogue. "I was so disappointed with how we handled that as a U.S. church," said Camosy, forty, now a professor of Christian ethics at Fordham University in New York. "The raw antagonism on both sides didn't allow for any nuance. It was the old battlegrounds again. It tore at the fabric of Notre Dame and our church. There were relationships that were destroyed. I was sitting there at the commencement and it felt like this was a moment to take advantage of. I knew Americans were not as polarized over abortion as the debate led us to believe. We had to do this differently. I felt we couldn't let the moment slip away."

When Camosy arrived at Fordham University to begin teaching, he threw himself into efforts to bridge divides and carve out space for dialogue. He became something of a one-man common-ground machine. Camosy teamed up with like-minded academics and activists across the country who were also fed up with false choices and stale narratives. They hosted a 2010 conference at Princeton University—titled "Open Hearts, Open Minds and Fair Minded Words"—with the goal of bringing together leaders on opposite sides of the abortion fight. "Pro-choice" and "pro-life" leaders, most of whom acknowledged the problems with those labels, held frank conversations about difficult topics—the moral status of a fetus, the benefits and limits of contraception, whether courts or legislatures are best equipped to address abortion, and how those who disagree over legalization might find common ground to reduce abortion. Both sides spoke honestly, disagreed, found points of convergence, and broke down stereotypes. An Indiana University law professor who used to represent the National Abortion Rights Action League called for policies "that reduce abortion through means that help women and their families avoid unintended pregnancy and choose healthy childbearing."[2] Several anti-abortion speakers acknowledged the limits of addressing the issue solely in the context of legalization/criminalization and expressed frustration with so-called pro-life politicians who rail against abortion even as they gut social safety nets that help pregnant women avoid desperate choices. There was some sniping on blogs afterward, but in large part the conference modeled the kind of civil space Camosy sees too rarely in the church today.

"So much of our church polarization gets read through Democratic and Republican polarization," he said. "There is a lot of idolatry of secular politics in the church on both sides. Media coverage fuels the illusion that there are only factions opposed to each other. People often look at Pope Francis through this lens. But you have to deal with the fact that he wants a poor church for the poor, *and* he believes that life begins at conception. If we just fight the culture wars through Pope Francis, we have a problem. I'm hopeful he can help us resist those kinds of categories. Much of what the pope has called for as far as social justice isn't new, but he's been able to get these messages out in a way that other popes and Vatican officials were not able to in the past. There was a different narrative that formed right away around Francis because he was largely unknown and didn't have the history that John Paul II or Ratzinger did. This creates a new conceptual space."

Camosy is not just waiting for church leaders to act. He is rolling up his sleeves and pulling people together. Along with the Princeton meeting, he organized a conference at Notre Dame in the spring of 2015—"Polarization in the Catholic Church: Naming the Wounds, Beginning to Heal"—that builds on the pope's insistence that what the church needs most today is the ability to "warm hearts and heal wounds." His new book, *Beyond the Abortion Wars: A Way Forward for a New Generation*, makes a compelling case that Americans are not as hopelessly divided over the issue as the shrillest commentators on both sides lead us to believe. A sizable chunk of Americans back policies that support pregnant women and reduce abortion. Younger voters, in particular, are increasingly frustrated with the way that labels reduce complex issues to bumper-sticker certainty. "Despite the prevalence of the 'us and them' meme in our abortion discourse and politicking," Camosy wrote in the *Los Angeles Times*, "Americans have already rejected the choice/life binary, and the next generation will find the notion positively antiquated."[3]

For the past five years, Camosy has also led the Catholic Conversation Project, which offers opportunities for early career theologians interested in rebooting common-ground efforts. "We pick people with diverse views who respect the complexity of issues," he said. "It helps that all of us were formed by something other than post–Vatican II culture wars. We came of age at a time when the baggage that weighed down previous generations doesn't weigh us down. People involved in the project don't fit into categories. One member supports women's ordination but thinks abortion is the greatest social injustice of all time. Another loves the Latin Mass and is a married gay man. Someone else defends church teaching on contraception but stopped eating meat for ethical reasons. It's all about building relationships."

When John Carr retired in 2012 after more than two decades as executive director of the Department of Justice, Peace and Human Development at the U.S. Conference of Catholic Bishops, he wanted to find constructive ways to defuse the simmering tensions dividing the church. Carr wants the Catholic tradition to be a resource for young Catholics in Congress, think tanks, government agencies, and nonprofits in the nation's capital. He also had a hunch that many faithful were weary of the artificial barriers put up between "pro-life" and "social justice" Catholics. In response, he founded the Initiative on Catholic Social Thought and Public Life at Georgetown University. Public dialogues featuring liberal and conservative Catholics leaders in politics, the media, and nonprofit organizations have been standing-room-only affairs since the initiative launched at a fortuitous time—just a few weeks after Pope Francis gave his bombshell interview in a Jesuit magazine that made headlines around the world. Carr thinks the pope is reminding politically active Catholics that our faith tradition is about "both-and," not an "either-or" dichotomy. "Catholics can make clear connections—defending human life and dignity, promoting human rights and responsibilities, protecting both the unborn and the poor," he said. "We can especially encourage the next generation of Catholic leaders so they see our faith as a gift, not a burden, and a call to participation in public life, not as an excuse for retreat or cynicism."[4] At the forum's "Francis Factor" kickoff event in 2013, speakers included Cardinal Donald Wuerl of the Archdiocese of Washington and Georgetown president John J. DeGioia, who clashed just the year before over an invitation to then Health and Human Services Secretary Kathleen Sebelius to speak at a graduation ceremony. A *Washington Post* profile noted that the cocktail reception after the event drew such a diverse crowd that "Opus Dei members sipped wine with lefties."[5]

At another forum hosted by the initiative, "Seeking the Common Good in a Time of Polarization," Carr asked editors from liberal and conservative Catholic publications—the *National Catholic Reporter*, *First Things*, *Our Sunday Visitor*, *Commonweal*, and *America* magazine—how Catholics can "find a common way to pursue the common good and whether Pope Francis is uniting or dividing us in a new way." Greg Erlandson, publisher of *Our Sunday Visitor* and a Vatican communications consultant, said that while he was "skeptical" that Francis was defusing tensions at this still early stage in his papacy, a Catholic vision of the common good that the pope articulates with freshness is a powerful antidote to the radical individualism of contemporary culture. "If you look at both parties, you see the influence of libertarianism," he said.

"There is an economic libertarianism on the right and a moral libertarianism on the left. Both are inherently at odds with Catholic social thought,
and our voice as Catholics needs to be heard." Catholic progressives and
conservatives, he noted, often tune out the wisdom from their own faith
tradition if it doesn't affirm their preexisting views. He described Pope
Benedict XVI's social encyclical, *Caritas in Veritate*, as a "profound and
complex document" that was ignored by some on the Catholic left and
right. "Conservatives of a certain ilk were uncomfortable with it and the
left wasn't going to concede anything to Benedict, so it got dropped," he
said.

R. R. Reno, the editor of *First Things*, sees a church united in fundamental ways and also splintered over how to apply core values in the
public square. "We should not overestimate the divisions. There is a
powerful and deep pro-life consensus in the Catholic Church," Reno said.
"We are also all committed to the preferential option for the poor. What
divides us is how do we interpret that, what is the best strategy to achieve
that? Is the primary affliction economic want or is it social decay? I've
written that gay marriage is a luxury that will be paid for by the poor. As
our marriage culture is degraded, people at the bottom are going to live
more difficult lives." At the same time, Reno noted that *First Things* has
strongly challenged economic libertarians, whom he called "the Ran-
dians," which has led to pushback from some donors to the conservative
journal. Overcoming polarization, he cautioned, should not be seen as
"some kind of holy grail." "Unity in Christ need not be unity in all
matters of policy. We do agree on core goals even if we fight, and fighting is not a bad thing as long as we fight fair and with charity."

When it comes to the church's role in witnessing to the faith in a
society increasingly less receptive to traditional Catholic teaching on
marriage, family, and sexuality, Reno describes a stark clash. "One side
wants to remove as many impediments as possible for people to come to
the faith, and that means downplaying some of the hard truths. My side,
and I will take sides, believes that a countercultural church that speaks
frankly and convincingly about hard truths will be more successful in
attracting people to the church." While Pope Francis has excited the
faithful, Reno doesn't see this pope as a unifying figure. "He is very
comfortable with condemnation. In the interview with *America* magazine,
he very quickly condemned traditionalist Catholics, and that's not always
helpful in overcoming divisions."

Caitlin Hendel, the president and CEO of the *National Catholic Reporter*, is a journalist who once covered politics in Washington. She concedes that covering the Catholic Church can feel a lot like reporting about a divided and dysfunctional Congress. But she thinks a new pope is breaking down old barriers. "Francis doesn't believe in parties," Hendel said. "He doesn't talk about two sides. He believes in service to the poor. Those are his people. If anybody can start to soften the edges of polarization, it could be Francis."

REVIVING THE CONSISTENT ETHIC OF LIFE

The consistent ethic of life vision championed by the late Cardinal Joseph Bernardin is getting a jumpstart under the Francis papacy. If the paradigm of American culture wars divides up issues of family values, economic justice, and abortion along an ideological spectrum that falls into predictable partisan categories, Francis is breathing new life into a robust Catholic tradition that refuses to accept those conventional terms of debate. The pope, for example, has addressed economic dignity and care for immigrants as sanctity-of-life issues. "Just as the commandment 'Thou shalt not kill' sets a clear limit in order to safeguard the value of human life," Pope Francis writes, "today we also have to say 'thou shalt not' to an economy of exclusion and inequality. Such an economy kills." Cardinal Sean O'Malley of Boston, the pope's top adviser in the United States, echoed that message during his homily before the 2014 March for Life in Washington. The cardinal called poverty a "dehumanizing force" and insisted "the Gospel of Life demands that we work for economic justice in our country and our world."[6]

Francis's first papal trip outside of Rome was to Lampedusa, a Mediterranean island where thousands of migrants and refugees from Africa have died at sea trying to enter Italy. The pope decried a "globalization of indifference" that turns away from suffering. "Yet God is asking each of us: 'Where is the blood of your brother which cries out to me?' Today no one in our world feels responsible." When Cardinal O'Malley led a delegation of bishops to the U.S.-Mexico border to bear witness to the suffering and death caused by our broken immigration system, he called comprehensive immigration reform "another pro-life issue."[7] In the leadup to the national anti-abortion March for Life rally in January 2015, one hundred Catholic leaders—including more than two dozen presidents of Catholic universities and a former pro-life spokeswoman for the U.S. bishops' conference—released a letter that called attention to the deaths of migrants at the U.S.-Mexico border and urged Catholic elected officials to pass comprehensive reform and "defend the sanctity of human lives at all stages." Five dioceses in Southern California held their first "One Life" march in 2015, drawing attention to not only abortion but also an array of justice issues, including homelessness and the treatment of the elderly. Archbishop José Gomez created the event, according to the archdiocese, in response to Pope Francis's efforts to address a broad spectrum of issues bearing on human life and dignity. More than ten thousand people attended the march in Los Angeles.[8]

The death penalty is also getting renewed attention as a "life issue," and in some cases it is bringing together unlikely collaborators. Four hundred Catholic and evangelical leaders issued a statement before the start of Holy Week in 2015 calling for an end to capital punishment. "All who reverence the sanctity of life, created in the image of God, must never remain silent when firing squads, lethal injections, electric chairs and other instruments of death are viewed as morally acceptable," Catholic theologians, women religious, and Christian evangelical leaders wrote.[9] Four national Catholic publications—a mix of conservative and liberal journals and newspapers—released a joint editorial in 2015 that called for "our nation to embody its commitment to the right to life by abolishing the death penalty once and for all." The editorial from the *National Catholic Reporter*, *Our Sunday Visitor*, *National Catholic Register*, and *America* magazine caught the attention of a *New York Times* religion columnist, who accurately described it as "an unusual show of unity among publications that speak for often antagonistic niches of Catholic public thought."

BUILDING A MORAL, PRO-FAMILY ECONOMY

This expansive consistent ethic framework could help spark a renewed commitment on the part of Catholics active in public life to find common ground when it comes to building a moral economy and strengthening families. In particular, Catholics across ideological divides can make a significant contribution by advocating for parental leave policies, paid

sick days, quality child care, an increase in the minimum wage, tax policies that help families, and stronger laws that end pregnancy discrimination in the workplace. All of these "pro-family" policies can find support
in Catholic social teaching.

The time is ripe for action. The United States is one of only three
countries to offer no paid maternity leave, according to the United Nation's International Labor Organization. Only 12 percent of U.S. workers
have access to paid family medical leave through their employers. Nearly
forty million working Americans have no access to even a single paid
sick day. In many cases, a parent with a minimum-wage job is trapped in
poverty despite working. Efforts to give the federal minimum wage a
modest boost have sputtered in the face of GOP opposition in Congress.
Catholic teaching has endorsed a living wage since 1891, when Pope Leo
XIII spoke out for workers to earn enough to support a family. Beyond
civil dialogue, there are tangible ways for Catholics to work together. The
Family Act, legislation that creates a national family leave and medical
program, among other things, allows employees time to care for a new
child or address a serious health issue. The Pregnant Workers Fairness
Act prevents employers from forcing pregnant women out of the workplace and ensures that employers provide reasonable accommodations to
pregnant women. A 2014 case before the U.S. Supreme Court shined a
light on pregnancy discrimination. A pregnant United Parcel Service
worker, advised by her doctor not to lift heavy packages, was refused
light duty by the company and put on unpaid leave. She lost her health
benefits. Progressive organizations such as the National Women's Law
Center and more than twenty pro-life organizations across the political
spectrum—including Concerned Women for America, the Southern Baptists, and Democrats for Life—filed friend-of-the-court briefs in support
of the worker. [10]

Kim Daniels, a former spokesperson for Cardinal Timothy Dolan of
New York and a onetime consultant to Sarah Palin, sees cases like this as
an example of how liberal and conservative Catholics can put aside in-
fighting to make a tangible impact. "There is a huge opening now. Pope
Francis is challenging the left and right to come out of our bunkers,"
Daniels said. "We add something distinctive to public life as Catholics
when we resist ideology and allow ourselves to be challenged by the
Gospel." The Catholic tradition, she emphasizes, is supposed to push us
all. "For liberals, that means how do you do a better job of building a

culture of life, and how do conservatives do more to address poverty and economic dignity by supporting things like raising the minimum wage. Our faith is relational and our social teachings focus on the common good. This should allow us to resist the libertarianism of the left and right." An attorney who specializes in health care conscience rights, Daniels also hopes Catholics can help disentangle the issue of religious liberty from the culture wars. "Religious liberty is a central part of the American liberal tradition," she said. "We have to protect the role of faith in public life, and the Catholic ministries of health care and education. I think there is broad agreement that we create a false architecture of religious liberty when we say our churches are deserving of religious liberty, but individuals and our social service ministries are not."

If you care about poverty and social justice, says Brad Wilcox, director of the National Marriage Project at the University of Virginia, you have to take seriously how family structure impacts economic opportunity. A Catholic and a senior fellow at the conservative American Enterprise Institute, Wilcox conducts research on the breakdown of traditional two-parent families and the impact of declining marriage rates on the poor and working class. There is a growing class divide when it comes to marriage. For the educated and more affluent, he said, divorce is down and marital quality is comparatively high. In contrast, lower-income and working-class Americans are less likely to marry, and when they do those relationships are more vulnerable.

"Pope Francis has cast a spotlight on inequality and what happens in the family has a lot to do with how justly our society is ordered," Wilcox said. "The retreat from marriage contributes to the growth of income inequality." Wilcox's 2014 report, "For Richer, For Poorer: How Family Structures Economic Success in America," estimates that 32 percent of the growth in family-income inequality since 1979 is linked to the decreasing number of Americans who form and maintain stable, married families.[11] "Marriage and family are in crisis," the pope said at a 2014 conference at the Vatican, pointing to the connections between what he described as "the decline of marriage culture" and rising poverty and other "social ills." Wilcox and other researchers highlight that children growing up in married, two-parent households are more likely to avoid risky behavior, graduate from high school, earn higher salaries, and delay parenthood until they are married. At the same time, Wilcox gave a presentation to Catholic bishops at a recent meeting in which he said that "the data suggests that same-sex couples—and this is really prelimi-nary—are more likely to have stable relationships when the legal regime is more supportive of their relationships." As a social scientist, he says, it will take several decades to evaluate the data on same-sex marriage fami-ly structures.

"There can be common ground if progressives and conservatives rec-ognize we both bring something to the table," Wilcox said. "One poten-tial is to have conservatives appreciate the way in which the progressive focus on economic foundations are so central, and for progressives to realize there are lots of different family types, but in the main families are more likely to flourish when there is a stable, two-parent family. Conser-vatives like me are concerned about employment trends, but something has to be done to reverse the erosion of stable jobs and wages. A family wage is needed. The question is, can we find a vehicle that would garner support?" He points to a host of policies that Catholics could rally behind to help strengthen families, including increasing the child tax credit and extending it to both income and payroll taxes. Eliminating or reducing the "marriage penalty" in the tax code, he says, is also important. Many of our tax and transfer policies—such as housing assistance and food stamps—unintentionally penalize marriage among lower-income couples because the addition of a second earner pushes couples just above the income threshold for public assistance.

Wilcox notes that President Obama has called on Congress "to strengthen families by removing the financial deterrents to marriage for low-income couples." He also thinks Catholic churches can improve out-reach to struggling families who are often disengaged from civic life, a form of social exclusion the pope addresses frequently. Wilcox says re-search from Robert Putnam of Harvard and others finds that the "Bowling Alone" phenomenon of civic disengagement is higher among lower-in-come Americans. The U.S. Conference of Catholic Bishops lists "call to family, community and participation" as one of the seven core themes of Catholic social teaching. "Since the 1970s, Catholic churches have not done a good job of reaching working class and poor communities," Wil-cox says.

The *Washington Post* columnist E. J. Dionne Jr., a liberal Catholic, agrees that the left and right must lower a few defenses. "The ideological resolution I'd suggest for the new year is that all sides stop fighting and pool their energies to easing the marriage and family crisis that is engulfing working-class Americans," Dionne wrote at the end of 2014. "This would require liberals to acknowledge what the vast majority of them already practice in their own lives: that, all things being equal, kids are better off with two loving and engaged parents. It would require conservatives to acknowledge that many of the pressures on families are economic and that the decline of well-paying blue-collar work is causing huge disruptions in family formation."[12]

Helen Alvare teaches family law at George Mason University and has represented the U.S. bishops' conference on congressional panels. A consultant to the Vatican's Pontifical Council on the Laity, she is a prominent speaker in the United States and around the world on issues of family, abortion, and contraception. "Birth control's worst enemy," the liberal online magazine *Salon* once barked in a headline.[13] "I'm not a Republican, I'm not a partisan," Alvare says by way of describing her frustration with the toxic climate that alienates her as a Catholic who doesn't feel at ease with either party. "Pope Francis was able to do in weeks what I couldn't do in decades, which is to communicate that Catholicism confounds political categories." Over the past decade, Alvare has been pushing lawmakers, students, the media, and anyone else who will listen that caring about strong marriages, the sanctity of life in the womb, and the moral scandal of poverty are all integral to building a flourishing culture. It's an unconventional message that she has found not many political leaders want to hear. In a 2005 law journal article, "The Consistent Ethic of Life: A Proposal for Improving Its Legislative Grasp," Alvare raised concerns about President Bill Clinton's welfare reform act, which introduced strict time limits on public support for low-income families, and also Republican proposals for privatizing a range of government social safety nets. "The consistent ethic proposed that the Church's positions on issues ranging from the taking of human life to attaining a dignified standard of living should be understood and spoken of as a morally coherent whole," Alvare wrote. "It was hoped that the consistent ethic would assist those laboring on diverse social justice issues to understand their common goals and the interdependence of their work. . . . The consistent ethic is justifiably a source of pride and inspiration for Catholics. Yet there is no concrete evidence that it has become a persuasive, motivating power in lawmaking."[14]

The deep-pocketed donors and interest group money that steer party agendas toward the ideological extremes have only grown more influential since then. Alvare still thinks enough Americans are disgusted with politics as usual, unsatisfied with a shallow culture of materialism, and hungry for community that new paths are possible. Pope Francis, she believes, offers political leaders and ordinary Catholics in the pews a model for breaking down barriers and going deeper. "We are so loud and argumentative in the United States. We are a nation of lawyers! Francis is a walking call to examination of conscience at all times," she said. "He encourages the difficult question. He is not afraid of taking up the messiness on the ground."

Ashley McGuire, a senior fellow with the Catholic Association whose commentary appears regularly in prominent media outlets, has sparred with liberals over contraception funding in health care reform and is a frequent critic of President Obama. Like any good talking head on cable news, she is ready with a punchy sound bite and isn't afraid to fight for her views. McGuire takes her pro-life activism in Washington policy and punditry circles seriously, but says the pope is helping her develop a broader perspective. "I think Pope Francis's challenge to both Republicans and Democrats who are Catholics is not to get so caught up in our advocacy that we forget about the people we are advocating for," she said.

> He has some strong language in *Evangelii Gaudium* about cocktail parties, for example, which struck a chord. So many of us outspoken Catholics live in the Acela corridor (New York–DC) where it is easy to go from party to party and speak and write and never come into contact with a single mom or someone living in destitute poverty. He constantly refers to this idea of accompanying others. This does not mean we all need to spend our days in the slums, but it does mean we all could spend a little less time blogging and a little more time in conversation with our friends and with those going through difficult times, witnessing to the Gospel through our own example. It also means making new friendships with people outside of our comfort zone. I think Pope Francis is not asking those of us involved in politics to abandon politics. To the contrary, he talks about politics as being one of the highest forms of serving the common good. But he just cautions us against getting too caught up in politics that we become rigid and lose sight of human beings.

McGuire is impressed with how the pope is able to frame hot-button issues in a new way that invites people into a conversation and challenges conventional thinking. "I've been struck by how Pope Francis speaks about the various issues that, at least in America, typically strike partisan chords," she said. "He talks about a 'throwaway culture,' both in regards to human life and the environment, for example. Even when he talks about the life issue, he talks about the unborn and the elderly, who are often forgotten when we are talking about a culture of life, or at least thought of separately." McGuire, age thirty, is part of a generation looking for fresh solutions to old challenges and wants to find unlikely allies open to common ground. "Catholics should be leading the conversation about seeking out a new pro-woman, pro-family, pro-life agenda. Reform conservatives have been leading the conversation about how Republicans can find new ways to help families," she said. "I also see a shared goal among young Catholics who want to end abortion and that has made liberal Catholics more willing to criticize their party's hard line on abortion, and conservative Catholics more open to thinking about policies that help the women most likely to seek out abortions feel empowered to choose life."

Charles Camosy of Fordham is optimistic that his many efforts at bridging ideological divides will yield results in part because of Catholics in McGuire's generation. "Common ground is there for the taking between pro-lifers and pro-choicers on paid leave, better protections for women in the workplace, and a whole host of issues that support families," he said. "What keeps us from finding it are the old 1970s binaries that tell us there are only two sides. My hope is with the Millennials and Latinos coming of age. They don't see the world in binaries. If those groups come into their own in the church and politics, we're in for a new way of thinking about things."

9

MILLENNIALS, LATINOS, AND THE FUTURE OF THE U.S. CHURCH

It's standing room only and getting hotter by the minute as more than a thousand young Catholics from Jesuit high schools and colleges pack into a hotel ballroom outside the nation's capital. "Anyone who says our generation is lazy, they're not here tonight!" a Creighton University student tells the amped-up crowd to affirming howls of approval. Students take selfies with a life-sized cardboard cutout of Pope Francis. Tables highlighting the work of Catholic Relief Services, the Catholic Mobilizing Network, Homeboy Ministries, and other social justice organizations fill the hallway. There are books about the slain Salvadoran archbishop Oscar Romero, heady conversations about structural injustice, and strategy sessions preparing for tomorrow's lobby visits on Capitol Hill. The popular Jesuit priest and writer, James Martin, who enjoys near celebrity status among young Catholic Millennials in their twenties who cheered his appearances as the "official chaplain" on the *Colbert Report*, is in the house. He can't walk more than a few feet before getting pulled in for another picture by groups of giddy students.

The annual Ignatian Family Teach-In—part organizing training, part spiritual retreat, and informal festival celebrating all things Jesuit—brings together students, professors, clergy, parish leaders, and activists for an intensive few days of what the late Jesuit Superior General Fr. Pedro Arrupe described as "a faith that does justice." This year the Teach-In is held as Catholics at Jesuit institutions around the world observe a somber anniversary. It was twenty-five years ago when members of the Salvadoran military gunned down five Jesuit priests, their housekeeper, and her daughter at the University of Central America in 1989. The Jesuit martyrs, who defied a U.S.-backed military government by educating and organizing the poor, became symbols of the perilous ministry that clergy and liberation theologians faced in El Salvador and across Latin America during a tumultuous period. "Our presence here today is an invitation to work in the spirit of the martyrs and to carry on their prophetic Gospel vision," Christopher Kerr, the executive director of the Ignatian Solidarity Network, which organizes the Teach-In, tells the gathering in his opening address.

At thirty-seven, Kerr is a coil of energy. He strides quickly through the conference with the youthful energy of students he comes to know during organizing trainings and public speaking on campuses. Growing up in a middle-class family in the Cleveland suburbs, Kerr had a conventional religious identity until his Jesuit teacher walked into class one morning and riveted the attention of a room full of jumpy ninth graders by conjuring a jarring scene. "What if you showed up at school one day and found me dead face down on the lawn?" the priest asked, provoking a discussion about the fate of the Salvadoran Jesuits killed a few years earlier. "Until then, I never really thought that my government could do anything wrong," Kerr said, referring to the role the United States played in financing and training Salvadoran military leaders that human rights organizations say were responsible for the torture and murder of tens of thousands during a twenty-three-year civil war that ended in 1992. Kerr worked in campus ministry and was active in Latin America human rights advocacy before becoming the executive director of the Ignatian Solidarity Network in 2011.

He is cautiously hopeful that the first Jesuit pope will begin to inspire bishops, Catholic educators, and clergy to give more priority to a set of issues that have not been emphasized in recent years. "Young people in Jesuit high schools and colleges were already coming to this understanding of the connection between justice and Catholic social teaching well before Francis," Kerr observes. "They were doing this through service learning, immersion experience and post-grad volunteer programs. But, sadly, they also became disenfranchised with a church beyond their campus or their community that had little interest in this passion for justice. For years, I have been asked to give presentations to high school and college students. I often start out by telling them that I'm going to talk about something that has been kept really 'top-secret' but that I'm giving them permission to share it. I just realized I might not be able to use that premise anymore. Pope Francis has brought significant awareness to the Gospel's call to encounter the reality of those who are poor and marginalized."

Lindsey Rennie was raised Catholic and attended the March for Life as a teenager, the annual anti-abortion rally that brings thousands—including busloads of high school students—to Washington every January on the anniversary of the *Roe v. Wade* decision. "What I saw was a lot of yelling and anger," the twenty-one-year-old senior at Loyola University in Maryland said during a break at the Teach-In. "I was turned off by all of it. It wasn't a movement I wanted to be a part of." Instead, she is passionate about prison reform and ending the death penalty. During her spring break, Rennie worked with other students and professors connecting ex-prisoners to resources that will help them find housing and work. White and middle class, Rennie says she has learned that along with protecting society from criminals, prisons have also become "warehouses for the poor that are rooted in racial and social injustice." When Pope Francis visited a youth prison to wash the feet of inmates during a Holy Thursday ceremony, Rennie watched the news coverage with rapt attention. She lights up when she talks about being in St. Peter's Square on Easter during a papal audience. She finds it refreshing that Pope Francis is open-minded and not afraid of discussion. Even so, the church often feels like a dry and distant institution to her. The faces in the pews are older, and she doesn't hear much about social justice from the pulpit. Rennie is also ashamed that the Catholic Church is leading the charge against same-sex marriage, a stance that, like most of her generation, she finds hard to accept. Though she may feel disillusioned, Rennie isn't ready to give up on her faith. "I feel estranged from the church," she says, "but I still pray and I'm committed to justice."

This sentiment is frequently shared by Millennials, the demographic cohort many researchers define as those between the ages of eighteen and thirty-three. A third of young adults under thirty do not have any affiliation with a religious denomination, and that number is growing.[1] Nearly seven in ten support same-sex marriage, and research has found that nearly a third of Millennials in the United States who have left the religion of their childhood did so because of what they regard as their church's negative treatment of gay, lesbian, bisexual, and transgender people.[2] At the same time, two-thirds of young people say they believe in God. More than a third identify themselves as "spiritual" but not "religious." One in five say they still pray every day. "The Millennial generation is forging a distinctive path into adulthood," according to a 2014 report from the Pew Research Center. These young Americans are "relatively unattached to organized politics and religion, linked by social media, burdened by debt . . . and optimistic about the future," the study found.[3]

This is the tricky audience that sits arrayed before Michael Lee at Fordham University in the Bronx, where he teaches theology to students who have a tenuous hold on the details of doctrine and tradition even as many carry a sincere pride in their Catholic identity. Lee is forty-seven, has a boyish face, and is a star in the field of liberation theology. He grew up in a large Puerto Rican Catholic family, went to Catholic schools from "kindergarten to PhD," and lived in a Catholic Worker community. His first book about Ignacio Ellacuría, one of the Salvadoran Jesuits killed in 1989, won a prestigious award from Princeton University. Lee acknowledges the struggle to connect with twenty-year-olds who are unmoored from Catholic institutions and rituals that shaped the dominant cultural experiences of their grandparents. "We as a church have not paved the way to help them find a real spirituality that isn't simply faddish," Lee admits. "The church doesn't need new branding but a deep spirituality for a digital age. The genius of St. Ignatius and St. Francis is they saw the old monastic model was not working, so you get this spirituality that begins to speak to people. The challenge is how do we channel what Francis is saying and doing and help young Catholics reconnect with the liturgy and other Catholic spiritual practices. They don't have these resources to fall back on."

Lee recognizes that some of the most vocal American Catholic leaders in the decades preceding the election of Pope Francis have alienated many of his students. "The most disturbing thing I see from even those who have a profound Catholic sensibility is what happens when they encounter the church as culture warrior in the media," he said. "They say if this is what it means to be Catholic, I must not be Catholic. A militant face of the church drives them away." If Pope Francis can help repair some of the damage caused by those who narrowly define Catholic identity in the context of sexual issues, Lee thinks, there may be potential to draw young Catholics into the church's rich tradition. "Faith and our Catholic tradition are about more than what's happening with your pelvis.

The pope's engaging and open persona is in many ways the opposite of the severe, closed face of the church most of them have experienced," he said.

In *Young Catholic America: Emerging Adults in, Out of, and Gone from the Church*, University of Notre Dame sociologist Christian Smith and his coauthors offer a detailed and sober portrait of Catholics leaving the faith. Informed by the National Study of Youth and Religion, the book draws on a sample of three thousand young Catholics beginning in 2002 when respondents were between thirteen and seventeen years old. The researchers followed up with them over the next decade, as they entered their late teens and early twenties. The results are discouraging, if unsurprising. Among the forty-one case studies of youth from Catholic families, the researchers found that by the third interview five years later only twelve were considered engaged with their faith. None were identified as devout—defined by the authors as consistently practicing, able to articulate church doctrine, believing most church teachings, and intending to live as Catholics in the future. Some 27 percent are "estranged" and distance themselves from the church. The glimmer of hope is that 29 percent are still defined as "engaged." These Millennials embrace a Catholic identity and "view faith as important and meaningful even if they don't believe everything that the church teaches." Smith and his coauthors found that most of the young people they followed left the church because their parents lost interest and showed little commitment to the faith. In addition, what Smith described as parishes that are "lame, uninteresting and convey nothing that feels appealing" have little ability to attract young Catholics. Finally, most who drifted away were poorly educated in the faith; as Smith explains, many "don't even understand what they are rejecting."

"KEEP IT CLOSE TO THE GOSPEL AND CLOSE TO THE GROUND"

Ray Kemp is a self-described "street priest" who grew up outside of Washington in what he called an Irish Catholic ghetto. "I got this crazy notion in my head that being a priest would be the coolest thing in the world," the seventy-four-year-old says with a sheepish grin framed by a white goatee. In the early 1960s, Kemp met Sulpician priests in Baltimore, where he was studying at the first Catholic seminary in the United States. Inspired by a Belgian priest who founded Young Christian Workers—a movement that eventually spread across Europe by bringing the radical message of the Gospels to the working class—the Sulpicians he knew were all about applying theology to the grittiness of daily life. Studying for the priesthood back then, Kemp recalls, could sometimes feel like being "locked up." As the world outside the walls of his seminary on Paca Street became charged with racial consciousness and struggles for civil rights, Kemp relished his occasional outings with activist clergy. He learned from the famed community organizer Saul Alinsky, who had Catholics at his side as he went block by block to help the poor confront absentee slumlords. He met Philip Berrigan, a Catholic priest who a few years later walked into a local draft board office with eight other Catholic clergy and activists and burned draft cards to protest what they saw as the church's silence over the Vietnam War. The "Catonsville 9" became heroes or traitors for Americans deeply divided over the fighting in the jungles of Southeast Asia. When Martin Luther King Jr. led the March on Washington in 1963, Kemp was warned by a priest at his seminary to stay away because there would be violence. He went anyway and describes the experience as "life changing." After his ordination, Kemp was assigned to St. Augustine's in Washington, considered the city's mother church for black Catholics since its founding by former slaves. A year after Kemp arrived, King was assassinated. The blocks around St. Augustine's exploded. Amid the tear gas and the fog of fear, the young priest learned practical lessons in how to be a witness to faith and justice on the street corners outside the safety of the sanctuary.

These days, Kemp shares those old stories and tries to help his students at Georgetown University make sense of contemporary racism, violence, and inequality through the lens of Catholic social teaching. For his mostly middle- and upper-class students, Kemp's "Church and the Poor" seminar is an immersion into a Catholic experience they rarely encountered growing up comfortably in suburbia. His students read Pope Francis's *The Joy of the Gospel*, meet community organizers, volunteer at the DC Central Kitchen, and hear from advocates trying to reform the criminal justice system.

"Part of it is just getting them the hell out of here," Kemp says wryly, gesturing toward a courtyard where students walk past stately buildings on a campus that is the nation's oldest Catholic and Jesuit university.

"Half of them have never been east of Rock Creek Park." If there is a theme that runs through the class, it's that the church isn't only concerned with charity. "I'm trying to teach them the biblical foundations for Hebrew and Christian justice," Kemp says. "My goal is to get them to do what the priest told L'Arche founder Jean Vanier when he was confronted with the horrible conditions of those living in asylums. Do a little something. I want them to do a little something. Volunteer with the Jesuit Volunteer Corps after graduating instead of taking a job right a way at a damn auditing firm! Keep it close to the Gospel and close to the ground."

The guest speaker today echoes that bottom-up message. Donald Kerwin ran track and studied theology here at Georgetown in the 1980s. He spent more than a decade as the executive director of the Catholic Legal Immigration Network (CLINIC). Now he runs the Center for Migration Studies in New York City. Soft-spoken and understated, Kerwin is one of the most respected and knowledgeable experts in his field. He is a policy wonk as comfortable testifying before Congress as he is in the field working with Haitian refugees. "The pope has warned about useless structures that are out of touch with real people," Kerwin tells Kemp's class of two dozen students. "We've been waiting to hear those kind of blunt words from the Vatican for a long time. I have nothing against high policy discussions, and I see Georgetown graduates at the United Nations and in Congress. But we need more of you in community organizing and direct service. We need you to get your hands dirty." Kerwin praises the movement built by young Dreamers, immigrants brought to the United States as children. He tells heartbreaking stories of migrants who have been deported and those who still live under what he vividly calls the "guillotine of family separation." The U.S. response to young migrants fleeing gang violence in Honduras, he laments, is "to build more detention centers." Kerwin quotes the pope, who just days after his election traveled to an island off the coast of Italy where thousands of migrants have died at sea trying to cross into Europe from northern Africa. At Lampedusa, the pope decried a "globalization of indifference." "We look upon the brother half dead by the roadside, perhaps we think 'poor guy,' and we continue on our way, it's none of our business," the pope said. Kerwin raises the parallel of migrants dying on the U.S.-Mexico border. "We can't be indifferent," Kerwin insists, "when the stakes are so high."

After class, Julia Hubbell calls Pope Francis "refreshing and energizing." The senior from Los Angeles even has a poster of the pope in her dorm room with a quote from *The Joy of the Gospel*: "Just as the commandment 'Thou shalt not kill' sets a clear limit in order to safeguard the value of human life, today we also have to say 'thou shalt not' to an economy of exclusion and inequality. Such an economy kills." She doesn't hear that kind of message enough from American Catholic leaders. "I would love to see more bishops who sound like Pope Francis," she said. "It always seems to be about abortion or gay marriage. It's one thing for the church to be countercultural and hold out a very beautiful idea about love, but you can be so countercultural at times it feels actively hostile to people who have different views." She has plenty of friends who are no longer Catholic. Hubbell understands why they have left, but she is sticking around, especially with a pope who is emphasizing a broad social justice vision. "The Catholic Church gives me a structure for my relationship with God, and Catholicism has 2,000 years of good things to say about human dignity and community."

Fr. Kemp worries many churches are not well positioned to take advantage of the newfound excitement Pope Francis is generating for his students. "We don't have enough priests who are ready for all of this. What I'm looking for is parishes that care enough about what the pope is talking about to build it into their structures," he said. "Francis wants every faith community to take solidarity seriously and get people physically involved with outreach to people on the margins. It's the structural work that in many ways we never got done after Vatican II." But Kemp sees hope in the interest many Millennials have in service, Ignatian spirituality, and organizing. "If we're totally dependent only on those who are ordained, we will be in real trouble," he says.

Robert Christian would offer a hearty amen to that assessment. The thirty-two-year-old doctoral student in politics at the Catholic University of America in Washington, who easily quotes papal encyclicals and is well read in church history, sees faith as the animating force in his life. Christian and his wife baptized their two young children with lofty ambitions. "Our number one goal as parents is to raise saints—not in the sense of sinless, otherworldly types, but people who live lives animated by love and who use their gifts to serve God and others, and seek communion," he says. "This is what the Catholic faith is all about to me—a quest for communion." Even with his strong Catholic identity, he has no trouble understanding why so many in his generation end up tuning out church leaders. "Many Millennials have been exposed to a lukewarm, bourgeois form of Christianity that really has little to offer," he said. "Their parishes had dull homilies that ignored the radicalism of Christ, boring music sung by people who sounded like they were in pain just having to sit through Mass, and an overall approach that separated religion from everyday life." Christian was raised Catholic, but after his parents divorced and stopped going to Mass he found himself grappling with hard theological questions at a secular university. He read voraciously, explored his faith tradition, and came to experience a deep spirituality in the Eucharist. In 2008, he joined about a million young Catholics at World Youth Day in Sydney, Australia, an experience that he remembers as both peaceful and energizing.

In 2010, Christian met up with friends at a restaurant in Washington to come up with a plan for responding to what they saw as a persistent problem in the church. The voices of Millennial Catholics were missing in public discussions about Catholicism. Someone in the group couldn't believe that a CNN special about Millennial Catholics featured mainly middle-age analysts. "The young people we did see in the press were often left wing or right wing, embracing either a social or economic libertarianism that we didn't really see as compatible with our under-standing of Catholicism and faithful citizenship," Christian said. "We wanted young Catholics who were pro-life progressives and social justice conservatives. We wanted to focus on faith in action and look outward, rather than get caught up in inside baseball and replaying the same old debates." A new online Catholic periodical, *Millennial*, which Christian edits with his wife, Sarah, grew out of that meeting. The online forum includes an eclectic mix of heady analysis from young theologians, personal essays from college students, reflections from clergy, and sharp commentary about the intersection of religion and politics. Not only are *Millennial* and its writers preaching to the Catholic choir, but they have also been featured in *Time*, *CNN*, the *Washington Post*, and *USA Today*. When Pope Francis was elected, the blog had more than fifty thousand hits that month alone, and their followers on social media continue to grow. When the *Boston Globe* hosted a panel discussion with church heavyweights in 2014 to celebrate the launch of *Crux*, the newspaper's publication covering Catholic issues, Christian was seated on the dais alongside Cardinal Sean O'Malley, one of the pope's key advisers in reforming the Vatican.

Every day, it seems, the pope offers an intriguing morning homily, a challenging speech, or an eye-popping quote that gives the publication a steady stream of material that not only drives traffic to the site but also serves as a source of spiritual wisdom for editors and readers. "Millennials really value authenticity and this is a pope who keeps it real," Christian says. "Everyone can see him live out the principles that he preaches. In terms of his message, I think young people like how radical it is. He is not saying 'be a little nicer and go to Church once a week and it's all good.' He has said, 'to live the faith is not to decorate life with a little religion, like a cake is decorated with a little frosting.' He's saying you've got to go all in. Young people like that passion and idealism. And they see him as warm and welcoming. They don't see him as a judgmental scold, but a man of love whom they respect even if they disagree with him on a political issue or two." Christian thinks American church leaders would be wise to pick up some pointers from Francis. "Speak to our everyday lives and connect," he says. "The pope's big themes and daily homilies are relevant to young people. Bishops and other leaders can do the same thing. Call young people to live extraordinary lives not just to follow a drab set of rules for reasons they don't really understand. Pope Francis is harnessing our idealism. Don't just talk at young people. Let them join the conversation."

If Catholic leaders are going to succeed in persuading Millennials that they have something compelling to offer, it will require making the case to Latinos who are increasingly the face of the church. Millennials between the ages of eighteen and thirty-three are the most racially and ethnically diverse generation in American history.[4] Some 34 percent of Catholics today are Latino, but more than half of Catholic Millennials born in 1982 or later are Latino.[5] In contrast, most Catholic clergy are white. About 6 percent of all Masses in the United States are celebrated in Spanish.[6] Of the 272 active bishops, only 29 are Latino.[7] Latinos will be a majority of U.S. Catholics in the coming decades. These changes, which present opportunities and myriad challenges for an institution often slow to adapt, will unfold as the first papacy grounded in the experience of Latin America takes shape.

Two major reports released within days of each other in the spring of 2014 should serve as a wakeup call for anyone tempted to believe that immigration trends alone will be enough to keep pews filled and parishes vibrant. Nearly a quarter of Hispanics in the United States are now former Catholics, according to the Pew Research Center. In 2013, the study found, 55 percent of U.S. Hispanics identified as Catholics, a swift decline from the 67 percent who did just three years earlier. Another recent report from the School of Theology and Ministry at Boston College provides the first comprehensive survey of Hispanic ministry in Catholic parishes. Results from that three-year study, produced in collaboration with the Center for Applied Research in the Apostolate at Georgetown University, paint a picture of a church that is struggling to keep pace with changing demographics. Indeed, the future strength of the Catholic Church in the United States will depend in part on whether parishes can do a better job keeping young Hispanics who are far less tethered to Catholic institutions than their parents and grandparents. The vast majority of Hispanic Catholic Millennials were born in the United States and are shaped by the secular cultural experiences that have left many Americans in their twenties and thirties increasingly disaffected from any religious denomination.

"We are at risk of losing a generation of Catholics," said Hosffman Ospino, a Boston College theologian who authored the report. Ospino immigrated to the United States in 1997 from Colombia, where he grew up with the missionary, in-the-street style of Catholicism that shapes Pope Francis. He laughs recalling one bishop who would sit on the stairs in front of his church so he could talk to people. It's this closeness and emphasis on *el pueblo de dios*, he said, that most young Hispanics don't experience from the church today. While dioceses have traditionally focused on Hispanics who came to the United States as immigrants, Ospino says the urgent challenge today is with second-generation Latinos born here. "Many of them live in a cultural or pastoral limbo. In many ways they are waiting for the church. But they are not going to wait long. We need to invest with this population and walk with them."

When Ricardo Veloz left Monterrey, Mexico, two decades ago and traveled to *El Norte* looking for work in the United States, he carried the same fears and hopes as most immigrants. He did landscaping, then construction, and tried to learn English when he wasn't exhausted from long hours. A Catholic church in Charlotte became a source of support, and his pastor asked him to help out with Hispanic youth in the parish. Veloz found he could connect with young people, organized several retreats, and started honing his skills by taking classes at the Southeast Pastoral Institute, which offers training to Hispanic ministry leaders in over two dozen Catholic dioceses in the region. Veloz is now the diocesan coordinator for Hispanic youth and *Pastoral Juvenil* in the Diocese of Raleigh. Hosffman Ospino of Boston College calls it a national model. When Veloz arrived in Raleigh in 2009, few Hispanics were showing up for diocesan youth events and retreats. Bishop Michael Burbidge wanted that to change and asked Veloz what was happening. Many of the Hispanic youth couldn't afford the weekend retreats, others were intimidated by language barriers, and most felt uncomfortable outside of their own small parish groups. Veloz and other diocesan leaders knew business as usual wasn't getting the job done.

"We worked really hard to create a bridge between the different cultures and start a process of integration," he said. This included training bilingual advisers who work closely with youth and young adults to better understand their family life, interests, and challenges. It meant putting structures in place to help them take on leadership roles in their parishes and on diocesan committees. Hispanic ministry is thriving in Raleigh, in large part because it's not treated as an addendum but as integral to diocesan life. As part of *Pastoral Juvenil*, bilingual advisers and Hispanic youth leaders meet every two months with diocesan staff setting a strategic direction around core areas: religious formation, spirituality, integration, communication, and apostolate (service). In the past five years, Veloz says, the number of Hispanic youth involved with diocesan activities has increased significantly. In 2010 when the diocese hosted a youth convention, a little more than two dozen Hispanics attended. More than three hundred young adults turned out for the convention in 2014.

The successful turnaround of Hispanic ministry in Raleigh is playing out against the backdrop of a larger demographic story that is reshaping the contours of the region and the Catholic Church. From 2000 to 2010, the percent of Hispanic immigrants in North Carolina nearly doubled.[8] The Catholic population in North Carolina and Georgia has increased at a time when dioceses in Ohio and Pennsylvania are closing parishes and schools. Fueled by immigrants from Europe, Rust Belt cities in the Midwest and urban centers in the Northeast were once the engines that fired Catholicism in the United States. It's now immigration from Latin America that is driving Catholic growth in places like Georgia, Texas, and Colorado.

In "The Changing Face of U.S. Catholic Parishes," the Center for Applied Research in the Apostolate details how these "dramatic demographic changes and evolving patterns of immigration" are forcing church leaders to respond to a new reality. Forty percent of all growth in registered parishioners in U.S. parishes from 2005 to 2010, the study found, came from Hispanic immigration. In Raleigh, Ricardo Veloz said the challenge now is how to move beyond expanding infrastructure to accommodate the influx of new immigrants in the church to making sure Hispanic youth who were born here see Catholic parishes as a welcoming home. "We have the buildings now, but if we don't reach these youth, who is going to be in these buildings in the future?" Veloz draws energy from a pope he says is connecting with young Catholics and so many other faithful. "They recognize he is calling them to do big things," Veloz said. "He is touching our hearts and giving us a new direction by inviting us to return to the basics and accompany people."

Indeed, Catholic leaders in the United States now have a road map from the top that shows the most effective way back to public relevance and spiritual renewal will be in prioritizing a faith that begins from below. "The Gospel of the marginalized is where our credibility is at stake, where it is found and where it is revealed," Pope Francis told hundreds of cardinals and bishops during a Mass at St. Peter's Basilica a day after naming twenty new cardinals from Myanmar, Cape Verde, Tonga, and other countries not typically viewed as prominent enough for membership in the world's most exclusive ecclesiastical club. "The way of the church is precisely to leave her four walls behind and to go out in search of those who are distant, those on the outskirts of life."

A CHURCH IN THE STREETS: BRINGING THE GOSPEL TO COMMUNITY ORGANIZING

Across the river from downtown Philadelphia's glittering skyline and familiar tourist attractions, a proud American city has been slowly dying for decades. The industrial muscle of Camden, New Jersey, once built hulking battleships used in World War II. Campbell Soup opened its first factory here. The Victor Talking Machine Company, later RCA Victor, cranked out phonographs. When Neil Armstrong landed on the moon and sent a message back to earth, he used a radio built in Camden. "In a dream I saw a city invincible," reads a verse from onetime resident Walt Whitman etched in marble at Camden's City Hall. These days much of Camden is a bleak landscape of abandoned houses and dreams deferred. One of the poorest and most violent cities in America, Philadelphia's forgotten neighbor is a case study in postindustrial decline and urban dysfunction. Whatever more well-connected and affluent places fight to keep out—sewer plants, scrap metal yards, jails—all find their way to Camden. When Pope Francis asks for a bruised and dirty church that is in the streets, he need look no further than a network of congregations here that take the Gospel seriously enough not to leave it in the sanctuary on Sunday morning.

On a frigid weekday in January, the heat doesn't seem to be working inside a drab community resource center a few miles from downtown Camden. A man recently released from prison slumps down with a tired face in front of James Rodriguez. A former meatpacker, the parishioner at St. Bartholomew has a muscular build, a gravely voice, and a fist bump ready for anyone he meets. "We're doing listening sessions and trying to find out the barriers that are holding people back," Rodriguez tells the man, who responds in barely a whisper: "I need a job. I need to eat. I have medical issues, asthma, a bad heart. I need medicine." Rodriguez slides a form over to him that will start the process of enrolling the former prisoner in Medicaid. "This is a positive way of moving forward and getting straight," Rodriguez tells him as another client steps to the table. Camden Churches Organized for People (CCOP)—a network of thirteen churches that work on issues of health care access, racial justice, and economic opportunity—started this "Welcome Center" for the previously incarcerated. The goal is to help the ex-prisoners find health care, mental health treatment, and jobs.

As part of this effort, Camden churches also led a "ban the box" campaign to prohibit businesses from conducting criminal background checks at the beginning of an application process. Those exiting prison frequently have trouble finding work because these restrictions on job applications prevent them from even getting an interview. A cycle of unemployment and criminal behavior is reinforced. CCOP, which has been leading faith-based activism here for three decades, is also pushing city officials and businesses to pay residents living wages as part of an "economic dignity" campaign and advocating for better health care so the working poor don't have to rely on emergency room visits. This Camden coalition that trains church members and clergy to do community organizing by putting Gospel values at the service of social change is a local affiliate of PICO National Network, which includes faith-based community organizations in 150 cities and 17 states. Founded by the Jesuit priest John Baumann in 1972, PICO is funded in part by the U.S. Catholic bishops' national anti-poverty initiative, the Catholic Campaign for Human Development.

If anyone understands the plight of those lined up before him at the "Welcome Center," it's the forty-three-year-old Rodriguez, who served jail time for drunk driving during a dark period when he wrestled with the demons of drug and alcohol addiction. He is counting the days until the ankle bracelet that monitors his movements is removed. Rodriguez grew up in a Catholic family, but by the age of twelve he was spending more time on the corner than in church. After years of addiction, prison, and a creeping despair in his soul, Rodriguez vowed to find a new road. He showed up at a Catholic church one day to start over. Rodriguez found a parish that, even as it lifted him up, asked something from him. Rodriguez sees his time spent helping ex-cons turn their life around not only as part of his own spiritual journey but also as a way of building a church that Pope Francis hopes will be what he calls a "field hospital after battle." Rodriguez finds his wounds bandaged by his parish and is now seeking out other casualties. "You have to know what people's struggles are to help them and you have to listen to their reality," he said. "I want the church to be out there on the corner. We have to bridge the gap between the church and the people."

At Rodriguez's church, Fr. Gerard Marable looks out the window of his rectory. A factory building across the street has stood abandoned for years, a quiet sentinel with gaping holes and scraggly weeds. The view is reminiscent of those old World War II photographs of bombed European cities reduced to rubble. A piece of art on Marable's wall depicts a black Jesus, bleeding and suffering, carrying his cross through the modern-day landscape of Camden. A onetime taxi driver from Atlantic City—"a great education for the priesthood," he quips—Marable is both grateful for Pope Francis and often bemused by those who seem dumbfounded that a pope is acting like Jesus would. "There was all this hoopla when he went to prison and washed those inmates' feet," Marable says with a chuckle as he prepares for a weekday Mass. "Some of us have been doing things like that for years! There is a certain validation." Something of a troublemaker

who once got kicked out of seminary for his Afro-centric garb and assertive racial identity—"I was too black for them," he deadpans—Marable
appreciates a pope who he views as disturbing consciences and forcing
the church to grapple more critically with social inequality.

"Charity is one thing but justice is different, and most people don't
want to change those structures that benefit their privilege," he says.
"Well, Francis is saying some of our structures mitigate against the Gospel. The question is, do you feel empowered by that or do you feel
threatened? In my experience, the energy behind Pope Francis is in the
grassroots. It's some bishops and priests who are uncomfortable. They
don't want to be out on the street. I was talking to a newly ordained
young priest, a nice guy. He is just confused. He's telling me that he spent
his whole formation in seminary thinking and going one way, and now
this pope is putting an emphasis on a whole different set of things."
Marable wants American Catholic leaders to catch up with the pope. "He
is creating an atmosphere in this country to talk about race, wealth and
capitalism. It's an opening at the highest level of the church. During
elections you see the bishops send out these helpful hints about voting.
But where is the church speaking out when it comes to the fruits of
racism? What about mass incarceration, white privilege, predatory capitalism? How about these as life issues? Sometimes it feels like poverty is
an afterthought."

Bishop Oscar Cantú of Las Cruces doesn't need convincing that Catholic leaders can do a better job of putting the "preferential option for the
poor" back at the forefront of the church's public commitments. "What
the pope is saying is not a new message, but there is a different emphasis," Cantú said a few days after returning from Iraq as the head of the
U.S. bishops' international justice and peace committee. "For the past
three decades after *Roe v. Wade*, a lot of the moral emphasis was understandably on the abortion debate. At the same time, the Gospel reminds
us to defend the poor and the marginalized," he said. "Pope Francis has
not shelved our commitment to the unborn, but he is highlighting that we
have become blind to and accepting of poverty and economic injustice.
We have grown callous. How do we change things that have calcified and
are built into political, economic and social structures? The pope is raising a strong voice." The forty-eight-year-old Cantú, who is the second
youngest bishop in the country, grew up straddling two worlds in what he
called the "shadow of the barrio" in inner-city Houston. As a student at a

Catholic prep school where most of his classmates were white and privi-
leged, Cantú knew what it felt like to be an outsider. "I understand the
bite of the immigrant experience," he says. His background fueled his
desire to become a priest who stands with those who lack power. Cantú
wants bishops and other Catholics to do more to strengthen faith-based
community organizing, which he sees as putting the Gospel into action.
This involves taking risks and engaging with an imperfect world. "The
Incarnation was messy," he says. "There was nothing clean about a stable
in Bethlehem 2,000 years ago. We sterilize that stable and lose the mystery of the Incarnation. We have to get our hands dirty." As discussed in
an earlier chapter, opposition to the church's involvement in organizing
has grown in recent years as a small but vocal network of pro-life groups
have pressured bishops to defund anti-poverty coalitions critics charge
with causing "scandal" by associating with groups that don't agree with
church teaching on every issue. "What about the scandal of not caring for
the poor?" Cantú asks. "That's the real scandal. Jesus ate with sinners and
went out to find the poor and the impure. When we have this fear of
associating with others, it's a fear of being contaminated, and that lets us
be bullied."

When a New Mexico anti-abortion group took out an advertisement in
the local Las Cruces newspaper attacking an interfaith organization for
allegedly using church funds to organize "pro-abortion rallies," Cantú
immediately responded. He rejected the claims that the interfaith organizing group funded by the U.S. bishops' anti-poverty campaign was taking
a stand on abortion and offered a stern rebuke to the Catholic pro-life
activists. "As your bishop, I do not take lightly to the efforts of anyone
driving a wedge between my flock and me, as this ad attempts to do," he
wrote in an op-ed. "I will not be bullied into compromising the legitimate
work of social justice of the church or allowing someone to lead the flock
astray." His vocal defense of faith-based organizing is inextricably tied to
a vision for a church that isn't confined to patrolling doctrinal borders.
Cantú understands that if Catholic clergy only wag a scolding finger and
withdraw behind walls of narrow religious legalism, the future for the
church is not bright. "Our own Catholics are tuning us out," Cantú acknowledges. "The world is watching us go into a museum mode where
we look out from a glass case. But that's not the Gospel and that's not our
church."

A sociologist of religion who has consulted with the U.S. bishops' anti-poverty campaign, Richard Wood sees the pope as that rare leader connecting with people unfulfilled by a materialistic culture, jaded by the cynicism of politics, and suspicious of institutions. "Francis embodies a church that is authentic to itself and our best tradition," says Wood, the author of *A Shared Future: Faith-Based Organizing for Racial Equity and Ethical Democracy*. "His vision is orthodox Christianity. It's the spirit of Jesus incarnate in the world in all its richness, rather than a church that seems to talk constantly about moral failings. Our political culture needs the joy that Francis embodies. The grimness of so much of our politics today on the left and right just doesn't pull people in. Francis offers something different: a public witness infused with spiritual joy." He cautions that if Catholic bishops and laity don't build off this unique papacy, entrenched habits will resurface to sap momentum for reform and renewal.

> The most important thing about Francis is how he is working to break open the church to new energies and gospel insight from the base of the church and the margins of society. He is reinvigorating powerful symbols that are deep in the Catholic tradition: the washing of feet, the embrace of the sick, a servant church incarnate in the real world. His joy in doing that revivifies a church that my students and my own kids had experienced as constantly lecturing them. Lots of young people had no ears to hear the church any more. They want and need moral insight from the tradition, but they need to hear that within the context of good news. The great temptation of this moment is to take Francis and accept him as the last great hope while we remain embedded in a one-dimensional hierarchical Catholicism. In that kind of Catholicism, all initiative and spiritual energy comes from above, and the laity is dependent on the hierarchy. That's not good for anybody, and not good for the church. What we do with Francis is at least as important as what Francis does.

In many ways, the church Pope Francis is calling for doesn't have to be invented from scratch but rediscovered and reemphasized. It can already be found in the work of faith-based organizing funded by bishops, Catholic Charities USA, Catholic Relief Services, Maryknoll lay missioners, and the contributions of women religious who literally helped build the church in the United States. The clergy abuse scandals and culture war battles that largely fixated on sexual morality in recent decades have prevented the church from accentuating the best public face of Catholicism. Catholic bishops should not be expected to be silent about contraception, marriage, and abortion. The church has both a right and an obligation to address these issues, especially as they impact the ministries of Catholic institutions. Our pluralistic public square would be weaker for the absence of the church's voice on matters of human life and family.

At the same time, a hierarchy that has failed to even persuade many of its own faithful in the pews on issues related to sex and marriage should enter public debates with greater humility and prudence. Winning hearts and minds has as much to do with listening as talking. During this unexpected period of renaissance for the church, bishops would be foolish not to embrace Pope Francis's call for a "new balance" that reorients Catholic identity and institutional priorities. Catholic institutions and movements that heal wounds and seek justice here and around the world inspire and attract. The Catholic social justice tradition must no longer be the church's "best kept secret," but rather the lead story bishops and lay faithful tell with renewed vigor.

Faith-based organizing could offer a particularly effective way for Catholic leaders to both reclaim a credible public voice and renew Catholic spirituality. "We gave good data that faith-based organizing done right can really impact parishes in meaningful ways," Wood says. "It can't be just a few lefty Catholics doing it on the margins; it has to be brought into the heart of the parish. You need clergy helping lay people interpret their experience so when they go advocate before the City Council they are thinking about that in light of Scripture and Catholic social teaching. This is traditional Catholic spirituality that incarnates the faith in the world. It's radically progressive and also deeply traditional in the best sense of both those things. When it's really rooted in the Gospel and the preached word and the music of the liturgy young people get the freshness and that's compelling."

Along with the potential for reviving parish life, research shows Catholics involved with faith-based organizing are more likely to cross racial and class lines than most Americans. These multiracial coalitions, essential to achieving public policy wins, will be increasingly important in the future, as the United States is expected to become a "majority minority" country by midcentury. Even with these religious and civic benefits, research shows that participation in faith-based organizing by Catholic parishes has decreased by nearly a fifth over the last decade. Especially hard hit were Hispanic parishes, which made up 20 percent of all organizing congregations in 1999 but only 6.5 percent of those joining between that year and 2011. "Might not the church in the United States benefit from directing more of its attention to its involvement in faith-based organizing—especially in light of the church's eroded position in American public life?" Wood asked in *Commonweal* magazine along with coauthors Brad Fulton, the lead researcher for the 2011 State of Organizing Study, and Christine Doby, a former diocesan social action director who is a program officer at the Charles Stewart Mott Foundation. At a time when Pope Francis is rallying the church to rediscover its ancient missionary spirit and wade into a messy world shattered by violence, savage inequalities, and environmental degradation, the answer to that timely question seems clear.

Sister Mary Scullion has a thick Philly accent, an infectious laugh, and a knack for raising millions of dollars to support Project HOME, a national model for homeless services and prevention she cofounded sixteen years ago. Named one of *Time* magazine's most influential people in 2009, Scullion is used to rubbing elbows with politicians and counts among her friends the rocker Jon Bon Jovi. When Scullion first started volunteering in the late 1970s at a women's shelter run by her religious order, the Sisters of Mercy, she could barely walk a block in this city without stumbling onto someone in need of shelter and food. State and local budgets were paltry compared to the scope of the crisis. Politicians rarely wanted to talk about a distressed population that didn't vote and whose myriad problems—addiction, mental illness, and dismal education—raised systemic challenges that defied even the most silver-tongued sound bite. The problems are still acute. Philadelphia has a poverty rate of 26 percent, the highest among the ten largest cities nationwide. But in large part because of Scullion, the homeless population has declined significantly. Elected officials line up to visit with her.

What started as a threadbare shelter is now a state-of-the art complex with seven hundred units of housing, a comprehensive health care center, and a workforce development program. The project is praised as one of the most effective homeless prevention initiatives in the country. Scullion and her team recently received a $30 million gift from a private donor.

"How can it be that it is not a news item when an elderly homeless person dies of exposure, but it is news when the stock market loses two points?" Pope Francis has asked. It's the kind of uncomfortable question that pricks the conscience and exposes skewed priorities. Scullion is beyond thrilled with a pope who is putting those on the margins at the center of his papacy. She also still finds herself amazed at the new tone and winds of change blowing from the Vatican. "This pope is opening the door for everyone to be part of the church," Scullion says. "It hasn't always felt like this. There have been times when I felt like an outsider in the church, and I'm a sister! He has made me feel at home again. The pope wants a big tent. It's not just about rules and regulations for him. He understands the fundamental dignity of people."

Vatican investigations of women religious, the silencing of theologians, and the mistrust that grew between some advocates and the hierarchy, she says, all left a cloud of suspicion hovering over those on the front lines of Catholic peace and justice efforts. "There was a lot of time and effort spent by the institutional church drawing lines. I didn't see many hands reaching across the aisle or a feeling of 'let's work together.' It was more like 'here's the rule book.' Even when it came to the poor, most of our support was from women religious and other people of faith. Church leaders usually weren't at the table. I think the church lost its way." Scullion still talks about the heady days in the years after the Second Vatican Council when she attended the International Eucharistic Congress in 1976. She was a college student at St. Joseph's in Philadelphia. Dorothy Day, the legendary Jesuit priest Pedro Arrupe, Mother Teresa, and the Brazilian bishop and liberation theologian Dom Hélder Câmera all came to the city for the event. "It was amazing. I had a chance to meet them all. I was on fire for the church and social justice," she says. Scullion still gets chills when she recalls the words of Pedro Arrupe: "If there is hunger anywhere in the world, then our celebration of the Eucharist is somehow incomplete everywhere in the world." A few decades later, Scullion founded Project HOME with a motto that sent a similar message: "None of us are home until all of us are home."

A papal visit is a blur of ceremonial pomp that is over before you blink. The streetwise Sister of Mercy knows photo-ops and speeches fade quickly. But Scullion also knows Pope Francis has proven he can break through to reach people in surprising and stirring ways. She is determined to take advantage of his presence to get politicians from both parties to visit her center and will be asking national leaders to sign on to a statement declaring their commitment to addressing inequality by supporting policies like living wages for workers. "I want them to come here and stand in line with the homeless," Scullion says. "It's important to leverage this visit so we're building momentum not just for service and charity but for social change."

A few hours south on Interstate 95, Ray East sips a strong cup of Salvadoran coffee inside a church rectory just down the hill from the house where abolitionist Frederick Douglass once lived. St. Teresa of Avila Catholic Church is a sturdy anchor in a long-troubled neighborhood in Washington that sits across the Anacostia River, an unofficial dividing line of race, class, and power in the nation's capital. In the late 1980s and early 1990s, the potent double punch of crack and AIDS brought this area to its knees. The church became a refuge. "We were the most violent precinct in the country for a while," says East, the grandson of Baptist missionaries who lived near the ancestral home of Nelson Mandela. "It was funeral city around here. We buried people every week." Anacostia is slowly improving as waterfront development near the city's major league baseball stadium moves closer and young professionals snatch up rehabbed homes and trendy condominiums not far from abandoned buildings. Even with the stirrings of gentrification, East pastors a church surrounded by extreme poverty, double-digit unemployment, and high schools with scandalously low graduation rates. The income gap in the District of Columbia is one of the highest in the nation.

East thinks Pope Francis would probably feel at home at his parish, where on Sunday a gospel choir and African traditions infuse the traditional Catholic liturgy with a charismatic style. "His idea of a church going to the margins is a great template for how we think about our ministry," says East, who grew up steeped in the social Gospel at a Jesuit parish in San Diego that offered sanctuary to sailors who refused to serve in Vietnam and where clergy were active in the farmworker movement. He remembers that church of his childhood, Christ the King, had a huge statue of Jesus. The hands broke off. They were never replaced, a reminder of St. Teresa of Avila's prayer that we must become Christ's hands and feet in this world. "We're always asking ourselves are we going to the edges and the peripheries? Around here that means right outside our door. Are we being prophetic? If we went out of business, would anyone miss us?" The parish runs a literacy program in the rectory basement where dropouts can earn a high school diploma. When a local nonprofit that specializes in conflict resolution and getting feuding gangs to call a truce couldn't find a space for a meeting with adjudicated youth in foster care, East opened the doors of St. Teresa's. He recently met an organizer at Barry Farms, a public housing complex on grounds that once served as the rural home to freed slaves. The organizer told him that clergy "preach a big game" but never come around the project.

"There needs to be more church in the street and more street in the church," East says as he steers his Volkswagen with tape on the dashboard and 170,000 miles on the odometer through Anacostia. "Instead of putting up the walls of the fort and building our moats deeper, the pope is telling us to drop down our drawbridge and walk out into the world. He's showing us how to do it." East turns onto the highway and heads downtown. The Nationals' baseball stadium sits empty over the frozen river. The dome of the U.S. Capitol, under construction, looms in the distance. "People are giving the Catholic Church a second look," the priest says in what almost sounds like a prayer. "This is a golden opportunity. Heaven help us if we miss it."

NOTES

I. THE FRANCIS REVOLUTION BEGINS

1. "No More Nice Words: The Resignation Is a Catastrophe," "Benedict XVI: Why Have You Abandoned Us?" *Rorate Caeli*, accessed April 28, 2015, http://rorate-caeli.blogspot.com/2013/02/no-more-nice-words-resignation-is.html.

2. "Audience to Representatives of the Communications Media: Address of the Holy Father Pope Francis, 16 March 2013," Vatican website, accessed April 28, 2015, https://w2.vatican.va/content/francesco/en/speeches/2013/march/documents/papa-francesco_20130316_rappresentanti-media.html.

3. Joel Connelly, "Pope Francis: I Need to Live Among People," Seattle-pi.com, June 10, 2013, http://blog.seattlepi.com/seattlepolitics/2013/06/10/pope-francis-i-need-to-live-among-people.

4. Cindy Wooden, "Pope Joins Homeless People for Private Tour of Sistine Chapel," Catholic News Service, March 27, 2015, http://www.catholicnews.com/data/stories/cns/1501338.htm.

5. Paul Vallely, *Pope Francis: Untying the Knots* (London: Bloomsbury Academic, 2013).

6. Antonio Spadaro, SJ, "A Big Heart Open to God," *America: The National Catholic Review*, September 30, 2013, http://americamagazine.org/pope-interview.

7. Spadaro, "A Big Heart Open to God."

8. Joseph A. Komonchak, "A Smaller but Purer Church?" *Commonweal*, October 21, 2010, https://www.commonwealmagazine.org/blog/smaller-purer-church.

9. Spadaro, "A Big Heart Open to God."

10. Thomas Reese, "The Hidden Exodus: Catholics Becoming Protestants," *National Catholic Reporter*, April 18, 2011, http://ncronline.org/news/faith-parish/hidden-exodus-catholics-becoming-protestants.

11. Spadaro, "A Big Heart Open to God."

12. Thomas Reese, "Pope Francis Wants Pastors as Bishops," *National Catholic Reporter*, June 21, 2013, http://ncronline.org/blogs/ncr-today/pope-francis-wants-pastors-bishops.

13. John Thavis, "A Pope Who Likes to Shake Things Up," JohnThavis.com, posted July 28, 2013, http://www.johnthavis.com/a-pope-who-likes-to-shake-things-up.

14. Robert W. McElroy, "A Church for the Poor," *America*, October 21, 2013, http://americamagazine.org/church-poor.

15. Gerard O'Connel, "Can the Catholic Church in the USA Be a 'Church for the Poor'?" *Vatican Insider*, October 24, 2013, http://vaticaninsider.lastampa.it/en/the-vatican/detail/articolo/church-chiesa-iglesia-mcelroy-28939/.

16. Rick Snizek, "Pope Francis: The First Six Months—Bishop Tobin Reflects on Pontiff's Impact," *Rhode Island Catholic*, September 12, 2013, http://www.thericatholic.com/news/detail.html?sub_id=6041.

17. Joan Frawley Desmond, "Bishop Thomas Tobin: Why I Switched to the Republican Party," *National Catholic Register*, August 22, 2013, http://www.ncregister.com/daily-news/bishop-thomas-tobin-why-i-switched-to-the-republican-party/.

18. Bishop Thomas John Paprocki, "Homily for Prayers of Supplication and Exorcism in Reparation for the Sin of Same-Sex Marriage," November 20, 2013, Diocesan Blog, Diocese of Springfield in Illinois, http://www.dio.org/blog/item/350-bishop-paprocki-s-homily-for-prayers-of-supplication-and-exorcism-in-reparation-for-the-sin-of-same-sex-marriage.html.

19. Mark Mueller, "Newark Archbishop's Pricey Retirement Home Spurs Backlash as Parishioners Withhold Donations," NJ.com, March 2, 2014, http://www.nj.com/news/index.ssf/2014/03/archbishops_pricey_retirement_home_spurs_backlash_as_parishioners_withhold_donations.html.

20. Nicholas G. Hahn III, "The Miracle of Madtown," Real Clear Religion, December 30, 2013, http://www.realclearreligion.org/articles/2013/12/30/the_miracle_of_madtown.html.

21. Doug Erickson, "Bishop Robert Morlino: Pope Francis Has Made Me a Stronger Culture Warrior," *Wisconsin State Journal*, March 10, 2014, http://host.madison.com/news/local/bishop-robert-morlino-pope-francis-has-made-me-a-stronger/article_a7e5def6-33d1-5b57-ab29-1f300cd6347b.html.

22. Charles J. Chaput, "Little Murders," *Public Discourse*, Witherspoon Institute, October 18, 2008, http://www.thepublicdiscourse.com/2008/10/127/.

23. Thomas C. Fox, "Boulder Pastor Says Jesus Turned Some Away," *National Catholic Reporter*, March 17, 2010, http://ncronline.org/news/faith-parish/boulder-pastor-says-jesus-turned-some-away; "Archdiocese Defends Decision to Deny Children Because of Lesbian Parents," CNN.com, March 10, 2010, http://www.cnn.com/2010/US/03/10/colorado.lesbians.church/.

24. John L. Allen Jr., "Right Wing 'Generally Not Happy' with Francis, Chaput Says," *National Catholic Reporter*, July 23, 2013, http://ncronline.org/blogs/ncr-today/right-wing-generally-not-happy-francis-chaput-says.

25. R. R. Reno, "Francis, Our Jesuit Pope," *First Things*, September 23, 2013, http://www.firstthings.com/web-exclusives/2013/09/francis-our-jesuit-pope.

26. Michael Sean Winters, "Germaine Grisez on Pope Francis," *National Catholic Reporter*, October 1, 2013, http://ncronline.org/blogs/distinctly-catholic/germaine-grisez-pope-francis.

27. Patrick Archbold, "There Is Something Very Un-Catholic About This," *Rorate Caeli*, March 17, 2013, http://rorate-caeli.blogspot.com/2013/03/there-is-something-very-un-catholic.html.

28. John Thavis, "Jesuit Officials Say *America* Editor Resigned After Vatican Complaints," Catholic News Service, May 9, 2005, http://www.catholicnews.com/data/stories/cns/0502817.htm.

29. Spadaro, "A Big Heart Open to God."

30. John Moody, "Pope Francis Should Stick to Doctrine, Stay Away from Economic 'Redistribution,'" FoxNews.com, May 9, 2014, http://www.foxnews.com/opinion/2014/05/09/pope-francis-should-stick-to-doctrine-stay-away-from-economic-redistribution/.

31. Fr. John Zuhlsdorf, "Pope Francis to UN Delegation: 'Legitimate Redistribution of Economic Benefits by the State,'" *Fr. Z's Blog*, May 9, 2014, http://wdtprs.com/blog/2014/05/pope-francis-to-un-delegation-legitimate-redistribution-of-economic-benefits-by-the-state/.

32. Bill Glauber, "Paul Ryan Signals Support for Kenosha Casino," *Milwaukee Journal Sentinel*, December 19, 2013, http://www.jsonline.com/news/statepolitics/paul-ryan-signals-support-for-kenosha-casino-b99167734z1-236595381.html.

33. Michelle Caruso-Cabrera, "Pope's Sharp Words Make a Wealthy Donor Hesitate," CNBC.com, December 30, 2013, http://www.cnbc.com/id/101302230.

34. Cardinal Timothy Dolan, "The Pope's Case for Virtuous Capitalism," *Wall Street Journal*, May 22, 2014, http://online.wsj.com/news/articles/SB10001424052702304198504579572571508689630.

35. "Larry Kudlow Wonders If Pope Francis Understands Economic Freedom," *Huffington Post*, August 12, 2013, http://www.huffingtonpost.com/2013/08/12/larry-kudlow-pope-francis_n_3743495.html.

36. Grant Gallicho, "Apostolic Nuncio to USCCB: Be Pastoral, Not Ideological," *Commonweal*, November 11, 2013, https://www.commonwealmagazine. org/blog/apostolic-nuncio-usccb-be-pastoral-not-ideological.

37. Joshua J. McElwee, "Archbishop Warns of 'Balkanization' in US Church," *National Catholic Reporter*, June 2, 2014, http://ncronline.org/news/ politics/archbishop-warns-balkanization-us-church.

38. Francis X. Rocca, "Pope Calls for Less 'Vatican-Centric,' More Socially Conscious Church," Catholic News Service, October 1, 2013, http://www. catholicnews.com/data/stories/cns/1304129.htm.

39. See "Letter of Pope Francis to Those Who Will Be Created Cardinals at the Upcoming Consistory of 22 February," Vatican website, January 12, 2014, http://w2.vatican.va/content/francesco/en/letters/2014/documents/papa- francesco_20140112_nuovi-cardinali.html.

40. James Martin, SJ, "The Tablet: Who Was Behind the LCWR Investigation?" *America*, May 3, 2013, http://americamagazine.org/content/all-things/ tablet-who-was-behind-lcwr-investigation.

41. Joshua J. McElwee, "Vatican Ends Controversial Three-Year Oversight of US Sisters' Leaders," *National Catholic Reporter*, April 16, 2015, http:// ncronline.org/news/vatican/vatican-and-lcwr-announce-end-controversial-three- year-oversight.

42. "Instruction on Certain Aspects of the 'Theology of Liberation,'" Vatican website, accessed May 12, 2015, http://www.vatican.va/roman_curia/ congregations/cfaith/documents/rc_con_cfaith_doc_19840806_theology- liberation_en.html.

43. Paul Vallely, "A Church for the Poor," *New York Times*, September 4, 2014, http://www.nytimes.com/2014/09/05/opinion/a-church-for-the-poor.html? _r=0.

44. Gustavo Gutiérrez and Gerhard Ludwig Müeller, *On the Side of the Poor: The Theology of Liberation* (Maryknoll, NY: Orbis Books, 2015).

2. THE MAKING OF A CULTURE WARRIOR CHURCH

1. George Weigel, "Moral Clarity in a Time of War," *First Things*, January 2003, http://www.firstthings.com/article/2003/01/001-moral-clarity-in-a-time- of-war.

2. George Weigel, "Who's Delegitimizing Whom?" Ethics and Public Policy Center, published in *The Catholic Difference*, October 27, 2004, http://eppc. org/publications/whos-delegitimizing-whom.

3. Michael Sean Winters, "New Heights of Hubris from George Wiegel," *America Magazine*, July 8, 2009, http://americamagazine.org/content/all-things/ new-heights-hubris-george-weigel.

4. Michael Sean Winters, "Weigel Criticizes O'Malley, Bishops Over Border Mass," *National Catholic Reporter*, April 7, 2014, http://ncronline.org/blogs/ distinctly-catholic/weigel-criticizes-omalley-bishops-over-border-mass.

5. George Weigel, "Beyond the Fortnight for Freedom," *National Review*, July 4, 2012, http://www.nationalreview.com/corner/304753/beyond-fortnight-freedom-george-weigel.

6. Richard John Neuhaus, "The Two Politics of Election 2000," *First Things*, February 2001, http://www.firstthings.com/article/2001/02/the-two-politics-of-election.

7. Damon Linker, "Richard John Neuhaus and the Perils of Theologically Motivated Hyper-Partisanship," *The Week*, March 13, 2015, http://theweek.com/ articles/543949/richard-john-neuhaus-perils-theologically-motivated-hyper partisanship.

8. Damon Linker, "The Republican Party's War with Pope Francis Has Finally Started," *The Week*, January 13, 2015, http://theweek.com/articles/532784/ republican-partys-warwith-pope-francishas-finally-started.

9. Bill Donohue, "America's Secular Saboteurs," FaithStreet.com, October 19, 2009, http://www.faithstreet.com/onfaith/2009/10/19/secular-saboteurs/ 4636.

10. Jeremy Cluchey, "Who Is Catholic League President William Donohue?" Media Matters, December 20, 2004, http://mediamatters.org/research/2004/12/ 20/who-is-catholic-league-president-william-donohu/132482.

11. John Allen Jr., "Why We Need the Catholic League," Archdiocese of New York website, December 16, 2010, http://blog.archny.org/index.php/why-we-need-the-catholic-league/.

12. "About Us," Catholic League for Religious and Civil Rights, accessed April 29, 2015, http://www.catholicleague.org/about-us/.

13. Grant Gallicho, "John Jay to U.S. Bishops: Homosexuality Is Not a Predictor of Clergy Abuse (Updated)," *Commonweal*, November 18, 2009, https:// www.commonwealmagazine.org/blog/john-jay-us-bishops-homosexuality-not-predictor-clergy-abuse-updated.

14. Ben Armbruster, "Bill Donohue to Foley: Most 15-Year-Old Boys Wouldn't Allow Themselves to Be Molested. So Why Did You?" Media Matters, October 4, 2006, http://mediamatters.org/research/2006/10/04/bill-donohue-to-foley-most-15-year-old-boys-wou/136833.

15. Bill Donohue, "Bishop Finn Agrees to Oversight Terms," Catholic League for Religious and Civil Rights, November 16, 2011, http://www.catholic league.org/bishop-finn-agrees-to-oversight-terms/.

16. Bill Donohue, "Bishop Robert Finn Resigns," Catholic League for Religious and Civil Rights, April 21, 2015, http://www.catholicleague.org/bishop-robert-finn-resigns/.

17. Matt Gertz, "Catholic League Fine with Rush Limbaugh's Attack on Pope Francis," Media Matters, December 16, 2013, http://mediamatters.org/blog/2013/12/16/catholic-league-fine-with-rush-limbaughs-attack/197288.

18. Father Matthew T. Gamber, SJ, "Legatus Celebrates 25 Years," *National Catholic Register*, February 14, 2012, http://www.ncregister.com/daily-news/legatus-celebrates-25-years.

19. Sabrina Arena Ferrisi, "Culture Warrior," *Legatus*, December 5, 2011, http://www.legatusmagazine.org/culture-warrior/.

20. William Donohue, "Caught in a Whirlwind," Catholic League for Religious and Civil Rights, March 2012, http://www.catholicleague.org/caught-in-a-whirlwind/.

21. Genevieve Pollack, "Legatus Honors President Bush, Cardinal George," *Zenit*, February 4, 2010, http://www.zenit.org/en/articles/legatus-honors-president-bush-cardinal-george.

22. Dan Vergano, "Half-Million Iraqis Died in the War, New Study Says," NationalGeographic.com, October 16, 2013, http://news.nationalgeographic.com/news/2013/10/131015-iraq-war-deaths-survey-2013/; "Names of the Dead," *New York Times,* February 27, 2012, http://www.nytimes.com/2012/02/28/us/us-military-deaths-in-iraq-and-afghanistan.html.

23. Lisa Bourne, "Fox News' Bret Baier Explains Why He Cancelled on Legatus," *LifeSite*, January 26, 2015, https://www.lifesitenews.com/news/fox-news-bret-baier-explains-why-he-cancelled-on-legatus.

24. National Catholic Prayer Breakfast, http://catholicprayerbreakfast.com/about/.

25. "Catechism of the Catholic Church," Vatican website, accessed May 8, 2015, http://www.vatican.va/archive/ccc_css/archive/catechism/p3s2c2a5.htm.

26. "Facts About the National 'Catholic' Prayer Breakfast," Catholics United, April 14, 2008, http://www.catholics-united.org/ncpb.

27. Brian Tashman, "Austin Ruse Says Left-Wing University Professors 'Should All Be Taken Out and Shot,'" Right Wing Watch, March 12, 2014, www.rightwingwatch.org/content/austin-ruse-says-left-wing-university-professors-should-all-be-taken-out-and-shot.

28. Dan Morris-Young, "Cardinal Newman Society Takes on Watchdog Role for Catholic Identity," *National Catholic Reporter*, November 21, 2012, http://ncronline.org/news/faith-parish/cardinal-newman-society-takes-watchdog-role-catholic-identity.

29. Mollie Wilson O'Reilly, "EWTN and Torture," *Commonweal*, February 19, 2010, https://www.commonwealmagazine.org/blog/ewtn-and-torture.

30. Mollie Wilson O'Reilly, "Power Corrupts," *Commonweal*, May 1, 2009, https://www.commonwealmagazine.org/blog/power-corrupts.

31. John-Henry Westen, "EWTN's Arroyo Takes Cardinal McCarrick to Task Over Kennedy and Pope Letters," *LifeSite*, September 1, 2009, http://www.lifesitenews.com/news/ewtns-arroyo-takes-cardinal-mccarrick-to-task-over-kennedy-pope-letters.

32. O'Reilly, "Power Corrupts."

33. Charles J. Chaput, "Little Murders," Witherspoon Institute Public Discourse, October 18, 2008, http://www.thepublicdiscourse.com/2008/10/127/.

34. Robert P. George, "A Clash of Orthodoxies," *First Things*, August 1999, http://www.firstthings.com/article/1999/08/a-clash-of-orthodoxies.

35. Anne Morse, "Conservative Heavyweight: The Remarkable Mind of Professor Robert P. George," *Crisis*, September 1, 2003, http://www.crisismagazine.com/2003/conservative-heavyweight-the-remarkable-mind-of-professor-robert-p-george.

36. David D. Kirkpatrick, "The Conservative-Christian Big Thinker," *New York Times Magazine*, December 16, 2009, http://www.nytimes.com/2009/12/20/magazine/20george-t.html?pagewanted=all&_r=0.

37. Barbara Bradley Hagerty, "Catholic Bishops Ramp Up Same-Sex Marriage Fight," NPR, September 27, 2012, http://www.npr.org/2012/09/27/161909566/catholic-bishops-ramp-up-same-sex-marriage-fight.

38. Jeremy Hooper, "Listen to the New Chair of US Commission on Intl. Religious Freedom Call for 'National Rebellion' Against Marriage Equality," GoodAsYou.com, July 25, 2013, http://www.goodasyou.org/good_as_you/2013/07/listen-to-new-chair-of-us-commission-on-intl-religious-freedom-call-for-national-rebellion-against-marriage-equality.html.

39. Robert P. George, "Who Will Stand?" *First Things*, April 5, 2015, http://www.firstthings.com/blogs/firstthoughts/2015/04/who-will-stand.

40. Charles J. Chaput, Robert P. George, William E. Lori, R. Albert Mohler Jr., and Russell Moore, "Now Is the Time to Talk About Religious Liberty," *Public Discourse*, April 3, 2015, http://www.thepublicdiscourse.com/2015/04/14748/.

41. Peter Jesserer Smith, "National Catholic Prayer Breakfast: Era of Comfortable Catholicism Is Over," *National Catholic Register*, May 14, 2014, http://www.ncregister.com/daily-news/national-catholic-prayer-breakfast-era-of-comfortable-catholicism-is-over.

42. "Manhattan Declaration," DeMoss.com, http://demoss.com/newsrooms/manhattandeclaration.

43. Kirkpatrick, "The Conservative-Christian Big Thinker."

44. Peter Steinfels, "Voters' Guides Define Moral Compromises to Take to Polls," *New York Times*, October 14, 2006. http://www.nytimes.com/2006/10/14/us/politics/14beliefs.html?_r=0.

45. Andrea Gagliarducci, "All Values Are Non-Negotiable, Pope Says in New Interview," Catholic News Agency, March 5, 2014, http://www.catholicnewsagency.com/news/all-values-are-non-negotiable-pope-says-in-new-interview/.

46. "Paul Ryan Challenged on Budget by Georgetown Faculty," *Huffington Post*, April 24, 2012, http://www.huffingtonpost.com/2012/04/24/paul-ryan-challenged-by-georgetown-faculty_n_1449437.html.

47. David Gibson, "Catholic Bishop Says Ryan Budget Fails Moral Test," *Huffington Post*, April 18, 2012, http://www.huffingtonpost.com/2012/04/18/ryan-budget-catholic_n_1434919.html.

48. Kathryn Jean Lopez, "Dolan: Ryan Is a 'Great Public Servant,'" *National Review*, August 17, 2012, http://www.nationalreview.com/article/314272/dolan-ryan-great-public-servant-kathryn-jean-lopez.

49. Rev. Timothy M. Dolan, letter to Rep. Paul Ryan, dated May 18, 2011, http://budget.house.gov/uploadedfiles/dolanresponsetoryan5_18.pdf.

50. Michael O'Brien, "Boehner and Ryan Tout Letter from Head of US Catholic Bishops," *The Hill*, May 19, 2011, http://thehill.com/blogs/blog-briefing-room/news/162239-boehner-and-ryan-tout-letter-from-head-of-us-catholic-bishops.

51. Jennifer Haberkorn, "Paul Ryan Gets Boost from Catholic Bishops," *Politico*, May 19, 2011, http://www.politico.com/news/stories/0511/55349.html.

52. "Bishop's Column: Subsidiarity, Solidarity, and the Lay Mission," Diocese of Madison *Catholic Herald*, August 16, 2012, http://madisoncatholicherald.org/bishopscolumns/3366-bishop-column.html.

53. David Cloutier, "Bishops, Budgets, and Getting Moral Theology Right," Catholic Moral Theology, August 18, 2012, http://catholicmoraltheology.com/bishops-budgets-and-getting-moral-theology-right/.

54. Steven Ertelt, "Chaput on Obama: 'I Can't Vote for Someone Who Is Pro-Abortion,'" LifeNews.com, September 17, 2012, http://www.lifenews.com/2012/09/17/chaput-on-obama-i-cant-vote-for-somebody-who-is-pro-abortion/; John L. Allen Jr., "Chaput in Philly Swims Against 'Nostalgia and Red Ink,'" *National Catholic Reporter*, September 14, 2012, http://ncronline.org/news/faith-parish/chaput-philly-swims-against-nostalgia-and-red-ink.

55. Francis Cardinal George, "The Wrong Side of History," *Catholic New World*, October 21, 2012, http://www.catholicnewworld.com/cnwonline/2012/1021/cardinal.aspx.

56. Cardinal James Francis Stafford, "Cardinal's Address to Catholic University of America," Catholic News Agency, accessed April 29, 2015, http://www.catholicnewsagency.com/document.php?n=780.

57. Cardinal James Francis Stafford, "Cardinal's Address to Catholic University of America."

58. "The Bishops and Obama," *Commonweal*, November 26, 2008, https://www.commonwealmagazine.org/bishops-obama-0.

59. "Archbishop Nienstedt Staunchly Opposes 'Travesty' of Obama Invite to Notre Dame Commencement," Catholic News Service, March 31, 2009, http://cns.winxweb.com/PressReleases/tabid/54/itemid/460/amid/452/archbishop-nienstedt-staunchly-opposes-travesty-of-obama-invite-to-notre-dame-c.aspx.

60. Liam Ford, "Barack Obama at Notre Dame: Chicago's Cardinal Francis George Slams Plan to Have President Speak," *Chicago Tribune*, April 3, 2009, http://articles.chicagotribune.com/2009-04-03/news/0904030083_1_catholic-bishops-chicago-archdiocese-commencement-address.

61. Donald R. McClarey, "Northwestern Indiana Humanist University," *The American Catholic*, April 3, 2009, http://the-american-catholic.com/2009/04/03/northwestern-indiana-humanist-university/.

62. "Archbishop Chaput: Obama Honor a Fitting Bookend to Catholic Higher Ed," *The Catholic Key*, May 18, 2009, http://catholickey.blogspot.com/2009/05/archbishop-chaput-obama-honor-fitting.html.

63. "Petition to Father Jenkins," NotreDameScandal.com, http://www.notredamescandal.com/PetitiontoFrJenkins/tabid/454/Default.aspx.

64. John R. Quinn, "The Public Duty of Bishops," *America*, August 31, 2009, http://americamagazine.org/issue/706/article/public-duty-bishops.

65. "Obama Signs Executive Order on Abortion Funding Limits," CNN.com, March 24, 2010, http://www.cnn.com/2010/POLITICS/03/24/obama.abortion/.

66. "Affordable Care Act Rules on Expanding Access to Preventive Services for Women," U.S. Department of Health and Human Services, last updated June 28, 2013, http://www.hhs.gov/healthcare/facts/factsheets/2011/08/womensprevention08012011a.html.

67. "Our First, Most Cherished Liberty," U.S. Conference of Catholic Bishops, accessed April 29, 2015, http://www.usccb.org/issues-and-action/religious-liberty/our-first-most-cherished-liberty.cfm.

68. David Gibson, "Star-Spangled Virgin: Blessed or Blasphemous?" Religion News Service, July 3, 2013, http://davidgibson.religionnews.com/2013/07/03/star-spangled-virgin-blessed-or-blasphemous.

69. Nick Sementelli, "Catholic Bishop Goes Off Script About Religious Liberty, Warns of U.S. Despotism," Faith in Public Life, June 6, 2012, www.faithinpubliclife.org/blog/catholic-bishop-goes-off-script-about-religious-liberty-warns-of-u-s-despotism/.

70. Michael Sean Winters, "DC Parishioners Push Back on Fortnight," *National Catholic Reporter*, June 13, 2012, http://ncronline.org/printpdf/blogs/distinctly-catholic/dc-parishioners-push-back-fortnight.

71. Igor Volsky, "Many Catholic Universities, Hospitals Already Cover Contraception in Their Health Insurance Plans," Think Progress, February 7, 2012, http://thinkprogress.org/health/2012/02/07/420114/many-catholic-universities-hospitals-already-offer-contraception-as-part-of-their-health-insurance-plans/.

72. Robert Mickens, "This Is Carl Anderson," *The Tablet*, June 16, 2012, http://archive.thetablet.co.uk/article/16th-june-2012/4/this-is-carl-anderson.

73. Dennis Sadowski, "Supreme Knight Anderson Invites Biden to Talk About Abortion Views," Catholic News Service, September 22, 2008, http://www.catholicnews.com/data/stories/cns/0804788.htm.

74. Tim Townsend, "Catholics to Rally Against Obama Birth Control Mandate," *St. Louis Post-Dispatch*, June 20, 2012, http://www.stltoday.com/news/local/metro/catholics-to-rally-against-obama-birth-control-mandate/article_45ee8fab-86bf-59ad-b8f5-3e0251ccf918.html.

75. Carl A. Anderson, "What Mexico Teaches Us," Knights of Columbus website, May 1, 2012, http://www.kofc.org/en/news/supreme/detail/fromthesk_20120501.html.

76. Steve Schneck, "Rifle with Crucifix," *U.S. Catholic*, accessed April 29, 2015, http://www.uscatholic.org/blog/2012/05/rifle-crucifix.

77. "Full Text of Bishop Jenky's Homily at Men's March and Mass," *The Catholic Post*, posted April 14, 2015, http://www.thecatholicpost.com/post/PostArticle.aspx?ID=2440.

78. Barbara Bradley Hagerty, "Bishops Launch 2-Week Campaign Against Health Law," NPR, June 20, 2012, http://www.npr.org/2012/06/20/155421644/bishops-launch-2-week-campaign-against-health-law.

79. Adam Cassandra, "Catholic Bishop: Democrats Embrace 'Intrinsic Evil' of Abortion," LifeNews.com, October 2, 2012, http://www.lifenews.com/2012/10/02/catholic-bishop-democrats-embrace-intrinsic-evil-of-abortion/.

80. Jim Dwyer, "Priest's Dip into Politics Raises Outcry," *New York Times*, September 18, 2012, http://www.nytimes.com/2012/09/19/nyregion/romney-endorsement-in-church-bulletin-raises-outcry.html?_r=0.

81. Michael Sean Winters, "Romney: 'I'm Pro-Life,'" *National Catholic Reporter*, January 12, 2012, http://ncronline.org/print/blogs/distinctly-catholic/romney-im-pro-life-0.

82. David Gibson, "Catholic Bishops Make Last-Minute Pitch for Romney," Religion News Service, November 1, 2012, https://www.religionnews.com/2012/11/01/catholic-bishops-make-last-minute-pitch-for-romney/.

83. "CREW Asks IRS to Investigate U.S. Conference of Catholic Bishops," Citizens for Responsibility and Ethics in Washington, November 2, 2012, http://www.citizensforethics.org/legal-filings/entry/crew-asks-irs-investigate-conference-catholic-bishops.

84. Rachel Weiner, "Romney Ad: Obama Waging 'War on Religion,'" *Washington Post*, August 9, 2012, http://www.washingtonpost.com/blogs/the-fix/post/romney-obama-waging-war-on-religion/2012/08/09/192c4e02-e213-11e1-a25e-15067bb31849_blog.html.

85. Pew Research Center, "America's Changing Religious Landscape," May 12, 2015, http://www.pewforum.org/2015/05/12/americas-changing-religious-landscape/.

86. David Breitenstein, "U.S. Catholics Face Shortage of Priests," *USA Today*, May 25, 2014, http://www.usatoday.com/story/news/2014/05/25/us-catholics-face-shortage-of-priests/9548931/.

87. "A Shifting Landscape," Public Religion Research Institute, February 26, 2014, http://publicreligion.org/research/2014/02/2014-lgbt-survey/.

88. Jerry Filteau, "Unusual Study Asks Former Catholics Why They Left Church," *National Catholic Reporter*, March 23, 2012, http://ncronline.org/news/faith-parish/unusual-study-asks-former-catholics-why-they-left-church.

89. Lilly Fowler, "Some Illinois Roman Catholics Weigh In on Why They Stopped Attending Mass," *St. Louis Post-Dispatch*, September 23, 2014, http://www.stltoday.com/lifestyles/faith-and-values/divine-dispatches/illinois-roman-catholics-weigh-in-on-why-have-they-stopped/article_2609ad20-180c-53ee-a76a-8fd9d2f1d4ff.html.

90. Michael Lipka, "Young U.S. Catholics Overwhelmingly Accepting of Homosexuality," Pew Research Center, October 16, 2014, http://www.pewresearch.org/fact-tank/2014/10/16/young-u-s-catholics-overwhelmingly-accepting-of-homosexuality/.

91. Antonio Spadaro, SJ, "A Big Heart Open to God," *America: The National Catholic Review*, September 30, 2013, http://americamagazine.org/pope-interview.

92. John L. Allen Jr., "Hard Questions About Francis in Argentina and a Lesson from Chile," *National Catholic Reporter*, April 12, 2013, http://ncronline.org/blogs/all-things-catholic/hard-questions-about-francis-argentina-and-lesson-chile.

93. Francis DeBernardo, "Cardinal Close to Pope Calls for Openness to Gay & Lesbian Couples," New Ways Ministry, accessed April 29, 2015, http://newwaysministryblog.wordpress.com/2014/08/27/cardinal-close-to-pope-calls-for-openness-to-gay-lesbian-couples/.

94. John A. Dick, "Belgian Bishop Advocates Church Recognition of Gay Relationships," *National Catholic Reporter*, December 30, 2014, http://

ncronline.org/news/faith-parish/belgian-bishop-advocates-church-recognition-gay-relationships.

95. Laurie Goodstein, "Knights of Columbus Donate Millions to Anti-Gay Marriage Effort, Report Says," *New York Times*, October 18, 2012, http://thecaucus.blogs.nytimes.com/2012/10/18/knights-of-columbus-donate-millions-to-anti-gay-marriage-effort-report-says/?_php=true&_type=blogs&_r=0.

96. Robert D. Putnam and David E. Campbell, "Walking Away from Church," *Los Angeles Times*, October 17, 2010, http://articles.latimes.com/2010/oct/17/opinion/la-oe-1017-putnam-religion-20101017.

3. CATHOLIC PROGRESSIVISM ON THE MARCH: THE NEW DEAL TO VATICAN II

1. Lew Daly, "In Search of the Common Good," *Boston Review*, May 1, 2007, http://www.bostonreview.net/lew-daly-in-search-of-the-common-good-catholic-roots-of-american-liberalism.

2. "*Rerum Novarum*: Encyclical of Pope Leo XIII on Capital and Labor," Vatican website, accessed April 29, 2015, http://w2.vatican.va/content/leo-xiii/en/encyclicals/documents/hf_l-xiii_enc_15051891_rerum-novarum.html.

3. "John Ryan, 'A Living Wage,' 1906," American Catholic History Classroom, Catholic University of America, accessed April 29, 2015, http://cuomeka.wrlc.org/exhibits/show/industrial/documents/cri-doc4.

4. David J. O'Brien, *American Catholics and Social Reform: The New Deal Years* (Oxford: Oxford University Press, 1968).

5. Michael Sean Winters, *Left at the Altar: How the Democrats Lost the Catholics and How the Catholics Can Save the Democrats* (New York: Basic Books, 2008).

6. Daly, "In Search of the Common Good."

7. "Historical Background and Development of Social Security: Pre-Social Security Period," Official Social Security Website, accessed April 29, 2015, http://www.ssa.gov/history/briefhistory3.html.

8. Winters, *Left at the Altar*.

9. Daly, "In Search of the Common Good."

10. Daly, "In Search of the Common Good."

11. Timothy A. Byrnes, *Catholic Bishops in American Politics* (Princeton, NJ: Princeton University Press, 1993).

12. Daly, "In Search of the Common Good."

13. "Dorothy Day—Catholic Worker Collection," Marquette University Raynor Memorial Libraries, accessed April 29, 2015, http://www.marquette.edu/library/archives/day.shtml.

14. Robert A. Slayton, "When a Catholic Terrified the Heartland," *New York Times*, December 10, 2011, http://campaignstops.blogs.nytimes.com/2011/12/10/when-a-catholic-terrified-the-heartland/.

15. Byrnes, *Catholic Bishops in American Politics.*

16. Byrnes, *Catholic Bishops in American Politics.*

17. Sharon Otterman, "For a 1950s TV Evangelist, a Step toward Sainthood," *New York Times*, June 29, 2012, http://www.nytimes.com/2012/06/30/nyregion/archbishop-fulton-j-sheen-advances-toward-sainthood.html?_r=0.

18. Byrnes, *Catholic Bishops in American Politics.*

19. "The Second Vatican Ecumenical Council," PapalEncyclicals.net, accessed April 29, 2015, http://www.papalencyclicals.net/vatican2.htm.

20. "Pastoral Constitution on the Church in the Modern World: *Gaudium et Spes*," Vatican website, accessed April 29, 2015, http://www.vatican.va/archive/hist_councils/ii_vatican_council/documents/vat-ii_const_19651207_gaudium-et-spes_en.html.

21. Curtis Wilkie, "Bishop Law: A Calming Factor in Tense Mississippi of the '60s," *Boston Globe*, January 27, 1984, http://www.boston.com/globe/spotlight/abuse/archives/012784_law_miss.htm.

22. John Gehring, "Be Not Afraid?" Faith in Public Life, June 2013, http://www.faithinpubliclife.org/wp-content/uploads/2013/06/FPL-CCHD-report.pdf.

23. Richard A. McCormick, "'Humanae Vitae' 25 Years Later," *America*, July 17, 1993, http://americamagazine.org/issue/100/humanae-vitae-25-years-later.

24. Peter Steinfels, "John Cardinal Krol, Pivotal Catholic Figure, Dies at 85," *New York Times*, March 4, 1996, http://www.nytimes.com/1996/03/04/us/john-cardinal-krol-pivotal-catholic-figure-dies-at-85.html.

4. THE RISE OF THE RELIGIOUS RIGHT AND A POWER STRUGGLE IN THE CHURCH

1. "The Protestant and Catholic Vote," Gallup.com, June 8, 2004, http://www.gallup.com/poll/11911/protestant-catholic-vote.aspx.

2. "Richard Nixon: Remarks at the Annual Convention of the National Catholic Education Association in Philadelphia, Pennsylvania, April 6, 1972," American Presidency Project, website of the University of California, Santa Barbara, accessed April 30, 2015, http://www.presidency.ucsb.edu/ws/?pid=3367.

3. Linda Greenhouse and Reva B. Siegel, eds., *Before* Roe v. Wade*: Voices That Shaped the Abortion Debate Before the Supreme Court's Ruling* (New York: Kaplan, 2010).

4. Timothy A. Byrnes, *Catholic Bishops in American Politics* (Princeton, NJ: Princeton University Press, 1993).

5. Byrnes, *Catholic Bishops in American Politics*.

6. Kristin Heyer, Mark Rozell, and Michael A. Genovese, eds., *Catholics and Politics: The Dynamic Tension Between Faith and Power* (Washington, DC: Georgetown University Press, 2008).

7. Byrnes, *Catholic Bishops in American Politics*.

8. Byrnes, *Catholic Bishops in American Politics*.

9. Deal W. Hudson, *Onward, Christian Soldiers: The Growing Political Power of Catholics and Evangelicals in the United States* (New York: Threshold Editions, 2010).

10. Jill Lepore, "Birthright: What's Next for Planned Parenthood?" *New Yorker*, November 14, 2011, http://www.newyorker.com/magazine/2011/11/14/birthright-2.

11. Greenhouse and Siegel, *Before* Roe v. Wade.

12. Lepore, "Birthright."

13. Greenhouse and Siegel, *Before* Roe v. Wade.

14. "Statement on Abortion: A Statement Issued by the National Conference of Catholic Bishops, April 22, 1970," Teachings of the Catholic Church, PriestsforLife.org, accessed April 30, 2015, http://www.priestsforlife.org/magisterium/bishops/70-04-22statementonabortionnccb.htm.

15. "Pastoral Constitution on the Church in the Modern World: *Gaudium et Spes*," Vatican website, accessed April 29, 2015, http://www.vatican.va/archive/hist_councils/ii_vatican_council/documents/vat-ii_const_19651207_gaudium-et-spes_en.html.

16. "Pastoral Constitution on the Church in the Modern World."

17. Amy Sullivan, *The Party Faithful: How and Why Democrats Are Closing the God Gap* (New York: Scribner, 2008).

18. Lepore, "Birthright."

19. Transcript of "God in America: Of God and Caesar," PBS.org, accessed April 30, 2015, http://www.pbs.org/godinamerica/transcripts/hour-six.html.

20. Randall Balmer, "The Real Origins of the Religious Right," *Politico*, May 27, 2014, http://www.politico.com/magazine/story/2014/05/religious-right-real-origins-107133.html.

21. Hudson, *Onward, Christian Soldiers*.

22. Lepore, "Birthright."

23. Joan Bokaer, "Paul Weyrich: The Man Who Framed the Republican Party," Talk to Action, August 9, 2006, http://www.talk2action.org/story/2006/8/9/55443/17515.

24. Bokaer, "Paul Weyrich."

25. Mary Hanna, "Catholics and the Moral Majority," *Crisis*, November 1, 1982, http://www.crisismagazine.com/1982/catholics-and-the-moral-majority.

26. Hrafnkell Haraldsson, "The Rise of American Fundamentalism: The Year 1980," PoliticusUSA.com, August 18, 2011, http://archives.politicususa.com/2011/08/18/the-rise-of-american-fundamentalism-the-year-1980.html.

27. Transcript of "God in America: Of God and Caesar."

28. Michael Sean Winters, *God's Right Hand: How Jerry Falwell Made God a Republican and Baptized the American Right* (New York: HarperOne, 2012).

29. Hanna, "Catholics and the Moral Majority."

30. Patricia Zapor, "Rev. Falwell's Moral Majority," Catholic News Service, May 18, 2007, http://www.catholicnews.com/data/stories/cns/0702860.htm.

31. Sullivan, *The Party Faithful*.

32. Peter Steinfels, "Cardinal Bernadin Dies at 68; Reconciling Voice in Church," *New York Times*, November 15, 1996, http://www.nytimes.com/1996/11/15/us/cardinal-bernardin-dies-at-68-reconciling-voice-in-church.html.

33. Joseph Louis Cardinal Bernadin, "A Consistent Ethic of Life: An American-Catholic Dialogue," Educational Resources, PriestsforLife.org, accessed April 30, 2015, http://www.priestsforlife.org/articles/884-a-consistent-ethic-of-life-an-american-catholic-dialogue.

34. Peter Steinfels, "Death of a Cardinal," *New York Times*, May 4, 2000, http://www.nytimes.com/2000/05/04/nyregion/death-of-a-cardinal-cardinal-o-connor-80-dies-forceful-voice-for-vatican.html.

35. Peter Steinfels, *A People Adrift: The Crisis of the Roman Catholic Church in America* (New York: Simon and Schuster, 2004).

36. "O'Connor Critical of Ferraro Views," *New York Times*, September 9, 1984, http://www.nytimes.com/1984/09/09/nyregion/o-connor-critical-of-ferraro-views.html.

37. Peter Steinfels, "Cardinal O'Connor, 80, Dies," *New York Times*, May 5, 2000, http://www.nytimes.com/learning/teachers/featured_articles/20000505friday.html.

38. Fox Butterfield, "Archbishop of Boston Cites Abortion as 'Critical' Issue," *New York Times*, September 6, 1984, http://www.nytimes.com/1984/09/06/us/archbishop-of-boston-cites-abortion-as-critical-issue.html.

39. Joe Klein, "Abortion and the Archbishop," *New York*, October 1, 1984, http://www.unz.org/Pub/NewYork-1984oct01-00036.

40. John L. Allen Jr., "He Was a Magnificent Pope Who Presided Over a Controversial Pontificate," *National Catholic Reporter*, accessed April 30, 2015, http://www.nationalcatholicreporter.org/update/conclave/jp_obit_main.htm.

41. Richard A. McCormick, "'Humanae Vitae' 25 Years Later," *America*, July 17, 1993, http://americamagazine.org/issue/100/humanae-vitae-25-years-later.

42. E. J. Dionne Jr., "The Vatican Finds a Fight in America," *New York Times*, March 16, 1986, http://www.nytimes.com/1986/03/16/weekinreview/the-vatican-finds-a-fight-in-america.html.

43. E. J. Dionne Jr., *Souled Out: Reclaiming Faith and Politics After the Religious Right* (Princeton, NJ: Princeton University Press, 2009).

44. Thomas J. Reese, "The Laghi Legacy," *America*, June 23, 1990, http://americamagazine.org/issue/100/laghi-legacy.

45. "Economic Justice for All," U.S. Conference of Catholic Bishops, accessed April 30, 2015, http://www.usccb.org/upload/economic_justice_for_all.pdf.

46. "Initial Reactions to *Centesimus Annus*," *Religion and Liberty*, Volume 1, Number 3, Acton Institute, accessed April 30, 2015, http://www.acton.org/pub/religion-liberty/volume-1-number-3/initial-reactions-centesimus-annus.

47. *Evangelium Vitae*, Vatican website, accessed April 30, 2015, http://www.vatican.va/holy_father/john_paul_ii/encyclicals/documents/hf_jp-ii_enc_2503 1995_evangelium-vitae_en.html.

48. Robert D. McFadden, "The Pope's Visit: The Overview," *New York Times*, October 8, 1995, http://www.nytimes.com/1995/10/08/nyregion/the-pope-s-visit-the-overview-125000-join-pope-at-mass-in-central-park-basilica.html.

49. Peter Steinfels, "Can We Talk About Abortion?" *Commonweal*, September 21, 2011, https://www.commonwealmagazine.org/can-we-talk-about-abortion.

50. "Called to Be Catholic," Catholic Common Ground Initiative, accessed April 30, 2015, http://www.catholiccommonground.org/called-be-catholic.

51. Steinfels, *A People Adrift*.

52. Steinfels, *A People Adrift*.

53. Steinfels, *A People Adrift*.

54. Thomas Reese, SJ, "New Leader for American Catholics," OnFaith.com, November 13, 2010, http://www.faithstreet.com/onfaith/2010/11/13/new-leader-for-american-catholics/2547.

55. "If It's November, It Must Be Baltimore," *Bishop's Blog: Thoughts and Reflections by Bishop Robert Lynch*, posted November 7, 2013, http://bishopsblog.dosp.org/?p=5956.

56. Tim Drake, "Elections Do Matter . . . Especially Among Bishops," *National Catholic Register*, November 11, 2010, http://www.ncregister.com/blog/tim-drake/elections-do-matter...especially-among-bishops.

57. "The Kicanas Conundrum," *LifeSite*, November 12, 2010, https://www.lifesitenews.com/news/updated-the-kicanas-conundrum-catholics-concerned-about-likely-new-us-bisho#.

58. Nancy Frazier O'Brien, "Rumors Aside, FOCA Legislation No Threat to Catholic Health Care," Catholic News Service, January 27, 2009, http://www.catholicnews.com/data/stories/cns/0900402.htm.

59. David Gibson, "Catholic Bishops Reject Moderate Leader, Elect New York's Timothy Dolan in a Shocker," *Politics Daily*, November 16, 2010, http://www.politicsdaily.com/2010/11/16/catholic-bishops-reject-moderate-elect-new-yorks-timothy-dolan/print/.

60. Russell Shaw, "The End of an Era," *Crisis*, November 22, 2010, http://www.crisismagazine.com/2010/the-end-of-an-era.

61. Nancy Frazier O'Brien, "Combined Years of Service Total 915 for Retiring USCCB Employees," Catholic News Service, February 6, 2007, http://www.catholicnews.com/data/stories/cns/0700706.htm.

62. George E. Curry, "Reagan Vetoes Civil Rights Bill," *Chicago Tribune*, March 17, 1988, http://articles.chicagotribune.com/1988-03-17/news/8803 010367_1_civil-rights-restoration-act-discrimination-act-rehabilitation-act.

63. "Family Research Council," Extremist Files, Southern Poverty Law Center, accessed April 30, 2015, http://www.splcenter.org/get-informed/intelligence-files/groups/family-research-council.

64. Evan McMorris-Santoro, "Family Research Council Labeled 'Hate Group' by SPLC over Anti-Gay Rhetoric," TalkingPointsMemo.com, November 24, 2010, http://talkingpointsmemo.com/dc/family-research-council-labeled-hate-group-by-splc-over-anti-gay-rhetoric.

65. Kevin Clarke, "Revolt of the Bishops?" *America*, November 13, 2012, http://americamagazine.org/content/all-things/revolt-bishops-statement-economy-voted-down.

66. David Gibson, "Catholic Bishops Divided on the Economy," *Salt Lake Tribune*, November 14, 2012, http://www.sltrib.com/sltrib/mobile/55270328-68/bishops-document-economic-bishop.html.csp.

67. John Gehring, "Vatican Rejects Deregulation, Trickle-Down Economics in Major Financial Reform Document," Faith in Public Life, October 24, 2011, http://www.faithinpubliclife.org/blog/vatican_rejects_deregulation_t/.

68. "USCCB Chairmen Oppose Senate Passage of ENDA," U.S. Conference of Catholic Bishops, November 7, 2013, http://www.usccb.org/news/2013/13-200.cfm.

69. "Catechism of the Catholic Church," Vatican website, accessed April 30, 2015, http://www.vatican.va/archive/ccc_css/archive/catechism/p3s2c2a6.htm.

70. "Catechism of the Catholic Church."

71. Michael Sean Winters, "USCCB Response to LGBT Nondiscrimination Order Worse Than Expected," *National Catholic Reporter*, July 22, 2014, http://ncronline.org/blogs/distinctly-catholic/usccb-response-worse-expected.

72. "USCCB Chairmen Express Grave Disappointment toward Supreme Court's Action," U.S. Conference of Catholic Bishops, October 6, 2014, http://www.usccb.org/news/2014/14-163.cfm.

73. David Morgan, "Catholic Bishops Pressured Komen over Planned Parenthood," Reuters.com, March 15, 2012, http://www.reuters.com/article/2012/03/15/us-usa-komen-catholic-idUSBRE82E12Q20120315.

74. John Gehring, "Ohio Catholic Conference Sits on Sidelines in Crucial Labor Fight," Faith in Public Life, September 1, 2011, http://www.faithin publiclife.org/blog/ohio_catholic_conference_sits/.

5. THE BATTLE FOR CATHOLIC IDENTITY

1. "Doctrinal Assessment of the Leadership Conference of Women Religious," Vatican website, accessed April 30, 2015, http://www.vatican.va/roman_curia/congregations/cfaith/documents/rc_con_cfaith_doc_20120418_assessment-lcwr_en.html.

2. Rocco Palmo, "Bishops on Health Bill: 'Regretfully, It Must Be Opposed,'" *Whispers in the Loggia*, March 15, 2010, http://whispersintheloggia.blogspot.com/2010/03/bishops-on-health-care-cost-too-high.html.

3. David Gibson, "Disgraced Cardinal Led Crackdown on Nuns," *St. Louis Post-Dispatch*, May 6, 2012, http://www.stltoday.com/lifestyles/faith-and-values/disgraced-cardinal-led-crackdown-on-nuns/article_fc1b39f7-64df-50e0-b278-fe49432e1ad8.html.

4. John L. Allen Jr., "LCWR Crackdown More Complicated Than 'Rome vs. America,'" *National Catholic Reporter*, May 3, 2012, http://ncronline.org/news/lcwr-crackdown-more-complicated-rome-vs-america.

5. Grant Gallicho, "Seeing Red," *Commonweal*, May 3, 2012, https://www.commonwealmagazine.org/blog/seeing-red.

6. Ann Rodgers, "Greensburg Bishop, Sisters at Odds over Health Bill," *Pittsburgh Post-Gazette*, April 16, 2010, http://www.post-gazette.com/local/east/2010/04/16/Greensburg-bishop-sisters-at-odds-over-health-bill/stories/201004160148.

7. "Bishop Tobin Cancels Hospital's CHA Membership," EWTN News, April 9, 2010, http://www.ewtnnews.com/catholic-news/US.php?id=348.

8. "Phoenix Bishop Removes Hospital's Catholic Status," *National Catholic Reporter*, December 21, 2010, http://ncronline.org/news/phoenix-bishop-removes-hospitals-catholic-status.

9. Jerry Filteau, "Catholic Health Association Backs Phoenix Hospital," *National Catholic Reporter*, December 22, 2010, http://ncronline.org/news/catholic-health-association-backs-phoenix-hospital.

10. Michelle Boorstein, "Arlington Diocese Parishioners Question Need for Fidelity Oath," *Washington Post*, July 11, 2012, http://www.washingtonpost.com/local/sunday-school-teachers-balk-at-oath-agreeing-to-all-church-teachings/2012/07/11/gJQAcAvGeW_story.html.

11. Bishop Robert F. Vasa, "Giving Testimony to the Truth," CatholicCulture.org, accessed May 11, 2015, http://www.catholicculture.org/culture/library/view.cfm?recnum=6060.

12. Deal W. Hudson, "Honoring a Bishop from the Northwest," *Crisis*, August 16, 2010, http://www.crisismagazine.com/2010/honoring-a-bishop-from-the-northwest.

13. Rev. Robert F. Vasa, Diocese of Baker website, letter dated December 3, 2006, http://www.dioceseofbaker.org/DIOCESAN_DOCUMENTS/Pastoral Guidelines08.2012.pdf.

14. Nicholas P. Cafardi, ed., *Voting and Holiness: Catholic Perspectives on Political Participation* (Mahwah, NJ: Paulist Press, 2012).

15. Brian Roewe, "Gay Ministry Group Refuses to Sign Oath," *National Catholic Reporter*, June 25, 2012, http://ncronline.org/news/spirituality/gay-ministry-group-refuses-sign-oath.

16. Michael D. Clark, "Catholic Teacher Backs Gay Son, Quits to Protest Contract," Cincinnati.com, May 10, 2014, http://www.cincinnati.com/story/news/education/2014/05/09/catholic-teacher-backs-gay-son-quitting-protest-controversial-contract/8898181/.

17. Michael D. Clark, "Catholic Teacher Contract Specifies Banned Practices," Cincinnati.com, March 26, 2014, http://www.cincinnati.com/story/news/education/2014/03/06/catholic-teacher-contract-specifies-banned-practices/6148399/.

18. "A Letter to the Archdiocese of Cincinnati," South West Ohio Catholic Educators Association, posted May 10, 2014, http://swocea.com/letter/.

19. Jim Rigg, "Catholic Teachers' Contracts and the Culture Wars," Cincinnati.com, March 31, 2014, http://www.cincinnati.com/story/opinion/contributors/2014/03/31/catholic-teachers-contracts-culture-wars/7145155/.

20. Charlette Report, "Gay Vice Principal Mark Zmuda Files Lawsuit Against Seattle Archbishop and Eastside Catholic School," Seattlepi.com, March 8, 2014, http://blog.seattlepi.com/capitolhill/2014/03/08/gay-vice-principal-mark-zmuda-files-lawsuit-against-seattle-archbishop-and-eastside-catholic-school/.

21. David Gibson, "Miami Catholic Archbishop Tells Employees If They Support Gay Marriage, They Could Be Fired," *Crux*, January 7, 2015, http://www.cruxnow.com/church/2015/01/07/miami-archbishop-warns-employees-against-supporting-gay-marriage-even-in-a-tweet/.

22. Francis DeBernardo, "Employees of Catholic Institutions Who Have Been Fired, Forced to Resign, Had Offers Rescinded, or Had Their Jobs Threatened

Because of LGBT Issues," New Ways Ministry, updated September 25, 2014, http://newwaysministryblog.wordpress.com/employment/.

23. Daniel Arkin, "'I Love You, Too': Cardinal Dolan Says Catholic Church Must Embrace Gays and Lesbians," NBCNews.com, March 31, 2013, http://usnews.nbcnews.com/_news/2013/03/31/17540236-i-love-you-too-cardinal-dolan-says-catholic-church-must-embrace-gays-and-lesbians?lite.

24. Kimberly Winter Stern, "Long Considered KC's Racial Dividing Line, Troost Avenue Is Diversifying," *Kansas City Star*, April 29, 2014, http://www.kansascity.com/mobile/m-top-stories/article347712/Long-considered-KC's-racial-dividing-line-Troost-Avenue-is-diversifying.html.

25. Nicholas Sciarappa, "Jesuit Leaves Church After Firings," *National Catholic Reporter*, September 22, 2014, http://ncronline.org/news/people/jesuit-leaves-church-after-firings.

26. Ben Brenkert, "I Thought I Could Be a Gay Jesuit Priest," *Washington Post*, September 17, 2014, http://www.washingtonpost.com/posteverything/wp/2014/09/17/i-thought-i-could-be-a-gay-jesuit-priest-i-cant-believe-how-wrong-i-was/.

27. "Always Our Children: A Pastoral Message to Parents of Homosexual Children and Suggestions for Pastoral Ministers," U.S. Conference of Catholic Bishops, accessed May 11, 2015, http://www.usccb.org/issues-and-action/human-life-and-dignity/homosexuality/always-our-children.cfm.

28. Lornet Turnbull, "Several Priests Shut Church Door to Petitions to Block Gay Marriage," *Seattle Times*, April 17, 2012, http://seattletimes.com/html/localnews/2017978133_catholics14m.html.

29. "Considerations Regarding Proposals to Give Legal Recognition to Unions Between Homosexual Persons," Vatican website, June 3, 2013, http://www.vatican.va/roman_curia/congregations/cfaith/documents/rc_con_cfaith_doc_20030731_homosexual-unions_en.html.

30. John Gehring, "The Boy Scouts, Gay Youth and Catholic Teaching," *Huffington Post*, June 3, 2013, http://www.huffingtonpost.com/john-gehring/the-boy-scouts-gay-youth-and-catholic-teaching_b_3379445.html.

31. Letter from Edward P. Martin, Scouting.org, May 29, 2013, http://www.scouting.org/filestore/MembershipStandards/Response-EPM.pdf.

32. James Martin, SJ, "Simply Loving," *America*, May 26–June 2, 2014, http://americamagazine.org/issue/simply-loving.

33. Mary Eberstadt, "The New Intolerance," *First Things*, accessed May 12, 2015, http://www.firstthings.com/events/the-new-intolerance.

34. Ryan Koronowski, "Most White Evangelicals Attribute Intense National Disasters to the Apocalypse, Not Climate Change," Climate Progress, posted November 22, 2014, http://thinkprogress.org/climate/2014/11/22/3596041/poll-religion-climate-end-times-evangelicals/.

35. "Public Sees Religion's Influence Waning," Pew Research Center, September 22, 2014, http://www.pewforum.org/2014/09/22/public-sees-religions-influence-waning-2/.

36. Alessandro Speciale, "Pope Warns U.S. Bishops on Threat of 'Radical Secularism' in America," *Huffington Post*, January 19, 2012, http://www.huffingtonpost.com/2012/01/19/pope-secularism-america_n_1217224.html.

37. Carl E. Olson, "Cardinal Pell: 'We're Not Giving in to the Secular Agenda; We're Not Collapsing in a Heap,'" *Catholic World Report*, October 16, 2014, http://www.catholicworldreport.com/Blog/3441/cardinal_pell_were_not_giving_in_to_the_secular_agenda_were_not_collapsing_in_a_heap.aspx.

38. Paul Strand, "Prayer Breakfast: Obama Admin. at War with Religion," CBNNews, April 20, 2012, http://www.cbn.com/cbnnews/us/2012/April/Catholic-Leader-Obama-Admin-at-War-with-Religion/.

39. Charles J. Chaput, "Strangers in a Strange Land," *First Things*, January 2015, http://www.firstthings.com/article/2015/01/strangers-in-a-strange-land.

40. John Gehring, "Be Not Afraid?" Faith in Public Life, June 2013, http://www.faithinpubliclife.org/wp-content/uploads/2013/06/FPL-CCHD-report.pdf.

41. John Gehring, "Immigrant Day Laborers Lose, Culture Wars Win," Faith in Public Life, July 17, 2014, http://www.faithinpubliclife.org/blog/immigrant-day-laborers-lose-culture-wars-win/.

42. Devin Dwyer, "Too Political? Minnesota Catholic Bishops Raise Marriage Issue Amid Governor's Race," ABCNews.com, October 4, 2010, http://abcnews.go.com/Politics/2010_Elections/catholic-church-launches-dvd-campaign-minnesota-governors-race/story?id=11793190.

43. Patricia Guilfoyle, Catholic News Service, "North Carolina Bishops to Exit Council over Same-Sex Marriage, Abortion," *National Catholic Reporter*, September 30, 2013, http://ncronline.org/news/faith-parish/north-carolina-bishops-exit-council-over-same-sex-marriage-abortion.

44. "Bishop Objects to Notre Dame Policy on Same-Sex Benefits," *South Bend Tribune*, October 18, 2014, http://www.southbendtribune.com/news/local/bishop-objects-to-notre-dame-policy-on-same-sex-benefits/article_f7029cb8-d290-5878-ba26-6ea72ca3b2ac.html.

45. David J. O'Brien, "The Land O'Lakes Statement," Boston College, accessed May 12, 2015, http://www.bc.edu/content/dam/files/offices/mission/pdf1/cu7.pdf.

46. O'Brien, "The Land O'Lakes Statement."

47. Neela Banerjee, "At Religious Universities, Disputes over Faith and Academic Freedom," *New York Times*, February 18, 2006, http://www.nytimes.com/2006/02/18/national/18notredame.html?pagewanted=all&_r=0.

48. Kathleen Gilbert, "Cardinal George: Notre Dame Obama Invite an 'Extreme Embarassment,'" Catholic.org, April 1, 2009, http://www.catholic.org/news/hf/home/story.php?id=32947.

49. Michael Kranish, "Group's Church Role Questioned," *Boston Globe*, August 28, 2005, http://www.boston.com/news/education/higher/articles/2005/08/28/groups_church_role_questioned/.

50. Dan Morris-Young, "Cardinal Newman Society Takes on Watchdog Role for Catholic Identity," *National Catholic Reporter*, November 21, 2012, http://ncronline.org/news/faith-parish/cardinal-newman-society-takes-watchdog-role-catholic-identity.

51. "Ellen Goodman Responds to Being Banned by Saint Francis University," AcademeBlog.com, accessed May 12, 2015, http://academeblog.org/2011/09/24/ellen-goodman-responds-to-being-banned-by-saint-francis-university/.

52. John Gehring, "Vicki Kennedy and Catholic McCarthyism," Faith in Public Life, April 9, 2012, http://www.faithinpubliclife.org/blog/vicki-kennedy-and-catholic-mccarthyism/.

53. Clare MacDonnell, "Archbishop Chaput Visits Christendom College," *Catholic Herald*, January 1, 1999, http://catholicherald.com/stories/Archbishop-Chaput-Visits-Christendom-College,4815.

54. "Bishop's Doctrine Committee Faults Book by Fordham Professor Sister Elizabeth Johnson," U.S. Conference of Catholic Bishops, March 30, 2011, https://deaconjohnspace.wordpress.com/2011/03/31/usccb-bishops-doctrine-committee-faults-book-by-fordham-professor-sister-elizabeth-johnson/.

55. Thomas C. Fox, "Johnson Letter to U.S. Bishop's Doctrine Committee," *National Catholic Reporter*, June 6, 2011, http://ncronline.org/news/faith-parish/johnson-letter-us-bishops-doctrine-committee.

56. Ann Carey, "Cardinal Müller: LCWR Stands in 'Open Provocation' of Holy See," *National Catholic Register*, May 5, 2014, http://www.ncregister.com/daily-news/cardinal-mueller-lcwr-stands-in-open-provocation-of-holy-see/.

57. David Gibson, "'Let a Female Speculate': Full Text of Sister Elizabeth Johnson's LCWR Talk," Religion News Service, August 17, 2014, http://www.religionnews.com/2014/08/17/let-female-speculate-full-text-sister-elizabeth-johnsons-talk-lcwr/.

58. "Statement by Mercy Sister Margaret A. Farley," *National Catholic Reporter*, June 4, 2012, http://ncronline.org/news/vatican/statement-mercy-sister-margaret-farley.

59. David Gibson, *The Rule of Benedict: Pope Benedict XVI and His Battle with the Modern World* (New York: HarperOne, 2007).

60. Peter J. Leithart, "Micro-Christendoms," *First Things*, April 11, 2014, http://www.firstthings.com/web-exclusives/2014/04/micro-christendoms; Joseph

Cardinal Ratzinger, *Salt of the Earth: The Church at the End of the Millennium* (San Francisco: Ignatius Press, 1997).

61. Ratzinger, *Salt of the Earth.*

62. "English Translation of Pope Francis' *Corriere della Sera* Interview," *Zenit*, March 5, 2014, http://www.zenit.org/en/articles/english-translation-of-pope-francis-corriere-della-sera-interview.

63. "Pope Francis' Address to Congregation for the Doctrine of the Faith," *Zenit*, January 31, 2014, http://www.zenit.org/en/articles/pope-francis-address-to-congregation-for-the-doctrine-of-the-faith.

6. THE FRANCIS ERA IN AMERICA

1. Blase J. Cupich, "Staying Civil," *America*, March 5, 2012, http://america magazine.org/issue/5131/article/staying-civil.

2. Daniel Walters, "Calling for Calm," *Inlander*, April 4, 2012, http://www. inlander.com/spokane/calling-for-calm/Content?oid=2137805.

3. David Gibson, "Catholic and Libertarian?" Religion News Service, June 3, 2014, http://www.religionnews.com/2014/06/03/catholic-libertarian-popes-top-adviser-says-theyre-incompatible/.

4. Daniel Burke, "New Chicago Archbishop Ditches $14 Million Mansion," *CNN Belief Blog*, October 22, 2014, http://religion.blogs.cnn.com/2014/10/22/report-chicagos-new-archbishop-wont-live-in-cardinals-mansion/.

5. John L. Allen Jr., "Are We Looking at the American Pope Francis in Chicago?" *Crux*, September 20, 2014, http://www.cruxnow.com/church/2014/09/20/are-we-looking-at-the-american-pope-francis-in-chicago/.

6. "Archbishop Blase Cupich's Installation Mass Homily," *Crux*, November 18, 2014, http://www.cruxnow.com/church/2014/11/18/archbishop-blase-cupichs-installation-mass-homily/.

7. Thomas C. Fox, "Quinn to Priest Group: Church Poised at a Moment of Far-Reaching Consequences," *National Catholic Reporter*, July 7, 2014, http://ncronline.org/news/people/quinn-priest-group-church-poised-moment-far-reaching-consequences.

8. E. J. Dionne Jr., "Blase Cupich Is Pope Francis' American Messenger," *Washington Post*, September 24, 2014, http://www.washingtonpost.com/opinions/ej-dionne-bishop-blase-cupich-is-pope-franciss-american-messenger/2014/09/24/1e9c1992-4424-11e4-b47c-f5889e061e5f_story.html.

9. "Exclusive—Cardinal Burke: Church Risks Serious Tensions in Months Ahead," Breitbart.com, November 5, 2014, http://www.breitbart.com/Big-Peace/2014/11/05/Exclusive-Cardinal-Burke-Church-Risks-Serious-Tensions-in%20Months-Ahead.

10. "Synod 14, Eleventh General Assembly: 'Relatio Post Disceptationem' of the General Rapporteur, Cardinal Péter Erdő, 13.10.2014," accessed May 8, 2015, http://press.vatican.va/content/salastampa/en/bollettino/pubblico/2014/10/13/0751/03037.html.

11. John Thavis, "A Pastoral Earthquake at the Synod," JohnThavis.com, October 13, 2014, http://www.johnthavis.com/a-pastoral-earthquake-at-the-synod.

12. Elisabetta Povoledo and Laurie Goodstein, "At the Vatican, a Shift in Tone Toward Gays and Divorce," New York Times, October 13, 2014, http://www.nytimes.com/2014/10/14/world/europe/vatican-signals-more-tolerance-toward-gays-and-remarriage.html.

13. Povoledo and Goodstein, "At the Vatican, a Shift in Tone."

14. "Pope Francis Speech at the Conclusion of the Synod," Vatican Radio, accessed May 8, 2015, http://en.radiovaticana.va/news/2014/10/18/pope_francis_speech_at_the_conclusion_of_the_synod/1108944.

15. Sylvia Poggioli, "Catholic Synod Highlights Divisions, Sets Stage for Further Battles," NPR, October 20, 2014, http://www.npr.org/blogs/parallels/2014/10/20/357508863/catholic-synod-highlights-divisions-sets-stage-for-future-battles.

16. Ross Douthat, "The Pope and the Precipice," New York Times, October 25, 2014, http://www.nytimes.com/2014/10/26/opinion/sunday/ross-douthat-the-pope-and-the-precipice.html?_r=0.

17. "From Bishop Tobin: Random Thoughts About the Synod on the Family," Roman Catholic Diocese of Providence website, October 21, 2014, http://www.diocesepvd.org/from-bishop-tobin-random-thoughts-about-the-synod-on-the-family/.

18. Josephine McKenna, "Cardinal Says Church Under Pope Francis Is a 'Rudderless Ship,'" Religion News Service, October 31, 2014, http://www.religionnews.com/2014/10/31/cardinal-catholic-church-pope-francis-ship-without-rudder/.

19. Michael O'Loughlin, "Archbishop Chaput Loves the Pope, Dislikes the Media," Crux, November 16, 2014, http://www.cruxnow.com/church/2014/11/16/archbishop-chaput-loves-the-pope-dislikes-the-media/.

20. Vince Rotondaro, "Cardinal Kasper: Pope Francis 'Does Not Represent a Liberal Position, but a Radical Position,'" National Catholic Reporter, November 7, 2014, http://ncronline.org/news/people/cardinal-kasper-pope-francis-does-not-represent-liberal-position-radical-position.

21. Laurie Goodstein, "U.S. Bishops Struggle to Follow Lead of Francis," New York Times, November 11, 2014, http://www.nytimes.com/2014/11/12/us/change-urged-by-pope-francis-is-rattling-hierarchy-of-roman-catholic-church.html.

22. Rachel Zoll, "US Bishops Struggling Under Francis' Pontificate," Associated Press, November 8, 2014, http://bigstory.ap.org/article/91b30e72b9494 860b25c6efbac6aebc5/us-bishops-struggling-under-francis-pontificate.

23. Michael O'Loughlin, Twitter post, November 10, 2014, 11:50 a.m., https://twitter.com/MikeOLoughlin/status/531896708331237376.

24. John Thavis, "Archbishop Kurtz Hits the Right Notes in Opening Talk to U.S. Bishops," JohnThavis.com, November 10, 2014, http://www.johnthavis.com/archbishop-kurtz-hits-the-right-notes-in-opening-talk-to-us-bishops.

25. Rotondaro, "Cardinal Kasper: Pope Francis 'Does Not Represent a Liberal Position, but a Radical Position.'"

26. Cardinal Sean P. O'Malley, "Reflections on My *60 Minutes* Interview," *Boston Pilot*, November 19, 2014, http://www.thebostonpilot.com/opinion/article.asp?ID=172548.

27. Melinda Henneberger, "Wuerl: Why I Won't Deny Pelosi Communion," *Politics Daily*, May 6, 2009, www.politicsdaily.com/2009/05/06/archbishop-wuerl-why-i-won-t-deny-pelosi-communion/.

28. Betsy Hiel, "New Pope Will Correct Church's 'Serious Problems,' Cardinal Wuerl Believes," TribLive.com, March 14, 2013, http://triblive.com/usworld/betsyhiel/3664110-74/story#axzz3JuqhxmQL.

29. Marc Santora, "Gay Groups to March in St. Patrick's Day Parade as a Ban Falls," *New York Times*, September 3, 2014, http://www.nytimes.com/2014/09/04/nyregion/new-york-st-patricks-day-parade-organizers-lift-ban-on-gay-groups.html.

30. Lisa Bourne, "Catholic Leaders Criticize Cardinal Dolan's Defense of Gay Group at St. Patrick's Parade," *LifeSite*, September 19, 2014, https://www.lifesitenews.com/news/catholic-leaders-criticize-cardinal-dolans-defense-of-gay-group-at-st.-patr.

31. Austin Ruse, "DC Priest Punished for Calling for End to Gay St. Patrick's Day Parade in New York City," Breitbart.com, September 7, 2014, http://www.breitbart.com/Big-Government/2014/09/07/DC-Priest-Punished-for-Calling-for-End-to-Gay-St-Pat-s-Parade-in-New-York-City?utm_source=twitterfeed&utm_medium=twitter.

32. John L. Allen Jr., "Dolan: Francis Should Call Out Moderate Muslims," *Crux*, September 4, 2014, http://www.cruxnow.com/church/2014/09/04/pope-francis-should-call-out-moderate-muslims-ny-cardinal-says/.

33. "Notification Regarding Sister Jeannine Gramick, SSND, and Father Robert Nugent, SDS," Vatican website, May 31, 1999, http://www.vatican.va/roman_curia/congregations/cfaith/documents/rc_con_cfaith_doc_19990531_gramick-nugent-notification_en.html.

34. Dan Morris-Young, "Influential Catholics Call for Removal of San Francisco Archbishop in Full-Page Ad," *National Catholic Reporter*, April 16, 2015,

http://ncronline.org/news/faith-parish/influential-catholics-call-removal-san-francisco-bishop-full-page-ad.

35. Francis DeBernardo, "New Ways Ministry Builds Bridges with Archbishop Cordileone," New Ways Ministry, accessed May 8, 2015, https://newways ministryblog.wordpress.com/2014/12/16/building-bridges-with-archbishop-cordileone/.

36. Kevin Clarke, "Francis Effect: Jesuits Report Surge in Vocation Inquiries," America, March 11, 2014, http://americamagazine.org/content/all-things/francis-effect-jesuits-report-surge-vocation-inquiries.

37. "Beginnings of a Francis Correction?" 1964, March 13, 2015, http://nineteensixty-four.blogspot.com/2015/03/beginnings-of-francis-correction-and.html.

38. Navar Watson, "Survey Shows Pope Francis Has Influenced Giving by U.S. Catholics," Catholic News Service, March 19, 2014, http://stlouisreview.com/article/2014-03-19/survey-shows-pope.

39. Daniel Burke, "How to Really Measure the 'Francis Effect,'" CNN, March 13, 2012, http://www.cnn.com/2014/03/08/living/pope-francis-effect-boston/.

40. Paul Baumann, "The Public Pope," Slate, March 11, 2014.

41. Jamie Manson, "When Does Our Hope for Francis Become Denial?" National Catholic Reporter, July 31, 2013, http://ncronline.org/blogs/grace-margins/when-does-our-hope-francis-become-denial.

42. "Bergoglio's Intervention: A Diagnosis of the Problems in the Church," Vatican Radio, March 27, 2013, http://en.radiovaticana.va/storico/2013/03/27/bergoglios_intervention_a_diagnosis_of_the_problems_in_the_church/en1-677269.

43. "Fr. Satish Reflects on the Synod on the Family," Ite Missa Est, accessed May 8, 2015, http://www.itemissaest.org/index.php/component/content/article/93-documents/the-discipleship-corner/4776-fr-satish-reflects-on-the-synod-on-the-family.

44. Rev. Dwight Longenecker, "Dear Pope Francis: Please Defend the Faith," Crux, October 17, 2014, http://www.cruxnow.com/faith/2014/10/17/dear-pope-francis-please-defend-the-faith/.

45. Richard R. Gaillardetz, "The 'Francis Moment': A New Kairos for Catholic Ecclesiology," accessed May 8, 2015, http://www.ctsa-online.org/Convention%202014/06%20-%20Plenary.Gaillardetz.pdf.

46. "Address to the Leadership of the Episcopal Conferences of Latin America During the General Coordination Meeting, 28 July 2013," Vatican website, accessed May 8, 2015, http://w2.vatican.va/content/francesco/en/speeches/2013/july/documents/papa-francesco_20130728_gmg-celam-rio.html.

47. Andrea Tornielli, "Aparecida: Where Francis' Pontificate Began," *Vatican Insider*, July 24, 2013, http://vaticaninsider.lastampa.it/en/world-news/detail/articolo/gmg-26681/.

48. Tornielli, "Aparecida: Where Francis' Pontificate Began."

49. "The Pope Defines the Mission of the Congregation for Bishops and the Characteristics of the Apostles' Successors," News.va, February 27, 2014, http://www.news.va/en/news/the-pope-defines-the-mission-of-the-congregation-f.

50. David Gibson, "Pope Francis: The Church Needs Better Bishops; Go Find Them," Religion News Service, February 27, 2014, http://www.religionnews.com/2014/02/27/pope-francis-church-needs-better-bishops-go-find/.

51. Daniel Burke, "The Lavish Homes of American Archbishops," CNN.com, accessed May 8, 2015, http://www.cnn.com/interactive/2014/08/us/american-archbishops-lavish-homes/.

52. Mark Mueller, "Newark, N.J., Archbishop's Retirement Home Includes $500K Addition," *National Catholic Reporter*, February 17, 2014, http://ncronline.org/news/faith-parish/newark-nj-archbishops-retirement-home-includes-500k-addition.

53. Sam Frizell, "Pope Francis Fires German 'Bling Bishop,'" *Time*, March 26, 2014, http://time.com/38336/pope-francis-bling-bishop-fires/.

54. Archbishop Wilton D. Gregory, "The Archbishop Responds," *Georgia Bulletin*, March 31, 2014, http://www.georgiabulletin.org/commentary/2014/03/the-archbishop-responds/.

55. Nicole Winfield, "Pope Francis: Priests Can Become 'Little Monsters,'" *USA Today*, January 4, 2014, http://www.usatoday.com/story/news/world/2014/01/04/pope-francis-priests-vatican/4316775/.

56. "Cardinal Burke: Synod's Mid-Term Report 'Lacks a Solid Foundation in the Sacred Scriptures and the Magisterium,'" *Catholic World Report*, October 14, 2014, http://www.catholicworldreport.com/Item/3429/cardinal_burke_synods_midterm_report_lacks_a_solid_foundation_in_the_sacred_scriptures_and_the_magisterium.aspx.

57. Joshua J. McElwee, "Francis Firmly Backs Equal Pay for Women, Citing Christian 'Radical Equality,'" *National Catholic Reporter*, April 29, 2015, http://ncronline.org/blogs/ncr-today/francis-firmly-backs-equal-pay-women-citing-christian-radical-equality.

58. Candida Moss and Joel Baden, "Pope Francis' Woman Problem," *Los Angeles Times*, December 7, 2014, http://www.latimes.com/opinion/la-oe-moss-pope-francis-women-20141208-story.html.

59. "Leaving Catholicism," Pew Research Center Religion and Public Life, revised February 2011, http://www.pewforum.org/2009/04/27/faith-in-flux3/.

60. Anne M. Butler, "Nuns on the Frontier," *New York Times*, May 15, 2012, http://www.nytimes.com/2012/05/16/opinion/nuns-on-the-frontier.html?_r=0.

7. A "FRANCIS EFFECT" ON U.S. POLITICS?

1. "Francis: 'A Good Catholic Meddles in Politics,'" *Vatican Insider*, September 16, 2013, http://vaticaninsider.lastampa.it/en/the-vatican/detail/articolo/27882/.

2. "Apostolic Exhortation *Evangelii Gaudium* of the Holy Father Francis to the Bishops, Clergy, Consecrated Persons, and the Lay Faithful on the Proclamation of the Gospel in Today's World," Vatican website, accessed May 8, 2015, http://w2.vatican.va/content/francesco/en/apost_exhortations/documents/papa-francesco_esortazione-ap_20131124_evangelii-gaudium.html.

3. Robert W. McElroy, "A Church for the Poor," *America*, October 21, 2013, http://americamagazine.org/church-poor.

4. "President Obama Quotes Pope Francis in Speech About Income Inequality," *Huffington Post*, December 4, 2013, http://www.huffingtonpost.com/2013/12/04/obama-quotes-pope-francis_n_4386622.html.

5. Molly K. Hooper, "Will Speaker Move Bill on the Pope?" *The Hill*, July 29, 2014, http://thehill.com/homenews/house/213588-will-speaker-move-bill-on-the-pope.

6. Joel Gehrke, "Rubio Challenges Pope Francis: 'Take Up the Cause of Freedom,'" *National Review*, December 17, 2014, http://www.nationalreview.com/corner/394896/rubio-challenges-pope-francis-take-cause-freedom-joel-gehrke.

7. Sheryl Gay Stolberg, "Popular Voice in the Capitol? It's the Pope's," *New York Times*, January 5, 2014, http://www.nytimes.com/2014/01/06/us/politics/popular-voice-in-the-capitol-its-the-popes.html?_r=0.

8. McKay Coppins, "Paul Ryan's Inner City Education," BuzzFeed, April 28, 2014, http://www.buzzfeed.com/mckaycoppins/paul-ryans-inner-city-education.

9. Stolberg, "Popular Voice in the Capitol? It's the Pope's."

10. Steve Moore, "Vatican's Turn to the Left Will Make the Poor Poorer," *Forbes*, January 5, 2015, http://www.forbes.com/sites/stevemoore/2015/01/05/vaticans-turn-to-the-left-will-make-the-poor-poorer/.

11. Maureen Mullarkey, "Francis & Political Illusion," *First Things*, January 5, 2015, http://www.firstthings.com/blogs/mullarkey/2015/01/francis-political-illusion.

12. Inés San Martín, "Key Advisor Blasts US Criticism of Pope's Environmental Stance," *Crux*, May 12, 2015, http://www.cruxnow.com/church/2015/05/12/key-advisor-blasts-us-blowback-to-popes-environmental-stance/.

13. Joe Romm, "Flashback: John Boehner Says on ABC: 'The Idea That Carbon Dioxide Is a Carcinogen That Is Harmful to Our Environment Is Almost

Comical,'" Climate Progress, January 5, 2011, http://thinkprogress.org/climate/2011/01/05/207289/john-boehner-carbon-dioxide-carcinogen-global-warming/.

14. Julie Kliegman, "Has Marco Rubio Backtracked on Climate Change?" PolitiFact.com, May 14, 2014, http://www.politifact.com/truth-o-meter/article/2014/may/14/has-marco-rubio-backtracked-climate-change/.

15. Clare Foran and Ben Geman, "How Jeb Bush's Environmental Record Could Hurt Him in 2016," *National Journal*, March 10, 2015, http://www.nationaljournal.com/energy/how-jeb-bush-s-environmental-record-could-hurt-him-in-2016-20150310.

16. "Bishops Welcome New Mercury and Air Toxics Standards to Protect Human Life and God's Creation," U.S. Conference of Catholic Bishops, December 21, 2011, http://www.usccb.org/news/2011/11-247.cfm.

17. "Message of His Holiness Pope John Paul II for the Celebration of the World Day of Peace, 1 January 1990," Vatican website, accessed May 8, 2015, http://w2.vatican.va/content/john-paul-ii/en/messages/peace/documents/hf_jp-ii_mes_19891208_xxiii-world-day-for-peace.html.

18. "Message of His Holiness Pope Benedict XVI for the Celebration of the World Day of Peace, 1 January 2010."

19. Coral Davenport and Laurie Goodstein, "Pope Francis Steps Up Campaign on Climate Change, to Conservatives' Alarm," *New York Times*, April 27, 2015, http://www.nytimes.com/2015/04/28/world/europe/pope-francis-steps-up-campaign-on-climate-change-to-conservatives-alarm.html?smid=tw-share.

20. David Kelly, "Bishop Adds Voters to Communion Ban," *Los Angeles Times*, May 15, 2004, http://articles.latimes.com/2004/may/15/nation/na-bishop15.

21. Paige Winfield Cunningham, "Pro-Life Democrats Ousted as Election Centers on the Economy," *Christianity Today*, November 3, 2010, http://www.christianitytoday.com/ct/2010/novemberweb-only/53-31.0.html.

22. Drew DeSilver, "U.S. Income Inequality, on Rise for Decades, Is Now Highest Since 1928," Pew Research Center, December 5, 2013, http://www.pewresearch.org/fact-tank/2013/12/05/u-s-income-inequality-on-rise-for-decades-is-now-highest-since-1928/.

23. Bryce Covert, "CEOs Earn Nearly 300 Times What Their Workers Make," Think Progress, June 12, 2014, http://thinkprogress.org/economy/2014/06/12/3448115/ceo-worker-pay-ratio/.

24. Laura Lorenzetti, "These 7 Companies Spent More on CEO Pay Than Federal Taxes," *Fortune*, November 19, 2014, http://fortune.com/2014/11/19/these-7-companies-spend-more-on-ceo-pay-than-federal-taxes/.

25. John L. Allen Jr., "CELAM Update: 'Option for the Poor' Alive and Well in Latin America," *National Catholic Reporter*, May 21, 2007, http://ncronline.org/news/celam-update-option-poor-alive-and-well-latin-america.

26. Laura Shin, "The 85 Richest People in the World Have as Much Wealth as the 3.5 Billion Poorest," *Forbes*, January 23, 2014, http://www.forbes.com/sites/laurashin/2014/01/23/the-85-richest-people-in-the-world-have-as-much-wealth-as-the-3-5-billion-poorest/.

27. "Pope to UN: Resist the Economy of Exclusion, Serve the Poor," News.VA, May 9, 2014, http://www.news.va/en/news/pope-to-un-resist-the-economy-of-exclusion-serve-t.

28. "Apostolic Exhortation *Evangelii Gaudium* of the Holy Father Francis."

29. Jane Mayer, "Covert Operations," *New Yorker*, August 30, 2010, http://www.newyorker.com/magazine/2010/08/30/covert-operations.

30. Michelle Boorstein, "50 Educators Sign Letter to Catholic University Protesting Koch Foundation's $1 Million Gift," *Washington Post*, December 16, 2013, http://www.washingtonpost.com/local/50-educators-sign-letter-to-catholic-university-protesting-koch-foundations-1-million-gift/2013/12/15/f53b9d4c-65c7-11e3-8b5b-a77187b716a3_story.html.

31. John and Carol Saeman, "Pope Francis, the Kochs, and How the Wealthy Can Help the Poor," *Washington Post*, November 28, 2014, http://www.washingtonpost.com/opinions/pope-francis-the-kochs-and-how-the-wealthy-can-help-the-poor/2014/11/28/958fbac2-770a-11e4-a755-e32227229e7b_story.html.

32. "Freedom Partners Chamber of Commerce," OpenSecrets.org, Center for Responsive Politics, accessed May 8, 2015, https://www.opensecrets.org/outsidespending/nonprof_contrib.php?id=453732750.

33. Alan Pyke, "Nation's Largest Food Bank Reduces Portions, Turns Away Needy After Massive Food Stamp Cuts," Think Progress, November 25, 2014, http://thinkprogress.org/economy/2014/11/25/3596689/food-bank-new-york-city-cuts/.

34. Thomas J. Healey, "Unsung Miracles," *America*, September 29, 2014, http://americamagazine.org/issue/unsung-miracles.

35. "History of Acton Institute," Acton Institute for the Study of Religion and Liberty, accessed May 8, 2015, http://www.acton.org/about/history-acton-institute.

36. Laurie Bennett, "The Ultra-Rich, Ultra-Conservative DeVos Family," *Forbes*, December 26, 2011, http://www.forbes.com/sites/lauriebennett/2011/12/26/the-ultra-rich-ultra-conservative-devos-family/.

37. Andy Kroll, "Meet the New Kochs: The DeVos Clan's Plan to Defund the Left," *Mother Jones*, January/February 2014, http://www.motherjones.com/politics/2014/01/devos-michigan-labor-politics-gop.

38. Rev. Robert Sirico, "Big Gains for the Union Liberation Movement," Action Institute PowerBlog, December 11, 2012, http://blog.acton.org/archives/46679-big-gains-for-the-union-liberation-movement.html.

39. Bishop Thomas Gumbleton, "Right-to-Work Laws Devastate Economic Justice," MLive.com, December 10, 2012, http://www.mlive.com/opinion/kalamazoo/index.ssf/2012/12/right-to-work_laws_devastate_e.html.

40. "Economic Justice for All: Pastoral Letter on Catholic Social Teaching and the U.S. Economy, 1986," U.S. Conference of Catholic Bishops, accessed May 8, 2015, http://www.usccb.org/upload/economic_justice_for_all.pdf.

41. "Acton University," Acton Institute, accessed May 8, 2015, http://university.acton.org.

42. Kishore Jayabalan, "Letter from Rome: Pope Francis and Truly Helping the Poor," Acton Institute, April 3, 2013, http://www.acton.org/global/article/letter-rome-pope-francis-truly-helping-poor.

43. Joshua J. McElwee, "Acton Conference Draws Ties Between Christian Persecution, Economic Liberalism," *National Catholic Reporter*, April 30, 2014, http://ncronline.org/news/global/acton-conference-draws-ties-between-christian-persecution-economic-liberalism.

44. Samuel Gregg, "Pope Francis and Poverty," *National Review*, November 26, 2013, http://www.nationalreview.com/corner/365004/pope-francis-and-poverty-samuel-gregg.

45. Michael Novak, "God Bless the Tea Party," American Enterprise Institute, November 8, 2010, https://www.aei.org/publication/god-bless-the-tea-party/.

46. Dan Morris-Young, "Napa Institute Gathers US Church's Well-Heeled and High-Ranking Devout," *National Catholic Reporter*, December 15, 2014, http://ncronline.org/print/news/faith-parish/your-face-catholicism-napa-institute-gathers-us-church-s-well-heeled-and-high.

8. THE SEARCH FOR COMMON GROUND

1. Domenico Agasso Jr., "Francis: 'The Church Is a Big and Varied Orchestra,'" *Vatican Insider*, October 9, 2013, http://vaticaninsider.lastampa.it/en/the-vatican/detail/articolo/-ed79dbb0e6/.

2. William Saletan, "Abortion Common Ground: A Pro-Choice Agenda," *Slate*, November 17, 2010, http://www.slate.com/articles/health_and_science/human_nature/2010/11/abortion_common_ground_a_prochoice_agenda.html.

3. Charles C. Camosy, "How the Abortion Wars Will End—With a Truce, Not a Bang," *Los Angeles Times*, March 20, 2015, http://www.latimes.com/opinion/op-ed/la-oe-0322-camosy-abortion-discourse-change-20150322-story.html.

4. Melinda Henneberger, "At Georgetown, Considering 'the Francis Factor,'" *Washington Post*, October 2, 2013, http://www.washingtonpost.com/national/2013/10/02/a8a30380-2b89-11e3-b139-029811dbb57f_story.html.

5. Henneberger, "At Georgetown, Considering 'the Francis Factor.'"

6. Michael Sean Winters, "Cardinal O'Malley's Sermon," *National Catholic Reporter*, January 22, 2014, http://ncronline.org/blogs/distinctly-catholic/cardinal-omalleys-sermon.

7. John L. Allen Jr., "O'Malley Preaches Support for Immigrants at US Border," *Boston Globe*, April 2, 2014, http://www.bostonglobe.com/metro/2014/04/01/cardinal/qVnbOwt2RE3Imym9P52JoL/story.html.

8. Michelle Boorstein, "Abortion Opponents Rally on Mall, Optimistic That Nation's Views Are Aligning with Theirs," *Washington Post*, January 22, 2015, http://www.washingtonpost.com/local/under-pope-francis-american-catholics-see-the-pro-life-label-as-broader-than-abortion/2015/01/22/621671dc-a1a7-11e4-b146-577832eafcb4_story.html.

9. "Christian Leaders Call for End to 'Profound Evil' of the Death Penalty," Catholic News Service, March 31, 2015, http://www.catholicnews.com/data/stories/cns/1501398.htm.

10. Thomas Berg, "Amicus Brief of Pro-Life Organizations Supporting Strong Protection for Pregnant Workers from Discrimination," *Mirror of Justice* blog, September 12, 2014, http://mirrorofjustice.blogs.com/mirrorofjustice/2014/09/amicus-brief-of-pro-life-organizations-re-pregnancy-discrimination.html.

11. W. Bradford Wilcox and Robert I. Lerman, "For Richer, For Poorer: How Family Structures Economic Success in America," American Enterprise Institute, October 28, 2014, https://www.aei.org/publication/for-richer-for-poorer-how-family-structures-economic-success-in-america/.

12. E .J. Dionne, "To a Healthier Democracy," *Washington Post*, December 28, 2014, http://www.washingtonpost.com/opinions/ej-dionne-to-a-healthier-democracy/2014/12/28/d53dba9c-8d18-11e4-a085-34e9b9f09a58_story.html.

13. Sarah Posner, "Birth Control's Worst Enemy," *Salon*, June 3, 2012, http://www.salon.com/2012/06/03/birth_controls_worst_enemy/.

14. Helen M. Alvare, "The Consistent Ethic of Life: A Proposal for Improving Its Legislative Grasp," *University of St. Thomas Law Journal* 2, no. 2 (2005), http://ir.stthomas.edu/cgi/viewcontent.cgi?article=1060&context=ustlj.

9. MILLENNIALS, LATINOS, AND
THE FUTURE OF THE U.S. CHURCH

1. Ben Fearnow, "Study: One-Third of Adults Under 30 Have No Religious Affiliation," CBS DC, October 9, 2015, http://washington.cbslocal.com/2012/10/09/study-one-third-of-adults-under-30-have-no-religious-affiliation/.

2. Cathy Lynn Grossman, "Survey: Americans Turn Sharply Favorable on Gay Issues," Religion News Service, February 26, 2014, http://www.religionnews.com/2014/02/26/gay-marriage-lgbt-prri-pew-religion/.

3. "Millennials in Adulthood: Detached from Institutions, Networked with Friends," Pew Research Center, March 7, 2014, http://www.pewsocialtrends.org/files/2014/03/2014-03-07_generations-report-version-for-web.pdf.

4. Samantha Raphelson, "Amid the Stereotypes, Some Facts About Millennials," NPR, November 18, 2014, http://www.npr.org/2014/11/18/354196302/amid-the-stereotypes-some-facts-about-millennials.

5. "Laity and Parishes," U.S. Conference of Catholic Bishops, accessed May 8, 2015, http://www.usccb.org/about/media-relations/statistics/laity-parishes.cfm.

6. Mark M. Gray, Mary L. Gautier, and Melissa A. Cidade, "The Changing Face of U.S. Catholic Parishes," 2011, http://cara.georgetown.edu/staff/webpages/Parishes Phase One.pdf.

7. "Cultural Diversity in the Catholic Church in the United States," U.S. Conference of Catholic Bishops, June 2014, http://www.usccb.org/issues-and-action/cultural-diversity/upload/cultural-diversity-cara-report-phase-1.pdf.

8. John Chesser, "Hispanics in N.C.: Big Numbers in Small Towns," UNC Charlotte Urban Institute, August 15, 2012, http://ui.uncc.edu/story/hispanic-latino-population-north-carolina-cities-census.

ACKNOWLEDGMENTS

This book would still be just an idea floating around in my mind without the consistent support of family, friends, and colleagues. I'm blessed to have parents, Rosemarie and Scott Gehring, who shared the gift of faith, made countless sacrifices, and still encourage me along the journey. I can never repay all that you have done except by how I live my life.

Writing a book is exhilarating and exhausting. This project started as our second child, Leo, came into the world and graced us with his joyful disposition. To my wife, Timi, your patience, pep talks, and sharp editing eye during a season in our lives when sleep was a stranger is something I will never forget. Your love and friendship these past fifteen years have made everything possible. To my daughter, Sophie, who always has a book under her nose, your curiosity, sass, and sweetness fill my heart every day.

The team at Rowman & Littlefield, especially my editor Sarah Stanton, guided this book with a steady hand. It was a privilege to work with you. A special word of gratitude to readers who took time out of their busy schedules to offer invaluable feedback on early drafts: Stephen Schneck at the Catholic University of America, Anthony Annett at Columbia University, and David Buckley at the University of Louisville. My colleagues at Faith in Public Life kept me laughing and sane. Your integrity and passion for justice make all of this more than a job.

Finally, I'm grateful for a pope who is not only the protagonist of this book but also a source of personal spiritual renewal. Along with so many Jesuits I've known over the years, you challenge me to serve, listen to the rumblings of the Holy Spirit, and put my faith into social action. The Catholic Church has a gift in your pontificate. May we learn from your example now and in the years to come.

ABOUT THE AUTHOR

John Gehring is Catholic program director at Faith in Public Life, an advocacy group in Washington, DC. His writing and analysis has appeared in the *Washington Post, New York Times, USA Today, Los Angeles Times*, CNN.com, *Crux*, and *National Catholic Reporter*, among other outlets. He is a former associate director for media relations at the U.S. Conference of Catholic Bishops and has been a staff writer at the *Catholic Review, Frederick Gazette*, and *Education Week*. He is a graduate of Mount Saint Mary's University in Emmitsburg, Maryland, and Columbia University's Graduate School of Journalism in New York City. He lives in Washington, DC, with his family.